International African Library 27
General Editors: J. D. Y. Peel, Colin Murray and Suzette Heald

'HALF-LONDON' IN ZAMBIA: CONTESTED IDENTITIES IN A CATHOLIC MISSION SCHOOL

The *International African Library* is a major monograph series from the International African Institute and complements its quarterly periodical *Africa,* the premier journal in the field of African studies. Theoretically informed ethnographies, studies of social relations 'on the ground' which are sensitive to local cultural forms, have long been central to the Institute's publications programme. The *IAL* maintains this strength but extends it into new areas of contemporary concern, both practical and intellectual. It includes works focused on problems of development, especially on the linkages between the local and national levels of society; studies along the interface between the social and environmental sciences; and historical studies, especially those of a social, cultural or interdisciplinary character.

International African Library

General Editors

J. D. Y. Peel, Colin Murray *and* Suzette Heald

'HALF-LONDON' IN ZAMBIA

CONTESTED IDENTITIES IN A CATHOLIC MISSION SCHOOL

ANTHONY SIMPSON

EDINBURGH UNIVERSITY PRESS
for the International African Institute, London

For my mother Lois and in memory of my father, John

© Anthony Simpson, 2003

Edinburgh University Press Ltd
22 George Square, Edinburgh

Typeset in Plantin
by Koinonia, Bury, and
printed and bound in Great Britain
by Antony Rowe Ltd, Chippenham, Wilts

A CIP record for this book is available
from the British Library

ISBN 0 7486 1804 X (paperback)

CONTENTS

ACKNOWLEDGEMENTS

Many people assisted me in the process of writing this ethnography. I would like to thank Richard Werbner who supervised with enthusiasm, humour and care the thesis on which this account is based. A three-month fellowship at the International Centre for Contemporary Cultural Research at Manchester University gave me the opportunity to begin revisions of the thesis. I am grateful also to Sara Delamont for advice on the ethnography of schooling. Jeanette Edwards, Harri Englund, James Ferguson, Sarah Green, Suzette Heald, Hugo Hinfelaar, Henrietta Moore, Pnina Werbner and Paul Willis all kindly read and constructively commented on earlier drafts. Judith Okely, who has been an inspirational teacher since I first encountered Social Anthropology at undergraduate level, offered helpful insights on parts of the text. Hector Blackhurst at John Rylands Library went well beyond the call of duty to help me in my search for Mudimbe's autobiography. The sensitive reading of IAI readers and editors has helped to make this a better book than it would otherwise have been.

Members of my family, my mother Lois, my sisters Susan, Maureen and Catherine and their partners George, Bill and Alex constantly provided me with all manner of encouragement and support. Catherine, in particular, worked tirelessly in assisting me in the various rounds of typing and retyping the original thesis and book manuscript. Marian Brothers of several Provinces assisted me at all stages of my fieldwork. The Brothers, workers, students and teachers at St Antony's, past and present, made me welcome and assisted me in my endeavours in ways too numerous to mention. Tom Scalway, the monks of Mount St Benedict in Trinidad, the monks of Pluscarden Abbey in Scotland, Patrick and Patricia Mwila in Lusaka, and Reuben and Annie Mondoka in Kalulushi each in very different ways provided me with environments conducive to rewriting and much practical assistance.

1

INTRODUCTION: 'HALF-LONDON'

This ethnography is about life in the 1990s in a Zambian boys' Catholic mission boarding school which I call St Antony's. The students called the school 'Half-London', a name that encapsulated all their great expectations of what a mission education should deliver. Indeed, their dream was that education would translate them beyond the difficult everyday Zambian world and transform them into new and 'educated' selves. The students were proud of the way in which the school compound was very different from the surrounding area and the homesteads that were found there. They said that the school was 'not in Zambia', 'not in Africa', 'another country', and they drew attention not only to the buildings, but also to the surroundings, especially the lawns and flower borders. St Antony's was not, then, a final resting place. Rather it was a space 'betwixt and between' (Turner 1967: 93) in which Zambian students were 'remade' and 'remade' themselves.

I taught at St Antony's through much of the 1970s and 1980s and in the early and mid-1990s. To have lived in Zambia through these years is to have witnessed at first-hand the harsh daily consequences of a period of dramatic economic decline. At Independence from Britain in 1964, the country was rated one of the most prosperous in sub-Saharan Africa, although one in which there were large inequalities in the distribution of income, and poverty was high (World Bank 1994; McCulloch et al. 2000: 4). In 1964, only 1,200 Zambians possessed a secondary school certificate and only 100 had university degrees. The United National Independence Party (UNIP), led by President Kenneth Kaunda, a former teacher whose father was a missionary from the Livingstonia Mission in Malawi, took control at Independence, later declaring Zambia a one-party state in 1972.[1]

The great expectations of Independence were soon dashed for the overwhelming majority of Zambians. The price of copper – the main export – collapsed, and the Zambian economy suffered from mismanagement, corruption and the first shock waves of the repercussions of the world market oil price increase in 1973, the detrimental effects of which were exacerbated by conflict in neighbouring countries. In the 1980s, shortages of basic foodstuffs such as mealie-meal (maize flour), sugar and cooking oil were commonplace, and queuing to buy essential commodities became the order of the day in urban areas. The Structural Adjustment Programmes of the 1980s proved an unpalatable remedy for many Zambians, some of whom took to the streets in food riots on the Copperbelt in 1986. In June 1991, with multiparty elections looming later in the year and in the face of widespread rioting in Lusaka and the Copperbelt in response to a 100 per cent increase in the price of high-grade maize meal – a condition of an agreement reached between the International Monetary Fund (IMF) and the Zambian government – Kaunda reneged on the agreement. In response the IMF suspended all financial disbursements in Zambia and the rate of inflation accelerated as the government printed money to finance UNIP's election campaign and to fund a civil service pay increase.

In October 1991, the Movement for Multi-party Democracy (MMD), led by Frederick Chiluba, swept to victory. On behalf of the state, the sermons of President Kaunda on the need for love and for recognising that everyone was a child of God, were replaced by the sermons of the Born-Again President Chiluba, for whom 'the hour had come'.[2] To celebrate the coming of this hour, President Chiluba held a Pentecostal celebration on the lawn of State House (prior to his taking up residence there). It was televised live on Zambian television. Thanking God for delivering the Zambian people from their 'slavery', ministers prayed that 'this continent may no longer be known as a dark continent', but as a place where Christian light and truth prevail. Chiluba declared Zambia a 'Christian nation'.[3]

The euphoria surrounding Kenneth Kaunda's departure was short-lived. Throughout most of Kaunda's rule, an overvalued exchange rate had been maintained. In the mid-1970s the local currency, the *kwacha*, was almost equivalent to the pound sterling. By 1990 the rate had fallen to approximately twenty *kwacha* to the pound and by the end of 1991 it was sliding towards 200 *kwacha* to the pound.[4] Inflation continued its upward trend in the early 1990s, peaking at 191 per cent at the end of 1992. Unemployment rose as mines closed and manufacturing industries failed to compete against the flood of imported goods from South Africa and elsewhere. The serious decline in healthcare provision, witnessed through the 1980s, continued as the country experienced repeated outbreaks of cholera. Malnutrition, infant mortality and maternal mortality rose. The HIV/AIDS pandemic moved from being largely a question of estimates of HIV prevalence to the reality of parents, siblings, other family members, teachers, neighbours and friends dying from AIDS-related conditions without access to antiretroviral therapy, priced far beyond their means. By the end of the decade life expectancy was estimated to have fallen below forty.

The new political regime exhibited all the signs of being as corrupt as or even more corrupt than what had preceded it. Zambians often blamed themselves for their economic woes (see Ferguson 1997: 146). Many of the students at St Antony's, surveying events in Zambia and elsewhere on the

African continent, compared themselves to the *'musungu'*, the white man, and found themselves and other Zambians sadly wanting. Many believed that their failure essentially lay with being *'umuntu'*, African. They longed for the good life that education might still deliver but they were haunted by a discourse of failure as the tangible effects of the collapse of the Zambian economy made themselves felt.

An early edition of the American Catholic New Testament used in teaching religious education at St Antony's was entitled *Good News for Modern Man*. The title encapsulates so much of the story that follows. As well as excluding women, the title ironically, although unintentionally, points to the ways in which various expressions of Christianity are often appropriated in Zambia as signs *par excellence* of all that is considered to be 'modern' and 'civilised'. Modernity at St Antony's was understood to be the prerogative of those who were 'educated', that is, had at least completed formal secondary education. They were urban Christian elites who could speak English, dress in Western fashions and variously exhibited in the presentation of their selves a style of life, a way of being that was predominantly associated with the *musungu* (the white man). It was an aesthetic that was also expressed in the distinction of taste (Bourdieu 1984), that is, in the possession of material goods and the consumption of items that urban life had to offer. It was most intriguingly revealed in the God the students chose to worship and the style and manner in which they transcended their everyday selves and their Zambian world in religious expression and ritual.

In their responses to the school regime students revealed how they readily engaged in education as a civilising process. Yet what were the consequences of schooling for those who spent many of their 'formative years' in institutions like St Antony's?

In his autobiography (1994a) Mudimbe, reading his early life through the prism of his study of Foucault, describes his education in a White Fathers' Catholic minor seminary in the Belgian Congo and his religious formation in a Benedictine monastery in Rwanda as an experience of domestication under the panoptic gaze of the institution where the student learnt how to become a 'docile body' in a project which aimed at 'radical conversion' (see also Mudimbe 1994b: 121–2). Yet how thoroughgoing was this process, even in Mudimbe's case? In the same autobiography, Mudimbe demonstrates how, as an adolescent, he was quite capable of resisting total entrapment. He describes, for instance, his weekly panic at being required to attend Confession when he felt he had nothing to confess (1994a: 23). Unable to get out of this ordeal but unwilling to invent imaginary sins, he got around the problem by choosing an elderly deaf confessor, to whom he regularly recited the Catholic prayer to the Virgin Mary, 'Hail Mary', instead of a litany of transgressions. In retrospect, he is uncertain whether the octogenarian priest was taken in or whether he readily colluded in this charade. Mudimbe also recounts an episode when in the minor seminary, driven by hunger, he stole down to the chapel after the night prayer of Compline, opened the tabernacle and devoured a whole ciborium of consecrated hosts (1994a: 71). This escapade seems not to have induced any realisation of having committed a sin. Indeed, Mudimbe stresses how, while accepting the Catholic church's teaching on the meaning and power of the Eucharist, he felt that he could always explain himself to God – his father and friend.

Like Mudimbe, I too find Foucault 'good to think with' but I also find him 'good to think against'. Foucault gives attention to institutions such as boarding schools, and Catholicism appears a source of enduring fascination for him. Foucault argues that institutional spaces such as prisons and schools effectively create 'docile bodies', constructed from discourses which inform the physical structure of the institution and the practices within it. The subject in Foucault's discourse is produced by the gaze of authority. Jay (1986) insightfully delineates the 'denigration of vision' in twentieth-century French thought and contextualises Foucault's position within this tradition, describing how ambiguous the role of sight can be when negatively portrayed as the fear of being watched by an omniscient God. In such projections, the individual's experience is portrayed as the object rather than the subject of the look. In contrast to theorists such as Simmel (1950), Weinstein and Weinstein (1984), or Levinas (1987) who stressed the importance of the reciprocal glance, Foucault in his depiction of the gaze 'resisted exploring its reciprocal, intersubjective, communicative function, that of the mutual glance' (Jay 1986: 185). In Foucault's early work, his 'lack of a rounded theory of subjectivity or agency' (McNay 1992: 3) is marked.

I follow Foucault's fine insights into attempts by the institution to impinge and inscribe itself upon the body and thus invisibly to achieve an interiorisation of control. However, I reject his essentially 'subjectless history' (Giddens 1982). In his early denial of agency and choice, Foucault often fails to allow sufficient space for revolts against the gaze (Foucault 1980: 162). In contrast to an early Foucauldian cultural matrix in which one is forced to play, at St Antony's there were myriad micro-practices, often conducted in 'back regions' (Goffman 1959), by which power and authority were subverted and where spaces were created for actors to try on other roles. Rather than being trapped within one discourse, students showed themselves capable of switching between discourses or part-discourses. They demonstrated a capacity for fashioning and presenting quite different selves, in a play of difference which was more Bakhtin (1984) than Foucault – and, indeed, perhaps more resonant of local culture, whether precolonial, colonial or postcolonial (see Ranger 1996). The varieties of schooling, by no means all of which was in the hands of the missionaries, might then be seen as an appropriate preparation for the conditions prevailing in the postcolony where, according to Mbembe (1992: 5), we will find, of necessity, a plurality of 'spheres' and arenas that can only be negotiated with several fluid identities rather than one single identity.

The focus Foucault places on constraint and the moulding of subjectivity within institutions such as boarding schools does not account for the multiple and frequently oppositional discourses which existed within St Antony's. The students used a variety of means, especially alternative religious discourses – particularly American-influenced Protestant fundamentalism – and various appropriations of time and space within the school, to challenge their 'domestication' and 'reconstruction' by the orthodox discourse of school authorities, such as the Catholic Marian Brothers, who managed the school and were now unsure of what their role should be.

Unlike Foucault's model panopticon, St Antony's presents us with a complex criss-crossing of hierarchies and discourses. These gave the students space in which to manipulate their own refashioning of their own subjectivity, informed not only by what the Brothers said and did, but also by multiple other voices and practices. St Antony's was thus a space characterised by both heteroglossia and disjunction.

My analysis therefore leads to a critique of one version of Foucault's *early* approach. Foucault had raised the fundamental issue of the appearance of Western man as a subject, the subject in and of his own discourse, a discourse which occults the very source of the subject's ontological status (compare Racevskis 1983: 26). However, in his last interview, Foucault explained that in his early work he had left aside the problem of the subject (Kritzman 1988: 243; 252). In his reintroduction of the subject, Foucault is prepared to allow that the procedure 'by which one obtains the constitution of a subject, or more precisely, of a subjectivity … *is of course only one of the given possibilities of organisation of a self-consciousness*' (Kritzman 1988: 253) [my emphasis].

Towards the end of his life, Foucault's later thinking gives evidence of a noticeable change of emphasis (see Boyne 1990: 144; McNay 1992). Noting the contradictions inherent in this apparent *volte-face*, Norris argues that Foucault's work 'swings between the opposite poles of a thoroughgoing determinist creed (the idea that subjectivity is entirely constructed in and through discourse) and an ethics – or even aesthetics – of autonomous self-creation which somehow escapes that limiting condition' (Norris 1993: 47). From a sociological perspective, Foucault rejects any notion of the 'deep self' or 'nature' that has to be deciphered (Taylor 1989: 488). However, the ethics and the aesthetics of the self that is faced with the challenge of reinvention are ideas that dominate Foucault's final period. Recognising that individuals always retain a space in which they resist the process of subjectification, the subject who was once conceived of as simply an effect of discursive power relations now achieves an active role. Thus the modern project is not the salvation of the soul, but the production of the self. In Foucault's late vision, modernity compels man to face the task of producing himself: 'Modern man, for Baudelaire, is not the man who goes off to discover himself, his secrets, his hidden truth; he is the man who tries to invent himself' (Foucault, quoted in Dreyfus and Rabinow 1986: 112).

Here then is Foucault, intrigued by the challenge of 'aestheticism' – 'the transformation of the self' (Kritzman 1988: 14). McNay (1994) notes how little attention has been paid to Foucault's later period. She cogently argues that Foucault's notion of an aesthetics of the self remains 'theoretically underdeveloped' (ibid.: 166), and questions Foucault's choice of the misogynist Baudelaire for his depiction of the heroisation of the self which 'relies on an unexamined and nostalgic fantasy of masculine agency' (ibid.: 153). Indeed, the spectacular absence of women in Foucault's work and the elision of the masculine with the general have been noted by a number of commentators (see, for example, Jones and Porter 1994: 10; Carrette 1999: 7). We are left to ponder how Foucault, had he lived, might have dealt with such a critique. What cannot be denied is that Foucault appears to ignore the social and political implications inextricably embedded in this notion of aesthetics. However, I still find the notion a fruitful one, and I use it to illuminate how young Zambians in a mission school drew upon diverse social, political and religious sources to face the challenges of living in postcolonial Africa.

The invention and presentation of self is a complex process in which all actors at St Antony's employed a variety of strategies to achieve their goals. In their encounters, there was continuous 'mutual monitoring' (Manning 1992: 167), a mutuality perhaps most controversial in the religious life of the school. In *Learning to Labour*, Willis demonstrates how the school is a site of 'the agency of face-to-face control par excellence' (1977: 65). I show that some of this monitoring and control is behind the backs of authorities, and if face-to-face among the students, it is not eye-to-eye but in the dark. While the teacher might be engaged upon the quest for truth, and have at his or her disposal elaborate means of surveillance and powers of discipline and punishment, the students were equally, if not better, equipped for this encounter. Students too, like their teachers, could draw from their presentation repertoires the techniques by which others might be 'taken in' (Goffman 1974: 83), thus in some ways wresting control, not only evading but achieving 'containment'. By a variety of means, they could, and did, create role distance and alternative spaces, managing information and impressions (Goffman 1959: 208f; 1969: 13), concealing and revealing aspects of the self in the different contexts of everyday life in the school.

To reflect upon the colonial experience in Africa is to recognise the manner in which, in Mudimbe's phrase, it 'signified a new historical form and the possibility of radically new types of discourses on African traditions and cultures' (1988: 1). The colonial project cast Africa and Africans as essentially Different and Other. Mudimbe identifies this enduring dichotomy in much twentieth-century African anthropology and African studies. This discursive formation, I argue, has indeed remained a powerful force in much postcolonial education in Africa. It could be witnessed in the way in which many students at St Antony's in the 1990s were seduced by the narrative of education as a civilising process, a process that inevitably entailed a profound sense of alienation and a pejorative evaluation of themselves as 'Africans'.

Sousa Jamba, who grew up and was educated in Zambia, speaks of this self-denigration as 'the African Disease' (1989: 9). He suggests that 'the feeling that all that is African is inferior runs very deep among the postcolonial generation' and gives examples from his own schooldays: reading Chinua Achebe was considered beneath one's dignity, whereas a James Hadley Chase novel was deemed the height of sophistication; the uncircumcised boys felt superior to the circumcised because they believed that no white men were circumcised. Although realising that there will be a variety of responses from different parts of Africa, Jamba concludes from his own Zambian experience: 'The true legacy of colonialism is that Africans – of all generations – make the mistake of looking at themselves through foreign spectacles' (ibid.: 10). St Antony's students felt the strong allure of the lifestyle exhibited, at least in their imagination, by all white men.

Some students asked why God had been so unfair as to curse Africans and yet to show his favour to *musungus*. Like Mudimbe's students in Africa, America and Europe (see Mudimbe 1994a:180), students at St Antony's suspected that the curse of the children of Ham – (Mudimbe attributes responsibility for the nineteenth-century perpetuation of this to official Christian and especially Catholic church hypocrisy) – remained inescapable for Black Africans in the twentieth century (Mudimbe 1994a: 183; 1988: 46). Yet how far-reaching has this process of alienation and self-denigration been and what resistance have African students offered? Speaking of West Africa, Stoller argues that Western education turned out to be the colonisers' 'most transformative policy' in that it had a widespread impact on West African conceptions of self and other (1995: 68). 'Through education the colonizers attempted,' Stoller suggests, 'to literally and figuratively capture the bodies of the colonized by systematically subverting an old way of learning' (ibid.: 72). They shaped minds by the inculcation of habits through a prescribed set of embodied practices.[5] Much African education continues to be in the hands of Christian missionary groups, but has it really had the power that Stoller and other commentators have ascribed to it? My ethnography portrays a more complex picture: an unending contest for the moral high ground, for the right to discern God's purpose, for the claim of 'true' conversion.

Missionaries in Zambia, as elsewhere in Africa, became involved in the provision of education because they considered the establishment of schools as a powerful tool by which they could bring about the conversion of indigenous people. The first Catholic missionaries to Zambia, the White Fathers, settled in North-East Rhodesia, arriving in the vanguard of British colonial expansion. While not being merely agents of colonialism, they undoubtedly facilitated the process (Gann 1968; Roberts 1973; Rotberg 1965; Fields 1985), not least because in large part they shared the notion of a civilising project with the colonialists who used this as a justification for the European exploitation of Africa. At first, there was little enthusiasm for mission education, whether it was offered by Protestants in the west (Caplan 1970; Ranger 1965) or by Catholics in the south (Carmody 1988), because the kind of education – in the vernacular and concentrating upon religious teaching and practical skills – seemed to be of little relevance in the colonial world that was unfolding. Once English was taught in the schools, attitudes changed and children flocked to receive an education that they and their parents judged would be of use to them. In the later period around and after Independence in 1964, the schools were given the task of forming future leaders. The stated aim of colonial education in Africa had been character formation (Jones 1925). At Independence the aim became, in the words of the Zambian Minister of Education, the formation of a national character so as to build a unified Zambia out of disparate ethnic groups (Mwanakatwe 1968: ix–x). Throughout this period Christian, and especially Catholic, missionary groups played a leading role in the provision of secondary education. The same is true today. Indeed, in a reversal of UNIP government policy, which resulted in the handover of all Catholic mission primary schools to government agencies in 1974, and increased government control over mission secondary schools, the MMD government has actively encouraged mission groups to 'take back' their schools and has given them greater freedom in their day-to-day administration.

St Antony's was founded in 1960 by French Canadian Catholic missionary Brothers dedicated to the Virgin Mary. The Brothers already had schools in Southern Rhodesia (now Zimbabwe) and in many other parts of Africa. In accordance with the spirit of their French Founder, who started the Congregation in the aftermath of the French Revolution of 1789, their aim was to produce Catholic leaders for the Zambian nation. In 1974, because of falling numbers, the French Canadian Brothers handed over the school to Spanish Brothers of the same Congregation.[6] The number of Brothers teaching at St Antony's has fluctuated over the years. In the 1970s and 1980s, they numbered eight or nine. In the early 1990s there were four Spanish Brothers, one Chinese and one Zambian Brother involved in the school. There were also four other Spanish Brothers in Zambia. Two taught at a skills centre that the Congregation had established on the Copperbelt.

Of the other two Spanish Brothers, one was engaged in the training of young Zambian men who had expressed an interest in joining the Congregation. The candidates underwent the first stage of a training programme, known as the postulancy, at the mission in a building adjacent to the Brothers' residence at St Antony's. The second Brother was the regional superior and vocations director. In the 1990s the Spanish Brothers at St Antony's were in a state of doubt about the reason for their presence. In Spain, as in the rest of Europe, in the aftermath of the Second Vatican Council, there were fewer and fewer vocations to religious life. In post-Franco Spain the place of the Catholic church in the life of the nation was profoundly altered. Those who felt called to the missionary vocation were as likely to be questioned as to their motives and even to be suspected of neo-colonialist intentions, as to be applauded and admired for their chosen way of life. Some Brothers at St Antony's felt they had been trapped into catering for an elite group, at a time when Catholic teaching urged a shift in emphasis to attend to the needs of the 'poorest of the poor'.

The student population, almost entirely male, was composed of about 500 students whose ages ranged from around sixteen to the early twenties. Like the missionary Brothers themselves who came from quite humble backgrounds in Spain, about 90 per cent of the students came from rural areas. Their parents were mainly subsistence or emergent farmers, although a significant number were primary school teachers. The rest came from homes in the compounds of Lusaka, Kabwe or the Copperbelt towns of Kitwe and Ndola or from the better-off parts of Lusaka.[7] From many different ethnic groups, like the Zambian teaching staff, students identified themselves as belonging to one of a variety of Christian denominations – Catholic, Seventh-Day Adventist, Born-Again Pentecostal, United Church, Jehovah's Witnesses and others – or none. Some students claimed a Christian identity, but acknowledged allegiance to no church. They had all been drawn to St Antony's by its reputation for outstanding exam results. While the national pass rate at secondary school leaving exams at the end of grade twelve was around 60 per cent, at Catholic schools the rate was consistently between 85 per cent and 90 per cent. St Antony's regularly produced some of the best results in the country – results which students and parents still dared to hope were the key to a bright future – and a step on the ladder to university or further education. Students had won their places in the face of fierce competition. There were only sufficient places in secondary schools for around 30 per cent of the pupils in the last grade of primary school – Grade Seven – and many of these secondary places were at government Basic Schools which lacked even the most elementary facilities and educational material. There were forty-one mission schools in the country, twenty-seven of them Catholic. Parents and students judged schools run by missionaries to be the best because, they explained, in church institutions discipline was maintained and hence an atmosphere conducive to study prevailed. Like the missionary Brothers in their own childhoods, St Antony's students had been selected from the mainstream and set apart. They formed a cohort of elites on the margins.

I first arrived at St Antony's in March 1974. It was not, I believe, because of any divine or human call. I had spent 1973 in an enclosed Benedictine monastery but had concluded that it was not the place for me. While pondering my next move, I decided to spend some time in the 'Third World' and applied to an organisation called Christians Abroad. I had no preference as to where I should go. I had studied English Language and Literature at university and there were apparently many places that could use an English teacher. I was offered a job in Zambia, teaching English at St Antony's. I readily accepted, although I had never taught before and had no idea where Zambia was.

Coming from England, I was unprepared for the way in which Christianity was such a 'hot' topic both in the school and in Zambia. Students regularly questioned me about my own beliefs. They were shocked to learn that not everyone in Britain attended church regularly, and yet the British were, they said, the 'owners of the religion'. 'Have they all gone mad?' I was repeatedly asked.

I pondered my own involvement with the missionaries who ran St Antony's and became more and more aware that the stereotypical representation of all-powerful missionaries, dismantling indigenous culture and replacing it with a Christian and a European one was an inadequate picture of the dynamics of the encounter. It allowed no space for African responses, for the way in which, far from being passive recipients, people in Zambia, as elsewhere, took the Christian story and made it their own, fashioning it to fit purposes other than those primarily intended by missionaries.

In 1990 I began fieldwork at St Antony's while working there as a part-time teacher. The period of my fieldwork coincided with a number of significant Catholic anniversaries. The Catholic church celebrated the first centenary of Catholicism in Zambia, and the Marian Brothers had just celebrated the bicentenary of the birth of their Founder. But the Spanish Brothers of St Antony's were hardly in a mood to celebrate: they were weighing up the painful consequences of a student strike, one result of which was the temporary withdrawal of the Brothers from the day-to-day running of school administration. Their partial retirement from the scene did not leave a vacuum. Rather, other competing voices, expressive of counter-discourses, rapidly filled the space created.

I engaged in participant observation over an eighteen-month period. I examined documents in the archive of the school administration from its beginnings. I kept a fieldwork diary, attended school activities both in and out of class and joined missionaries and students at the various religious services available in the school. I interviewed a number of Brothers, workers, students, former students, and teachers. In some interviews I took extensive notes, in others I taped discussions. My account of the school, like my accounting for myself, can never be final, of course, but I must speak of myself as part of the school, to offer a glimpse of the standpoint which informs my ethnography. I am well aware of the need to attempt to historicise the encounter I narrate, because this 'magician' is certainly part of the plot (cf. Hastrup 1992: 118).

In presenting others, how do I present myself? I must become 'autobiographical' (Leach 1989: 45). But which differing narratives of self do I choose to reveal? To which audience criteria should I shape my story? I need to explore, if only briefly, how at least one version of my own biography bears upon the life histories of others in the school, of the missionaries, workers, teachers and students, past and present, who appear in my text; 'our past is present in us as a project' (Fabian 1983: 93). Some of their life histories and some of their voices are heard, admittedly very selectively, at times more obviously than at others. All ethnography is the product of multiple voices (Bakhtin 1981) of course. However, I am only too aware that their voices never fully break through my discursive speech (Hastrup 1992: 121). Additionally, their telling was to me, a person about whom they had constructed their own narrative throughout our shared involvement in the life of the school, as students or as colleagues, or as first one and then the other, over many years, as each of us had progressed through the lifecycle.

In some of their accounts to me, I figured in their memory, acting in a certain way, saying something that they could recall, although their account of our shared past often did not match mine. A former student, then a teacher at St Antony's, remembered seeing me, in my capacity as housemaster, eating Sunday lunch in the student dining-hall. He recalled his unhappy first days in the school: 'I was homesick and I didn't like the food. But then I saw you eating it, and I said to myself, "If that white man can eat it, then so can I."' An apparently trivial example, but which 'white man' is this? It's me, half-British, half-West Indian, descended from British working-class stock on my father's side and Carib, Portuguese plantation owner and African slave on my mother's side.

My ethnography begins with a demonstration of how missionary uncertainty and doubt were in evidence in the challenge to give the school a Catholic and Marian atmosphere, conspicuously so in the face of fundamentalist contestation from some students and teachers. There has been some recent debate about the term 'fundamentalism' and about which expressions of Christianity should warrant the term 'fundamentalist' (see Bruce 2000; Martin 2002: x). Martin sets out the case for rejecting the label 'fundamentalist' to describe Pentecostalism, especially because of the manner in which the term 'fundamentalism' is employed in broad terms to describe recent shifts in Christianity, Islam and other religious systems. Among other points, Martin highlights the fact that 'while Pentecostalism is indeed attached to Christian "fundamentals", and to a conservative under-standing of Scripture, the heart of its distinctive appeal lies in empowerment through spiritual gifts offered to all' (2002: 1). However, I have retained the term 'fundamentalist' to describe the Seventh-Day Adventist, Pentecostal or 'Born Again' as well as to other students of St Antony's who claimed allegiance to no church but who, like those others, opposed the Catholicism of the Marian Brothers and claimed for themselves the identity of 'true Christians'. These students who formed the religious opposition to the Marian Brothers experienced empowerment and embodied 'modern' self-presentations in their religious worship, yet shared a conservative attitude to Scripture and hostility to modern theology and to Catholicism. An apoca-lyptic tone informed their preaching and teaching at St Antony's; a millennial mood prevailed in their religious worship.

'Making Mary known and loved', in accordance with the Founder's vision, appeared an impossible task to many Brothers in a context where virginity was equated with infertility, and among a male student population which relegated young women to inferior roles. Given the Marian Founder's original teaching regarding the education of youth, the early history of the school shows that, from its beginnings, St Antony's attempted, in discursive and non-discursive modes, to have a long-term impact upon its students. Viewing the missionaries' domestic space reveals a life of order and discipline in which the Brothers realised a rhythm of prayer and work into which everyday Zambian realities rarely intruded as a disordered and disorderly physical world. The Brothers, despite their generosity, with their celibate life and their material power were often read by Zambians as ambi-guous figures.

But what were the everyday regimes of the formal academic spaces? And how were student lives fulfilled beyond the classroom? Mission education, conceived as a formation process, was imparted and received in the 1990s through the placement and inspection of students, through attempts to control speech, movement and posture, to produce, in Bourdieu's terms, a particular kind of habitus. Much of this formation work was placed in the hands of the prefects. Yet fundamentalist prefects, at times, acted *ultra vires* in accord with their own values and beliefs and counter to Catholic ones. Other students, especially Grade Nines, furnished another counter-discourse. They acted upon the bodies of newcomers, through mockery, to fashion a new identity, a different sense of self, at times reinforcing and at times undermining the institutions' master narrative. Throughout these discourses, it was clear that in many respects 'these black men want[ed] to be white' (Fanon 1972: 9).

A very important part of the moral and religious training as 'Christian formation' at St Antony's was in the hands of the students and not the missionaries. There were places within the school which sustained not only other types of religious formation – fundamentalist and Pentecostal – but also an apocalyptic discourse on authority, time and evil. Varying tropes of the 'civilising mission' were further enunciated within different sites of St Antony's, among them the school chapel and the student dormitories. The space created through counter discourse promoted the creation and recreation of identity. Alternative aesthetics of the self, which always entailed a system of ethics, were revealed in religious worship and everyday speech and practice. In their sermons fundamentalist student preachers refigured their selves through unmediated appropriation of Christian narrative. Discipline and order came once more to the fore. Members of each fundamentalist fellowship strove to convert other students and to remain pure, undefiled, while being required to live among those who had not won salvation. In this manner, they achieved a reversal of Catholic order, creating in effect schools within the school. Through fellowship, students situated themselves in new relations of religious kinship, in novel orientations to the world. It was both mutual recognition through mimesis shared with some, and the location of difference from others. St Antony's is merely one of the many sites in the postmodern world in which strangers gather in a context of dislocation and disjunction.

2

CATHOLIC FORMATION: CHANGE AND CONTEST

For the Brothers' religious superiors in their home province in Spain, the mission's primary purpose in Zambia, following the spirit of their Founder, was catechetical. In Zambia, however, at least a few of the Brothers were uncertain, and were reluctant to see their mission in that light. For them, the nature of a 'Catholic' school in contemporary, postcolonial Zambia was problematic. Two contrasts were striking. The first was the contrast between the contemporary Community's sense of mission and that of the French-Canadian pioneer Brothers who arrived in Northern Rhodesia in the late 1950s when the Catholic hierarchy unequivocally promoted the need to convert others to the Catholic church. Although the Canadian Brothers' experience subsequently changed their understanding of their presence, they had not doubted the value of dedicating themselves to the creation and development of a successful Catholic mission boarding school. By contrast, the Community of Spanish Brothers was highly ambivalent. They wondered about their presence and their goals. They felt a tension: should they remain at St Antony's or start another mission elsewhere, among 'the poorest of the poor'? The Brothers, among themselves, constantly debated the purpose of their work, and defended different perspectives, different concepts of 'mission' and 'presence'. The second contrast was to the mission of the Protestant fundamentalist students who, partly because of the Brothers' uncertainties, found a great deal of space within which to seek the Protestant fundamentalist conversion of other students. Where the fundamentalist students whom they encountered on a daily basis were confident, the Brothers were remarkably muted. Their diffidence about the purpose of their endeavours was striking. In fact, Brothers seen as prevaricating in religious matters were taken, in fundamentalist student sermons, as exemplars of 'tepid' Christians subject to damnation.

THE ORIGINAL MISSION PROJECT

The intentions of the pioneer Brothers I interviewed were quite clear. They knew what they intended to achieve by going to Northern Rhodesia (now Zambia) to establish the school. They spoke of the certainties of religious life prior to the Second Vatican Council; their intention was 'to educate and to help'. For some, conversion to Catholicism was an important concern, for others it was not. Brother Jean-Pierre, originally from Quebec and now in his sixties, spoke of his intention to be an exemplar for the conversion of others: 'OK. I wanted to give my life for ... well, we are talking about the very early sixties – to try to bring more people to the church, to *my* beliefs. You know, I felt, "No, I'm young, I can mix with them ..." So that was my idea all along' [emphasis in the original].

Brother Phillippe, in his mid-fifties, reflecting upon the intensely Catholic environment of the Quebec of his childhood and upon his desire for his father to practise the Catholic religion, identified the conversion of Africans as his reason for requesting to work in the mission field. However, he went on to describe how the lived experience of life at St Antony's caused him to re-examine his motives for remaining:

> As you get older, you see it in a different way. Otherwise you would not stay in the country ... All the dreams you have when you are young, you know, going to convert the people, things like that, and you find out that is not what has been happening ... What you expected to get out of it – well, you don't get it, – like this conversion ... You want to make Christians out of them; you find out they are different – even their way of thinking. It may be as good as your own, but it is different.

The Spanish Brothers' crisis of confidence and, indeed, of identity, made itself felt in many ways. Several Brothers reluctantly avoided teaching Religious Education, and concentrated upon secular subjects. Even here, they doubted the value of teaching such academic matters, given the everyday Zambian realities of poverty and hardship. They feared the institution of the school trapped them into catering for an elite. Their attitudes about conversion were equally complex. Brother Miguel, the master of postulants who had previously acted as both deputy and headmaster, strongly denied any intention to convert anyone:

> I have always been disgusted by the term 'conversion' or the term 'pagan', which, very often, at least in the past I used to hear. I have not come here to convert anybody. I have come to share what I consider are some of my values and ways of living, and to share people's values and ways of living. Each culture has its own rotten part and its wonderful aspects ...

Brother Miguel considered that Zambians lived in fear of one another and he wanted to share 'development', especially modern farming techniques. Brother Francisco was equally scathing about attempts to convert others to Catholicism. He also spoke of the fear he found among many Zambians. Although convinced that Christianity had much to offer, he repeatedly remarked, 'I am a teacher, not a pastoral worker, not a preacher'. He explained:

I think I have nothing to offer, to tell you the truth. Just what I am, of course, in a material way. I guess some people will appreciate that I can work with them and I can teach, but I don't find myself having anything ... Christianity – it's the religion I have, the one I believe in, the figure of Christ, the incarnation, the power of love, the fact that you can be a new person and can overcome yourself and be a new man because of that ... the presentation, I feel very sad about this message not getting through, especially on the part of the insecurity of the person ... The fears of the person, how strong they are! They haven't been overcome. It means that Christianity is not appealing to them, or it really hasn't got the power to overcome that.

While the Spanish Brothers were prepared to 'give instruction' to students who sought to become Catholics, they did not proselytise in any direct manner in the school. One particular focus of the crisis of confidence and identity within the Catholic mission was the place of Mary at St Antony's, and the contested nature of the Virgin's role in Salvation and the recognition that was due to her. Dedicated to the Virgin and sensitive to the neglect of the education of young women, the Brothers met opposition from students and staff when they tried to promote the admission of girls into the formerly all-male environment at St Antony's.

Numerous religious denominations were represented in the school. Students who identified themselves as Catholics made up little more than 30 per cent of the school population. In 1991 among the 480 students, the distribution of denominations was as follows: Catholic, 31 per cent, Seventh-Day Adventist 28 per cent, United Church of Zambia, 17 per cent, Watchtower, 7 per cent and New Apostolic Church, 6 per cent. Among the remaining 11 per cent were Anglican, Reformed Church, Salvation Army, Baptist, Pentecostal, Church of Israel, Lutheran, Evangelical Church of Zambia, Church of Christ, Methodist, Christian Missions to Many Lands, Pilgrim Wesleyan, and Rastafarian. Some students who were Born Again preferred to describe themselves as belonging to one of the above churches. Other members of the Born-Again fellowship declared they belonged to no church. Almost all students stated affiliation to one or other of the Christian denominations, with the exception of one student who said he was Moslem. Among the twenty lay members of staff, twelve were Catholic, and four were Seventh-Day Adventist. Others were members of Pentecostal, United Church of Zambia and Christian Missions to Many Lands.

In the light of these facts, one may well ask, in what sense was St Antony's a Catholic school? From the early days of substantial Catholic involvement in secondary schooling in Zambia, Catholic missionary agencies pondered whether they should consider themselves genuinely 'Catholic' schools and usually decided they should not on the grounds that their student population was not wholly Catholic.[1] The Catholic Archbishop who invited the Brothers to Zambia explained to me that he wanted a school 'with a Catholic atmosphere'. This may appear a rather nebulous concept. By contrast, the Second Vatican Council document concerning Catholic education, *Gravissimum educationis*, sets out the nature and character of a Catholic school very clearly.[2] In the orthodox discourse, all was clear; the practical discourse told another story.

Although managed by Catholic Brothers, St Antony's was a grant-maintained school and thus under the direction of the Zambian Ministry of Education. There was considerable confusion among students about the status of St Antony's and the agreement between the government and mission agencies, especially with regard to their respective financial contributions to the running of the school. The Catholic agency neither selected pupils nor hired and fired staff. In no respect did the school curriculum differ from that of other secondary schools in the country. Students had freedom of worship, although all were required to attend school prayers and assemblies. In addition, Catholic students were expected to attend Sunday Mass, and others were required to attend the alternative Sunday service, normally conducted by students of the fundamentalist groups in the school hall. Morning prayer and Mass were conducted in the school chapel, a large, imposing building. It had no statues, but two icons in the side chapels, one of Christ and one of the Virgin Mary. Against the altar wall hung a huge crucifix carved in wood, to which Adventist and Born-Again students took particular exception.

The stereotypical response of students to the question, 'What is a missionary?' was 'Someone who preaches the word of God'. Clearly, according to this formulation, the Brothers were not missionaries; they did not preach. They had deliberately chosen not to be priests. They saw themselves as teachers: doers of the Word, men of action. In Catholic ritual, they remained ordinary members of the congregation, and attended daily Mass like other Catholics.

The Sunday Mass was celebrated by a priest who also acted as the school chaplain. There were two Masses on Sunday: the first, in English, for students, and the second, in Bemba or in a mixture of Bemba and Nyanja, for 'villagers'. The student Mass was a rather desultory affair. It often failed to engage the students, many of whom followed the service in a distracted manner. This was in stark contrast to the atmosphere at the Mass for 'villagers' which followed. This was a lively service with a great deal of participation, especially by the younger members of the congregation, in singing, offertory dances and reading.

However, many Catholic students enjoyed being altar boys. They explained to me that they enjoyed dressing up and liked being at the front, seen by others. Several of them said that on the sanctuary they felt 'closer to God'. In addition, a small choir made valiant attempts to enliven proceedings, singing hymns to drum accompaniment in English, Bemba and Nyanja. Attendance usually varied between seventy and ninety students, but numbered less than forty on occasion, especially on Sundays following school celebrations. Clearly, not all self-identified Catholics were faithful in their Sunday observance; many preferred the alternative service Protestant students held in the school hall, or went 'dodging' by remaining in the dormitories or going out-of-bounds. No more than a small minority of Catholic students received Communion, never more than thirty at any Mass that I attended. The Brothers made no attempt to record or to encourage attendance, although from time to time during school assemblies, the Zambian lay Headmaster, Mr Mwila, reminded Catholic students of their obligations.

No student ever stated that he or she applied to St Antony's because of its specifically religious character. The usual student reason for coming was that St Antony's achieved good results in public exams. Boys said, also, that it had a good reputation for discipline and that they had understood that, being 'in the bush' and 'single-sex', St Antony's would offer few distractions from study (see Simpson 1990).

Students at St Antony's identified the Brothers by certain aspects of their faith, especially their devotion to the Virgin Mary.

THE VIRGIN MARY IN THE ORTHODOX AND THE PRACTICAL DISCOURSE

Mary's role in the life of Jesus and the life of the Brothers' Founder is woven throughout the texts of the Brothers' Rule. The Founder's realisation of Jesus and Mary's love for him led him to start the Congregation and place the Brothers in Mary's special care. The life of the Founder is refracted for the Brothers through the life of Mary. The Founder experienced her assistance and love at every stage in the work of establishing the Brothers' Congregation in the face of many hardships and local opposition; hence, he called her 'our First Superior'. Through Mary, God gave His Son to the world, and thus the Brothers wished to make her known and loved 'as one who will lead us to Jesus'. This is the explicit reason for the Congregation's motto: 'All to Jesus through Mary, all to Mary for Jesus'. The three Marian virtues are humility, simplicity and modesty, all exemplified by the Founder himself. Jesus was the very focus of Mary's whole life; so, too, He is to be the focus of each Brother's life. Throughout the day, Brothers all over the world have recourse to Mary in both Community and private prayer. The local address joined that of the global family of Marian religious. The figure of Mary framed the Brothers' day. In the Community, morning prayer opened and evening prayer closed with a sung rendition of one of the antiphons dedicated to the Virgin. The most common hymn was the 'Salve Regina',[3] normally sung in Latin if only the expatriate Brothers were present, or recited or sung in English for the benefit of Zambians who did not know the Latin version. Whatever language was used, the tune remained that of the solemn plaintive plainchant. The words speak of the Christian's sorrowful exile on earth, an exile that can be mitigated by the loving gaze of the Virgin:

> Hail, Holy Queen, Mother of Mercy! Hail, Our Life, Our Sweetness, and Our Hope. To thee do we cry, poor banished children of Eve. To thee, do we send up our sighs, mourning and weeping in this valley of tears. Turn then, most gracious advocate, your eyes of mercy towards us. And after this, our exile, show unto us the Blessed Fruit of thy womb, Jesus. Oh clement, oh loving, oh sweet Virgin Mary.

Mary was officially proclaimed Queen of Heaven by Pope Pius XII in 1954, four years after the proclamation of the Assumption. It has been pointed out that the sovereignty of Mary and its cult could be read as a great distortion of Christ's idealism as expressed in the Sermon on the Mount (Warner 1990). Yet this is but one aspect of Mary. Yes, she is depicted as triumphant, but her triumph is not merely temporal. Its essence, according to Warner, is the victory over human weakness and evil, a conquest no more clearly depicted than in her virginity and through her own immaculate conception. It is in this aspect that Mary provides a model for celibate religious to follow for a life of chastity.

Every evening the Brothers assembled before evening prayer to recite the rosary, a meditation on certain aspects of Christ's life, 'the Joyful, Sorrowful and Glorious Mysteries', at crucial moments of which Mary is always discreetly present. Conscious of the care that Mary has for her children, the Brothers' Rule encourages them to go to Mary 'as children' and to place in her a 'child-like confidence'. Here is just one of the many opportunities the Brothers have to seek the intercession of the Virgin Mary, the mother whose son, Christ, can deny her nothing (cf. Christian 1989: 175). Each decade begins with one 'Our Father', and is concluded with the doxology, the 'Glory be'. In between these prayers are ten 'Aves' or 'Hail Marys'. The Hail Mary begins with Gabriel's greeting at the Annunciation and ends with a plea for assistance: 'Hail Mary, Full of Grace, The Lord is with thee. Blessed are you among women and blessed is the fruit of your womb, Jesus. Holy Mary, Mother of God, Pray for us sinners, Now and at the hour of our death. Amen.'

According to Warner (1990: 316), the Virgin gives Christ a human face because she can be so hailed. Further, in the Catholic tradition, where no one is promised a millennium and each awaits his or her own judgement at the end of linear time, the Mother of Mercy can circumvent God's justice: she can plead humanity's cause before the judgement seat (ibid.: 323).

The rosary was recited antiphonally, each member of the Community taking it in turn to say the first half of the 'Ave', the rest of the Community completing the second half. Thus the prayer was passed from one to the other. The Brothers were conscious both of the individual members of the Community and also of their corporate existence as they moved together through the private space of the grounds of their residence. They recited this prayer while walking up and down their garden, aided by a set of rosary beads or, by preference, a ring with a crown of ten points on it.[4] It was an activity that intrigued many students unfamiliar with the rosary. The ring may well have been preferred, I suggest, because it was less obtrusive and presented a more 'masculine' image, although, of course, it may also have acted as a symbol of the Brother's 'marriage' to religious life, if not to the Virgin. Some Brothers appeared to be sensitive to any action that might cast doubt upon their machismo, that might threaten their manhood. Was this, perhaps, all the more salient because the vow of celibacy in religious life denied them the avenues of expressions of sexuality and responsibilities of fatherhood, which other men could use to demonstrate their potency to others? It seemed almost as if Mary, declared 'Mother of the Church' at the Second Vatican Council, had the potential to embarrass, like mothers attending Sports Day or Prizegiving at school.

The Spanish Brothers had a surprising degree of ambivalence towards Mary, or at least the Marian cult, expressed in the rosary and elsewhere. This was all the more unexpected for the Brothers whose family origins lay in northern Spain, an area formerly noted for its particular devotion to Mary (Christian 1989). William Christian documents that metaphors of parenthood and models of family, especially in relation to Mary and God the Father, have developed over hundreds of years during which, in contrast, the cult of saints has markedly declined. Marian devotion has encouraged a sense of intimacy and affection for Mary (ibid.: 172). Even the post-Second Vatican Council period, which sought to encourage a different sense of church and a greater awareness of social issues, has done nothing to dent the popularity of the role of Mary as mother (ibid.: 184).

The other fixed point of the day when the Virgin was vividly recalled was during the evening prayer, towards the end of which is the 'Magnificat' canticle, Mary's triumphant hymn, recorded in Luke's Gospel:

> My soul proclaims the greatness of the Lord, my spirit rejoices in God my Saviour; for he has looked with favour on his lowly servant, and from this day all nations will call me blessed. The Almighty has done great things for me; holy is his name. He has mercy on those who fear him in every generation. He has shown the strength of his arm, he has scattered the proud in their conceit. He has cast down the mighty from their thrones, and has lifted up the lowly. He has filled the hungry with good things, and has sent the rich away empty. He has come to the help of his servant Israel for he has remembered his promise of mercy, the promise he made to our fathers, to Abraham and his children forever.

The prayer is an intricate set of biblical motifs, images and echoes, but one theme predominates: the ultimate triumph of humility. Linked to the virtues of docility and simplicity, humility is the virtue *par excellence* that the young Brothers should cultivate, according to the Brothers' Constitutions and Statutes and the Formation Guide. Mary brought up Jesus at Nazareth, 'hidden and unknown in the world'; the same simplicity, enthusiasm and love should inform the Brothers' apostolic work with young people.

Mary played a complex role in the life of the Brothers, as she does in the life of the Catholic Church. Despite, or perhaps because of, the negligible amount of information that exists in the Gospels and elsewhere about her, she is a rich symbolic source. The Founder's love for Mary is said to have equalled his love for Jesus. Despite this image of harmony and balance, there was a paradox. These Spanish religious clearly asserted and exhibited an ethos of machismo and yet they dedicated their bodies, lives and wills to the imitation of Mary as a feminine ideal. Their residence was tightly gendered as a male space and being strong, being 'real men' seemed important to them. Some would even go to the extent of disguising quite serious illness, rather than be thought to be weak. Possibly, this may be a more general feature of Catholic religious Community life: Burke (1990) has observed similar reactions to illness among Catholic nuns in Zaire.

When illness or temporary incapacity rendered a Brother dependent upon other members of the Community, the phrase most often ironically used was that the others who ministered to his needs were 'like mothers' to him. It was an irony that, in some cases, I read as an attempt to mask the expression of what might be regarded as inappropriately expressed feelings of care and concern. Mothers featured very prominently in the life narratives that the Brothers shared with me in interviews, where they idealised their mothers' love and care. Each mother was notably portrayed as a woman of faith who transmitted that faith to her child, a faithful woman who had to be strong to keep a large family together, in often difficult circumstances. Although, or perhaps because, several of the Brothers left home at an early age, all recalled childhoods marked by much closeness with their mothers. The continuing strength of their attachments invigorated their communications with their families back home in Spain. Mothers were often said by the Brothers to feel acutely the absence of their sons so far away. If a parent visited a Brother on the mission, it was his mother who was the one more likely to make the journey. Fathers usually figured less prominently in the Brothers' life stories and, at times, Brothers recollected some difficult relationships with male parental figures.

According to the ethos of their Congregation, the Brothers strove to work in a self-effacing way, like Mary largely 'hidden and unknown' in everyday life at St Antony's. The school itself had no statue of Mary; statues of her were in the postulants' and the school Community's chapels. The Community chapel also had a large painting of the Madonna, by a former member of the Community. The school chapel had but one small icon of Mary, discreetly placed in a side chapel, not by the Brothers but by a former school chaplain.[5]

For the Brothers, Mary was a figure of importance because of her role in the history of the 'Divine Economy' of Salvation and because she was, in the Founder's phrase, their 'Ordinary Resource'; they might thus have daily recourse to her in prayer. They were acutely aware, however, that Protestant denominations at St Antony's read their devotion to Mary as little short of blasphemy. Catholics were accused by the Seventh-Day Adventists and the Born Agains of 'worshipping' Mary.

In general, the Brothers expressed great reluctance to bring up the devotion to Mary in their everyday communication with the students. One or two Brothers even commented that, despite their presence at St Antony's, there was 'nothing Marian' about their school. They explained that in such a context they thought their devotion would be misunderstood: students would mistake devotion to Mary to be the 'worship' of her, worship that belonged to God alone. It was, they feared, not only the students who might misunderstand them. When a visiting Polish priest, zealous in his devotion to Mary, persuaded Catholic and non-Catholic in-patients at the clinic to recite the rosary, the Brothers were embarrassed by what they judged to be the manipulation of a captive audience. Brother Tomas, upset by what he considered to be an unacceptable intrusion and embarrassed by the fact that I had become aware of the event, commented to me, 'Well, now – there's something for your diary!'

Brothers were also aware that it was extremely difficult to allow a woman, even the mother of God, such prominence in a context in which girls and women were judged to be inferior to boys and men. The Brothers were critical of the prevailing attitudes towards the position of women held by many students, some teachers and indeed by many male African religious. As a result, they considered it almost impossible to promote a feminine model to be admired and emulated.

The way in which devotion to Mary was understood at St Antony's was part of a more general process. It is the process in which the mission project becomes muted or changed because of the dynamics of the field in which the missionaries operate (cf. Huber 1988: xi). Each mission station, because of its internal composition and because of the dynamics of the cultural field in which it seeks to operate, becomes a distinct mission of its own (see Huber 1988: 81 and 200). Marian Catholic 'tradition', so inflexible in ortho-dox discourse, was in practical discourse continually up for reinterpretation. Some aspects were clearly articulated while others were muted or, indeed, at an individual level rejected altogether. This is not to deny evident contin-uities, but merely to recognise the complexities of the interaction between the missionaries themselves and between missionaries and 'missionised'.

The postulant master, Brother Miguel, made an abortive attempt in May, a month dedicated to Mary, to encourage some Catholic students to join him in reciting the rosary. At the first meeting, he discovered that the students did not know the words of the prayer; on the second, no one turned up. The parish had a group of the Legion of Mary, but the expatriate Brothers played no role within this group.[6] This absence may have reflected their reluctance to get involved in local religious life. It may also, however, have indicated the ambivalence and embarrassment that some of the Spanish Brothers experienced towards the person and cult of Mary. She was at once a devotional subject, a trusted and distrusted mother, a religious focus of contention, and, for some Spanish Brothers, an index of a crisis of confidence and identity.

Mary was a contested figure even within the Brothers' Communities, especially with regard to devotion to her in ritual practice. She was seen by some Spanish Brothers as merely a historical figure, but one who provided a model of how to live the Christian life. Brother Francisco, critical of the Formation programme, the religious induction offered to young Zambians who desired to join the Brothers' Congregation, mentioned that while he was 'off all devotions', he still had a sense of relation to Mary. He had to 'confess', nevertheless, that he saw Mary 'more in the shade', a historical figure who offered a model of life to be followed, and thus cast doubt on the value of praying to her for assistance. Even though he was a Brother, he explained, this did not make him 'a defender of Mary'. He made no secret of his lack of enthusiasm for Marian devotion, often absenting himself from the Community rosary or arriving very late and not joining in the prayer.

Brother Roberto, an experienced formator charged with the induction of new Brothers and the discernment of their vocation, admitted that he did not know how he saw her. He was 'still a bit confused'; he had the experience of her presence although he could not articulate it. When teaching Mariology to young African Brothers, he found it best to speak of her as 'the Beloved One among the Good Spirits', in this way drawing upon his understanding of the African 'tradition' of belief in the positive active role of ancestral spirits.

Brother Miguel called Mary 'the heart of it all'. He was attracted to her 'as the slave of the Lord'. For him, being a Brother meant belonging to Mary. This gave him 'an attitude of mind, confidence, peace and a way of living'. She was always there, and he felt confident in the decisions he made because he knew that Mary was the one really making the decisions, not him. The person of Mary and the person of God appeared to collapse into one: 'In other words, it is not me acting in the deep [that is, in his innermost self], it is her. It is God.'

Another formator, Brother Juan, preferred to see Mary both in the aspect of mother and in that of 'the woman of our dreams', a 'girlfriend' with whom, as a celibate religious, he could have a 'pure relationship'. He also suggested that Brothers could also be mothers to others. However, he was conscious of how difficult it would be to suggest such an idea to young African Brothers.

For many Brothers, Mary was the good mother who could be trusted by those who placed their trust in her. Some Zambian Brothers were already familiar with Marian devotion because of their mother's membership of the Legion of Mary, but others often had initial difficulty concerning the use of statues and images of Mary. Brother Paul, a novice, explained how he was beginning to understand Marian devotion:

> At first I was very much against it – like going to a statue of Mary. Maybe you kneel there and you start praying. I was taking it as praying to that small thing there ... Even now I don't understand it very much, but I do understand that when we are there we don't really pray to that statue there. That statue is maybe just to help us.

After such initial difficulty, young candidates did not appear to have problems accepting Mary in the way she was presented to them. They often reported that they had discovered Mary and understood her role for the first time. Former members of other churches, such as the Seventh-Day Adventists, declared that, prior to their initiation, they had been very much against any devotion to the Virgin. Once discovered, the aspect of Mary as mother, as protectress of the child Jesus, had greatest resonance for them; so, too, did the fact she was said to have been always at his side throughout his life. For those who venerated her, she would also be a mother and protectress. Linked to the notion of maternal care was that of respect. They spoke of how all mothers should be respected and how the mother of Jesus was worthy of much greater respect.

Here local constructions of personhood and local categories of value came into play. To respect an individual, one had to give respect to that individual's parents. In the words of one of the novices, Brother Peter:

> The point is that Mary is the mother of Christ and we cannot respect only Jesus and then we forget about Mary who is his mother. Like, I cannot respect you and forget about your parents and say they are nothing. If I really want to please you and to respect you fully, I have to respect your parents as well, for you to be happy.

In spite of being 'only a woman', Mary was said to have been able to do great things. Several of the young Brothers told how they experienced Mary's love and care in their everyday lives, especially in the support she gave them to persevere in their vocation.

Among Catholic students, the person of Mary had little or no appeal. They saw no value in the notion of her virginity. In their terms, infertility went with virginity, and they rejected it because of the great value they placed on fertility and reproduction.[7] Others, like the Born Agains, cited 'worshipping Mary' and the use of 'idols' such as statues, pictures and rosary beads, as one of the most serious faults in the Catholic Church. Christ was the sole mediator. What was important was to be saved. Mary was 'only a woman' and could not act as an intercessor. Constructing a special place for Mary was completely unscriptural. She did not remain a virgin all her life. Jehovah's Witnesses also centred attacks on the problem of Mary. She was simply the means through which Jesus came to earth. If he had come 'straight from heaven', he would not have been accepted. Seventh-Day Adventists expressed similar views: for them she had no role in the story of Salvation and it was a grave error to 'worship' her. The construction of Mary's biography, and the relevance of this biography to individual lives, provided an area of contestation. Behind this was an array of different readings of the Christian narrative, and of how this narrative should be appropriated by the 'true' Christian.

ATTITUDES TO WOMEN AT ST ANTONY'S

The general and most widely shared public attitude towards girls and women in the formerly all-male school environment was extremely negative. Nevertheless, the Brothers insisted on admitting girls as day-scholars. Former students told me that, when they learned of this, they felt the school had been 'somehow contaminated'. Toilets and showers were constructed for the girls, and the common reaction in the school was that the Brothers were 'wasting money on useless girls'. Male students and many male Zambian teachers alike attributed the recent decline in examination performance solely to the presence of girls.[8] This perception of affairs was quite at variance with the facts. The school had very few girls, never more than about a dozen at any one time, and none passed the exam which, at the end of the first two years, would have enabled them to proceed into the senior school. However, four girls, relatives of teachers, had transferred into the senior school from elsewhere. Indeed, few girls actually presented themselves for the exams: they tended to drop out in the course of the first two years, either because of lack of family support or, more frequently, because of pregnancy.

The young women spoke of the difficulties they experienced in trying to get a secondary education and of the work they were expected to do, once their school day was over. The boys had mocked them a great deal, when they had first come to school. Being few, they had felt 'awkward' surrounded by so many boys. Emelia, a Grade Nine day scholar, recounted, 'We used to feel shy. And they used to mock us. They used to tell us, "You're not supposed to be here. You are in the wrong school. This school is a boys' school. And we don't expect one in a skirt to be here!"' The girls also told of the enormous pressure they felt under from some students and certain teachers; several of their contemporaries had been misled by promises of marriage into relationships that had left them pregnant and abandoned.

Two of the school's female teachers were Catholics, one from Eastern Province and the other from North-Western Province. The third, from Southern Province, was a member of the Seventh-Day Adventist Church. One of the Catholics, Mrs Phiri, was married to another teacher and had two young children; the other, Mrs Kimbinyi, was a widow with three young children. The third teacher, Miss Milambo, was a single mother. All spoke of the difficulties they experienced in making their voices heard in the male-dominated environment of the school. They had found the boys at first reluctant to trust them as competent teachers. Their own biographies revealed the difficulties they had experienced in gaining an education, in families where it was thought much more important to educate their brothers. Mrs Kimbinyi said that among her people, the Kaonde, a man who produced 'only' daughters would not win the respect of the community – girls were thought to be much inferior to boys. Hence her needs were only attended to after her brothers had all been taken care of. Her father, she said, preferred to spend time with his sons, 'praising them', rather than his daughters. According to the other Catholic, Mrs Phiri, girls were 'not given much respect' in the family. The slogan was: 'Boys leave a name but girls don't'. She gave the example of her own mother: 'When my sister got married, my mother used to say, "These are not my children, my grandchildren, but those who will come from a man, a son, they are my grandchildren. These are for somebody else."'

Miss Milambo, the Adventist, attributed the fact that she had received her education to the influence of missionaries in the area who had taught the importance of educating women. Her own father had been in favour of her going to secondary school, in the face of considerable opposition within her extended family. Miss Milambo described this opposition in some detail:

> The relatives of my father would come and demand that I stop schooling. Yes! Even on the opening day, they would come. If my father hadn't received his cheque from the cooperative, he would select one of his animals and sell it and give me the money I needed for boarding school. Now, you see, for the Tongas to do that, it's a taboo! What are the other relatives going to inherit? So they would come and shout at us, shout at my mother. Just on the day of going to school. They wanted just my brothers to go to school, but then my father had to struggle and say 'No!'

The three women all said their mothers had not encouraged them to desire education, for 'traditionally' the mothers would be wrong 'to speak out in the family'. Furthermore, their mothers, who 'didn't like girls', believed their daughters should 'pass through' where they in turn had passed, that is, they should marry early. Their daughters' desire for school was interpreted within the family as a sign of indiscipline. In two cases, the mothers were blamed for producing daughters instead of sons. Still, these teachers thought that in general the position of women in Zambia was slowly improving. They felt that within their own relationships with men, it was up to them to 'struggle for respect'. It was not something that would be automatically given to them.

Despite the lack of 'respect' publicly given to the girls, the boys explained that the introduction of girls had also brought unwanted distractions into the school. The presence of girls in the classroom was said to make it very difficult to concentrate. Boys also said many of them had to pay more attention to, and thus spend more time on, their own personal appearance because they now had to compete for the girls' attention. Their limited financial resources were also stretched because of this.

Girls and women were generally said by the male students to be weak-willed, lacking in intelligence and physical strength, and easily possessed by spirits. Most importantly of all, girls and women were said to be both 'unpredictable' and 'treacherous' and therefore not to be trusted in relation-ships, however innocent they might appear. It was said that a boy might think he was engaged in an exclusive relationship with a particular girl, only to discover later that he was merely one of several partners. The majority of students found that the idea of a platonic relationship with a woman made no sense. When Zambian priests were observed by students waiting at the back of the church at the end of services to greet the congregation on their way out, they were commonly suspected of arranging assignations with a number of women.

The theme of 'treacherous' women was frequently depicted in the students' drama club performances and formed the substance of many tales told and retold in the dormitories at night. 'Good-looking' boys, those said to 'look like girls', or those whose manner was judged to be effeminate took the female parts. Girls did not appear on stage. One drama sketch, impro-vised by students for Africa Freedom Day celebrations, depicted a young woman, called Rhoda, who decided to cheat on her husband when he was called away to visit his sick grandfather. She arranged a series of visits by men she had contacted in advance, during a shopping trip to town. They promised her money in return for her favours and she dreamt of all the things she would do with her gains. To howls of delight from the student audience, Rhoda's plans fell apart when all the men arrived at the same time and her husband also returned unexpectedly. At the end of the sketch, in which the husband died in a fight with one of the visitors, the club chairman returned to the stage to emphasise the moral to be learnt. His address to the audience neatly juxtaposed alleged differences in black and white attitudes towards women: 'Guys, never trust a woman. You go to town, you find a beautiful girl. Watch out! She may not be alone! Though the white man says, "A woman is for loving", be careful!'

At St Antony's, the Brothers, dedicated to the Virgin Mary, strove in some respects to be like her. Because of this, they tried to bring more female students into the school, and they drew attention to, and expressed great sympathy with, the plight of many of the young mothers who lived nearby. The Brothers judged their lives to be particularly difficult since they were often left with the care and education of their children with little or no support from the children's fathers. The Brothers also considered that women in Zambia carried the greater burden in the daily struggle for survival and yet their contribution often went unrecognised. The missionaries sought to alleviate this burden and encouraged young women's potential through offering them mission education. Again and again they met with opposition from students and teachers of all denominations, who were convinced that 'education' at St Antony's should remain a 'male' endeavour, free from the pollution of women.

VOCATION AND RECRUITMENT AT ST ANTONY'S

An area of contestation at St Antony's that was more theological in nature was the question of vocation. From their earliest days in Zambia, the Brothers attempted to recruit young Zambians to their Congregation, but their first attempts came to nothing (Simpson 1996: 232ff.). At the beginning of the 1980s the interest in attracting vocations to Catholic religious life was renewed. Vocations Directors were appointed among all religious Congregations and diocesan clergy, and they formed an association in which they could pool ideas and experiences. The result was that a number of them decided to go on recruitment exercises together in the central part of Zambia, and they visited St Antony's each year.

Designed to attract young Zambians to Catholic religious life, the recruitment exercise was conducted within an environment where the hostility was only partially veiled. While Catholic students, on the whole, remained largely unmoved, the exercise opened up a space in which fundamentalist students, more or less gently, challenged the Catholic narrative of vocation and formation. In doing this, they defined themselves, at least in part, by what they were not. It was subjective definition through the polemical negation of rival others.

An important part of my knowledge of Catholic vocation at St Antony's came from the Brothers' Vocations Director, Brother Lara, who was also the Regional Superior and an active member of the Vocations Team. Each year he hosted the visit of the team to the school and travelled with them extensively in Lusaka and Southern Province. I accompanied him on some of his recruitment exercises, both when he was working with the team and when he was operating alone. In the second term of 1991 the team came to St Antony's.

The recruitment exercise bore certain resemblances to a jobs fair. The meeting was held in the school hall, during the period timetabled for evening study. Students had the choice of remaining in class or going to the meeting. The visit was announced to the students by Brother Henry, the sole young Zambian Brother on the school staff at the time of my fieldwork. Head of the Religious Education Department, he was himself soon to leave the Brothers. From the start, he made it clear, at the prompting of the Vocations Director, that the meeting was primarily for Catholics, although Christians of other denominations could attend if they wished. In the event, among the few senior students in attendance, the majority were indeed from other denominations: Seventh-Day Adventists and Born-Agains.

The Vocations Team included three nuns: a Zambian from the Congregation set up by the former archbishop of Lusaka, Archbishop Milingo,[9] called the Daughters of the Redeemer, an English Franciscan Sister and a German Dominican nun. Having travelled together, they arrived early in the afternoon, had ample time to approach the few girls in the school, and left after sharing supper with the rest of the Vocations Team and the Brothers' Community. The Brothers themselves were not unequivocally enthusiastic about the team's visit, although they did not show this to the visitors.

Among the men's Congregations, only five groups had representatives present at St Antony's: three of them belonging to Brothers' Congregations or to Congregations that had both Brothers and priests, plus the school Community's own Vocations Director. The fifth member was a Zambian Jesuit novice, the only one to represent the priesthood explicitly. The Zambian priest who was the diocesan recruiter had decided to stay behind in the nearby town.

Spread out around the hall were a number of stands with information about each religious Congregation and about the diocesan clergy. One or two stands had been put up by members of the team on behalf of team members who were not present. The stands had a number of posters and a large number of photographs, where possible depicting local religious communities in which there were a reasonable number of black faces. Some information was more imaginatively displayed. The American member of the team, Brother Bob, representing a religious Congregation with both priests and Brothers, had on his stand a range of visual aids including mobiles, a mock television and a mock computer complete with flashing lights. Brother Bob's inventiveness and enthusiasm had not, however, been rewarded by a flood of vocations. Despite years of dedicated recruitment work, his community had yet to retain a Zambian recruit.

Approximately eighty students and three Zambian teachers were present. The students were from all grades in the school, but the highest grade, the 'school leavers' of Grade Twelve, was poorly represented by only half a dozen students. None of the Grade Twelve students present could be thought of as a 'likely candidate' because they were leaders in either the Seventh-Day Adventists or Born-Again groups. Their affiliation was not known by any of the members of the Vocations Team, apart from the local Vocations Director who would have been able to identify at least one or two of them. The presence of these particular groups of non-Catholics seemed to result from a desire on their part to monitor the activities and strategies of the 'opposition'. If muted, they effectively sustained the covert side of the religious contestation in which they were daily involved. Their own positions were to be more clearly observed in their efforts to recruit and initiate students. This work of conversion had both public and less public faces within the school compound.

Brother Lara started the meeting by introducing briefly all the members of the Vocations Team and adding that they would explain 'what vocation is all about'. He then handed over to Brother Bob, who gave a lengthy explanation of the meaning of vocation to religious life. It was, Brother Bob stressed, a call from God to follow one of three possible vocation routes. These also included the vocation to marriage and the vocation to priesthood. Drawing explicit parallels with marriage, a wedding ring repeatedly symbolised commitment. Brother Bob explained that one way to follow Jesus, religious life, was made up of three stages: initiation, engagement when one took first or temporary vows, and final commitment when one took vows for life. At stages one and two, the young brother was always free to leave and, if it was decided that this was best for the individual and for the Community, there would be 'no shame' on either himself or his family.

Brother Bob extolled the communal nature of religious life. It offered a common life of prayer and work in a Community, the members of which 'share everything' including, as a practical example, the resident Vocations Director's double-cab vannette. When Brother Lara left Zambia, said Brother Bob, he would not be taking the vannette with him as the vehicle belonged to the Community, even though he had the temporary use of it. A number of students groaned, and some laughed, as a cynic in the audience muttered audibly, 'Perhaps he *will* take it with him. How do we know?' Indeed, the students had never seen any other Brother drive this vehicle.

Brother Bob went on to outline the entrance requirements. For acceptance to one of the sixteen Catholic religious Congregations, one needed to be a practising Catholic, both baptised and confirmed, single and without children, physically fit, 'balanced', with a reasonably good Grade Twelve certificate, with no financial obligations or debts, and with parental consent.

After this lengthy general introduction, each member of the team was called upon to give an outline of his group, their charism – the particular spirit of their founder and their Congregation – and their work in Zambia and beyond. All started with the biography of their Founder, highlighting the moment of revelation which led to the foundation of their particular Congregation. The person and charism of the Founder were given particular emphasis, as was the notion that those who became his followers did so in order to continue his work. Identification and continuity were key themes. With the exception of the Jesuit, all the other team members belonged to Congregations founded in France in the wake of the French Revolution, which was characterised by Brother Lara, when his turn came to describe the Brothers' Congregation and their work, as 'against religion'.

In his description, the local Vocations Director was at pains to stress that, although the Brothers were dedicated to the Virgin Mary, they did not, despite claims to the contrary by others, treat her as a goddess. The unnamed others were, of course, the Seventh-Day Adventists and the Born-Agains. Brother Lara repeated, 'We don't worship Mary: we honour her. She is the means to go to Jesus and to bring youth to Jesus.' Brother Lara went on to emphasise the international aspects of the Congregation, working in over seventy countries including seventeen in Africa. The training itself was outlined with the same attractive international flavour as were the training programmes of other groups.

For these Brothers, after a period of candidacy including attendance at one or more workshops at the Juniorate, came a period of postulancy at the Juniorate in Zambia. Successful completion of the postulancy led to a two-year novitiate at the Regional Novitiate in Zimbabwe, at the end of which the young Brother took temporary vows. Next came a three-year post-novitiate Formation programme at the Brothers' International Centre in Nairobi, and on completion of that either a degree or a diploma validated by a Roman university.

The vows Brother Lara named were chastity, obedience and simplicity, 'simplicity' being substituted for the more usual name of 'poverty'. The substitution was indicative of the problems that the notion of 'religious poverty' posed for Zambians, and for at least some of the Spanish missionaries. Throughout the evening, Brother Lara maintained unmistakably the authoritative stance, voice, gaze and manner of a rather stern teacher; consequently, the message he offered was felt to be cold, distant and somewhat offputting. His strategy was perhaps defensive, anticipating and guarding against possible expressions of hostility from sections of his audience. No one could doubt that he was determined to remain in control of proceedings which might easily get out of hand. He concluded by announcing a time for questions, adding the proviso, evidently based on past experience, that students should keep 'to the topics under discussion'. He would not have questions about 'Why Mary? Why the Pope?', questions he would be prepared to discuss on another occasion.

There were few questions, none of them about the 'forbidden' topics.

One Grade Eleven Catholic student asked what would happen if his Grade Twelve results were not good enough to meet the entry requirements, when he 'really wanted to serve God'. The issue of entry requirements was a contentious one among the Brothers themselves. While some insisted that all who joined had to have sufficient academic ability for teacher training, others pointed to the Founder, who had been very weak at school, and the first Brothers, who were barely literate. By direct resort to the Founder's biography, the early history of the Congregation and the biographies of the first Brothers, some sought to demonstrate that insisting on qualifications was directly against the spirit of the Founder. It was a moot point, one among a number of others, in which members of the Community disputed the lessons to be drawn from the life of the Founder. What was at issue was fidelity to his charism. What would the Founder have done if he had been in the Brothers' position? The situation was further complicated by the fact that Brothers in neighbouring Malawi required much lower educational qualifications and on the surface appeared to be much more successful in recruiting young Brothers, although the issue of qualifications was only one aspect in a complicated picture.

The youth who asked the question was told by Brother Bob that he would have to repeat Grade Twelve and resit his exams. This suggestion was greeted by loud groans from the students, who evidently felt that in such a situation the Brothers should help. The student went on to ask whether, if the Brothers thought that he was interested in joining, they would help him in his studies? In response, Brother Bob told the student that he might or might not receive help, but he should not count on it because 'you are offering something to God, you are not looking for help'. More groans and murmurs came from the students who evidently judged the Brother's response to be unreasonable. Some Communities had, in fact, offered academic assistance and board and lodging to help students to resit exams, but had been disappointed by the failure of even one of those assisted to become a Brother.

A Grade Twelve Seventh-Day Adventist choir member, confined to a wheelchair, commented in a challenging tone, 'So, there is no place for people like me, then?' He was assured that, provided his disability did not prevent him from making an active contribution to the particular work of the Congregation, then no obstacle need bar his joining them. One of the teachers present, a young Zambian bachelor Seventh-Day Adventist who had been educated by Catholic Brothers in Western Province, asked why there were so many different Catholic religious Congregations. Would it not be better to have just one or two? Brother Bob countered by explaining that the different groups stressed different aspects and witnessed in different ways. This, he argued, was 'the richness of the Catholic Church, a richness that many other churches have lost'.

A Grade Eleven student followed up the teacher's observation by saying:

'It's confusing! How are we to know which is the right one for us?' Brother Lara responded rather stridently with a series of questions: 'What is your inclination? What is God pushing you to do in life?' He went on to emphasise that, in the Spanish Brothers' case, their emphasis was on educating young people, especially the disadvantaged. He then rather abruptly brought the question-and-answer session to an end by asking the students to stand and recite the prayer for vocations which had been distributed on small cards and which the students were encouraged to take away and to recite privately. The prayer read as follows:

> Lord make me a better person, more considerate towards others, more honest with myself, more faithful to you. Help me to find my true vocation in life, and grant that through it I may find happiness myself and bring happiness to others. Grant, Lord, that those whom you call to enter the priesthood or the religious life may have the generosity to answer your call, so that those who need your help may always find it. We ask this through Christ our Lord. Amen.

Printed below this was a slogan and the name and address of a priest in England from whom further information about vocations might be obtained. The slogan read:

GOD'S PATH FOR YOUR LIFE IS MADE ESPECIALLY FOR YOU AND NO ONE ELSE BUT YOU CAN TRAVEL IT!

After the prayer, Brother Lara announced there was time for another look at the stands and for a talk, on an individual basis, with any member of the Vocations Team. Although students did ask questions to clarify certain points, no one present was sufficiently moved on this occasion to present himself as a potential candidate.

CONCLUSION

In the recruitment of new members, Catholic missionaries, even in their own schools, did not have it all their own way. The discernment of God's call, the movement of the Spirit, devotion to the Virgin Mary and the role of the Pope were all contested issues, at times openly, at times covertly, within the school. Religious interest came in the main not from Catholic students but from critical others – fundamentalist and Pentecostal students – ready and able to interpret the Word of God and to debate the question of a truly Christian vocation. While willingly accepting the discipline and order of the programmes of study in the Catholic school, fundamentalist students reserved the right to challenge the teaching and practice of the diffident Brothers. Catholic religious discourse offered one avenue for reconstructing, reforming and resituating the self in Christian narrative. As just one among many, that discourse was under constant threat of fragmentation.

3

ORDER AND DISCIPLINE

'God sees me at all times and in all places.'
Founder's motto to be taught to all children

St Antony's in its reality is an educational hybrid of the French Catholic ideals of the Brothers' Founder and of the English public school, a system of education exported to British colonies and dependencies, whether in Africa or elsewhere. The school is the meeting of two traditions: the Marian and the Brotherly, on the one hand, and, on the other, the boarding school. What needs to be borne in mind is that order and discipline were what students said attracted them to Catholic mission schools such as St Antony's.

The Brothers' Founder established his schools in the aftermath of the Revolution in France. Historically, his vision is from an era of radical change in discipline and surveillance, and thus in subjectivity. If Foucault's reading of the history of the period is correct,[1] the Founder, who was born in the South of France two months before the Revolution of 1789 and started the Congregation of Brothers in 1817, would seem, in his faith in the 'prophylactic power of surveillance' (Jay 1986: 192), to have been paradoxically the very child and servant of that Revolution which had appeared to him so harmful. Foucault remarks:

> A new aspect of the problem of justice for the Revolution was not so much to punish wrongdoers as to prevent even the possibility of wrongdoing, by immersing people in a field of total visibility where the opinion, observation and discourse of others would restrain them from harmful acts. This idea is constantly present in the texts of the Revolution.
> (Foucault 1980: 153)

In Foucault's account, it was the Catholic Church in France that was uniquely placed as a social body to make available to the state 'the foremen and overseers' (ibid.: 157) indispensable for the task of schooling hundreds of thousands of children.

Historians' descriptions illuminate the complexities surrounding developments in educational institutions in eighteenth and nineteenth-century France, descriptions which assist in contextualising the Founder's educational vision.[2] Indeed, there was, both in Europe and North America, 'a visible 19th-century public discourse ... [in which] the school was seen as a politically productive space for the creation of human subjects' (Corrigan et al. 1986: 25).

Eighteenth-century France probably had a greater range of educational institutions, from 'little schools' to universities, than any other European country, although the institutions were 'badly distributed and lacked any central co-ordination' (Jones, R. 1990: 82). The spread of primary schooling had been a gradual process mainly administered by the Catholic Church (Goubert 1991: 245; Heffernan 1992: 150). Schools run by religious Congregations had been subject to tight Church controls (Gemie 1992: 131). While the Revolution had seemed to achieve nothing definitive in the field of education, it did initiate significant steps of continuing importance both to Catholic schools and to the French system of education, when the responsibility for schools shifted back and forth between church and state towards the end of the eighteenth century (McMahon 1992: 114; Piveteau 1967).

Under Napoleon a certain uniformity began to emerge, especially with the introduction in 1808 of a national examination system (Jones, R. 1990: 85). By this time, the De La Salle Brothers and numerous other groups of teaching Sisters had been restored (Piveteau 1967: 7). Teaching methods during this period shifted through a series of innovations. First came the 'individual' method, in which each child was given individual tuition in turn. Later, the 'mutual' method was introduced. Approved by the Imperial University, it relied on monitors to undertake teaching work. Next was the 'simultaneous' method, made popular by the De La Salle Brothers, which employed a complex system of signs and signals to enable a single teacher to control classes of up to 150 pupils. An alternative was the 'mixed' method which combined elements of the two (Gemie 1992: 142; Hamilton 1989: 60, and see Foucault 1977).

McMahon (1992: 118) draws attention to a document (cited in Gemie 1992), drawn up by the Lyon *arrondissement* committee, which typifies the manner in which teachers were expected to perform and highlights the importance of order and discipline. Of the eighty rules listed, thirty-seven concerned 'instruction', which included such topics as catechism classes, merit cards and the length of time the school was to be opened; thirty-one outlined disciplinary practices; twelve described the physical setting of the ideal classroom; and six concerned religious and moral instruction:

> According to their rules, school rooms were to be large, well lit and airy, with their benches secured to the floor, and a bust of the king and a crucifix prominently displayed above the teacher's desk. Furniture and other fittings were to be arranged in such a way that the pupils would never escape the teacher's eye ... The committee firmly forbade the use of corporal punishment, arguing that a teacher who hit a pupil was clearly a poor teacher.
> (Gemie 1992: 142–3)

The Founder strongly favoured the 'simultaneous' method. On at least one occasion, he withdrew his Brothers from a school rather than abandon this technique (Farrell 1984; McMahon 1988). His educational philosophy, especially with regard to method, and his religious Rule and Constitutions drew heavily upon those of the De La Salle Brothers.[3] Jean-Baptiste de la Salle, like many other founders of religious orders and Congregations, paid great attention to the minutest detail. His *Conduct of Christian Schools*, published in 1720, the year after his death, is a 220-page manual dealing with all aspects of school life. In it are many parallels with the Founder's educational vision; in it too is the expectation that the educational gaze should act with precision upon the bodies, the hearts and the minds of the children in the Brothers' care.

According to the orthodox biography of the Founder, *The Life of Father Founder* (1947), a text studied by all Brothers and given to young Zambians when they embark upon their induction into Brotherhood, the Founder taught the Brothers that the education of children had one sole purpose: preparation for eternal life. The Brothers were to work towards this goal through the teaching of the catechism, which would prepare the children in their care for the reception of baptism, Communion and the other sacraments. It was a task ideally to be discharged by parents but one that was neglected by the parents of the rural children he encountered. In teaching the catechism, the Founder told his Brothers: 'You perform a duty which the angels contemplate with envy' (Marian Brothers 1947: 539). The Brothers should offer other subjects as 'baits' to attract the children and their parents, but no subject was as important as catechism. A Brother who neglected the study of catechism in the classroom was guilty of serious fault; such neglect rendered the school 'altogether secular' (ibid.: 455). If children made a 'good First Communion', they already had 'one foot in heaven'. In addition, the 'true Brother' always strove to make the Virgin Mary 'loved and served by all his pupils' (ibid.: 546, 551).

The Brothers' pedagogy of simplicity, work, presence and discipline draws its inspiration from the Virgin. The Brothers' 'educational attitudes', elaborated in various documents of the Congregation, flow from Mary in three ways. First is the example of Mary as Mother, which inspires the Brothers to foster 'family values, family attitudes, family-type relationships'. In this spirit, the Brothers express their 'respectful concern' for young people, especially 'those most in need'. Mary, in the way she brought up Jesus at Nazareth, is the model from whom the Brothers learn to express patience, to bear witness, to work 'hidden and unknown', to be leaders who focus everything on Jesus.

The purpose of education was first to make the child 'a good *Christian*' and thereby also 'a virtuous *citizen*' (my emphasis). The Founder elaborated a set of methods to achieve the salvation of both the children's and the

Brothers' souls. The children must be led to understand that without the fear of God they could never be happy (ibid.: 544). The Brother, in turn, should remember that on the Day of Judgement God would demand from each Brother an account of the children placed in his care. The Founder, who often referred to his Brothers as his 'children', taught that order and discipline were the keys to success for the child and for the Brother, both in his religious life and in his role as an educator:

> Discipline constitutes half the education of the child, and, if that half is missing, then, most of the time, the other half is useless ... A Brother who has the art of securing discipline in a class, even though he may not be capable of much else, is preferable to one who may be very learned, but who either does not understand the importance of discipline, or is incapable of achieving it.
> (Marian Brothers 1947: 526)

Order and discipline were the keys to success both in the classroom and outside it. While these were the very things that the children feared most (ibid.: 579), they must be taught to realise, 'All men love order, and disorder displeases everyone, even the children themselves' (ibid.: 599). The 'greatest pest' of the day was 'the spirit of independence'; children were imperfect beings in constant need of correction, and the Brothers must be diligent in 'combating sins'. This correction, and the inculcation of piety and obedience, were never to take the form of corporal punishment, but were to be achieved through the use of reason, nurtured in a 'family spirit'.

As a child, the Founder had resolved on his first day at the village school never to return after witnessing the harsh regime inflicted upon the children in his class by the village teacher. Slow at learning academic things himself, he urged his Brothers to pay special attention to the poorest children and those who experienced the greatest difficulties in their studies. The Brothers should never employ rough tactics.

The teacher's love, although essential, was problematic for the Founder. One of his most quoted maxims is 'To educate children, one must love them, and love them all alike'. This love was to be expressed in the gentleness of the Brother's approach to those in his care. But there were to be no nicknames, nor undue familiarity. The Brother must guard himself particularly against transgressions in this regard, identified by the Founder as the greatest evil and which caused him the greatest distress. Not only was the Brother to keep watch over himself and his own inclinations towards evil; each member of the Community was to keep watch over his Brothers and report any failures to the Brother Superior. The Founder noted:

> Nothing is more opposed to the true and sincere love we owe those children than unbecoming familiarity, partiality and particular friendships ... the wise and prudent teacher never touches his pupils

with his hands, either to caress them or to punish them.
(Marian Brothers 1947: 592, 598)

A child's faults should never be exaggerated, as such a procedure was 'one of the most dangerous snares of the devil', designed to 'drive children into the devil's arms'. The antidote to the temptations of the Evil One was the example of the Brother himself, 'the guardian angel of his children' (ibid.: 583). The Virgin Mary should be the Brother's guide in the way that she brought up the Child Jesus, teaching Jesus not by word but by the example of her 'presence'. The Brother must be constantly 'present' to his charges, exercising unwearied vigilance over them: 'The Brother should never lose sight of his children by day or by night' (ibid.: 549). If he had to choose between the superintendence of the children and receiving Communion, the former should take precedence. By constant surveillance, the Brother should strive 'to render it impossible to commit evil'. The children, 'weak beings', should never be allowed to be alone or unsupervised because it was at such moments that, 'through the perverse inclinations of nature ... vice may spread ... through vicious children' (ibid.: 586–7). Furthermore, to assist in the unending struggle against the devil's wiles, all children should be taught to recite often the maxim, 'God sees me at all times and in all places'. There was to be no escape from the omniscient, omnipotent gaze. That was the vision, as it is transmitted in the Founder's official biography.

THE BEGINNINGS OF ST ANTONY'S AND ITS EARLY FORMATION

The Brothers, both French-Canadian pioneers and later Spanish missionaries, encountered a system of education somewhat different to the one they had experienced themselves, especially in matters of discipline and order. However, from their experience of teaching in Southern Rhodesia, the pioneer Brothers sent to Northern Rhodesia had already come to know schools which, although segregated, were run along the lines of the English public school.

Although this type of boarding school had its origins in Europe before the Middle Ages (Gathorne-Hardy 1979), only in the nineteenth century did it emerge as a public school *system* (Wakeford 1969: 19). This period saw 'the rise of athleticism, the intensifying disciplines, the wire entanglements of sexual obsession, the development of that rigid, uniform, totalitarian, Church-centred, class-creating, Empire-fuelling body – "the Monolith"' (Gathorne-Hardy 1979: 476). Victorian British public school education, as exemplified at Arnold's Rugby, had as its professed aim the production of 'Christian gentlemen' (Bullivant 1978: 32). The emphasis was upon sport, which Lytton Strachey termed the 'games fetish' (ibid.). The formation of the 'whole man', who was also to be a 'Christian leader', was attempted in accordance with the ethos of muscular Christianity (see Eickelman 1985:

166). As British popular education developed, the ideal of service was as important, if not more important than, the ideal of creating leaders. In this, the gentleman was schooled into knowing his place within the wider order, subordinating his own interests to 'a larger good' (Williams 1958: 329); thus such education was 'devoted to the training of servants' (ibid.).

Within this tradition, character was to be formed 'by transforming the small stuff of life into tests of character, into dramas of moral choice' (Kleinfeld 1979: 64). Control, through the maintenance of order and discipline, was felt to be a necessary prerequisite. It was for this reason that public schools took on their distinctive structure, delineating the types of social relationships among members of the student body and between students and staff. Such a structure was also to be found within Catholic religious orders and Congregations. Northern Rhodesia was thus one of many sites at which the two traditions of order and discipline became intertwined and fed off one another.

In interviews with me, pioneer Brothers foregrounded the organisational aspects of the schools, especially the house and prefect system, as fundamental aspects of discipline and order.[4] Comments, either approving or disapproving, furnished evidence of early differences between French-Canadian and Spanish Brothers. The Canadian Brothers were fulsome in their admiration of the efficiency and effectiveness of 'the British system'; the Spanish Brothers at times expressed dislike for a structure that put so much stress on hierarchy and created a distance between them and the students. Brother Francois commented, 'We were influenced by the British system right from the beginning. We found it in Southern Rhodesia. We just grew up with it. The whole system — well, we thought it was great.'

The Spanish Brothers' attitude was rather mixed. Brother Roberto was at first full of praise, commenting of his experience in Southern Rhodesia:

> Coming from Spain, we found many elements very positive – the prefect system, the academic side, the emphasis on sport. You know, also, the uniform, the tie and the white shirt at St Antony's. And in Southern Rhodesia the swimming galas – it was so typically English. After the gala, the *brai* [barbecue] – the whole thing, you know, in spite of the fact that the Rhodesians were fighting against the British – you know they were keeping their identity – totally British!

Brother Carlos explained that he was deeply disturbed by the distance between the Brothers and the students in Southern Rhodesia, suggesting that this had much to do with the Brothers' unconscious identification with the Smith regime:

> I think there was an unconscious attitude, looking to the Africans with superiority. You know, 'We are the boss' and the white men at the same time. And I think that is why most of the relationships of the

Brothers were with Whites – I found it very difficult to swallow … You know, we Spanish were much called by the concept of liberation theology. One of the main principles is that you don't help people from above, you don't teach from above. You do it by being *with* them. And this is a very strong clear point with all the Spanish Brothers.

A former headmaster, Brother Jean-Pierre, explained that it was the Zambian Deputy Principal who taught him the system: 'When I came, I had no idea at all what a prefect system would be'. He improved his own surveillance techniques with the assistance of a pair of binoculars, and spoke enthusiastically about the prefects whom he called the 'headmaster's spy system':

I mean, you may have four or five hundred students and twenty staff, and you and your staff can't be everywhere in the school. I'm not saying you shouldn't try to keep an eye. To run a school, you have to know what is happening. So I think the prefects were doing a wonderful job … I used to have meetings with prefects – to advise them – sometimes up to midnight or one in the morning. But the prefects were very good. You just had to encourage them.

Brother Roberto, while admiring the system in Southern Rhodesia, came to find the distance between the Headmaster and the students at St Antony's, and the prefect system itself, barriers when he wanted to get to know the students: 'The approach to the boys – it was all very official. In 'the boarding' the prefects were totally in charge, in the dining room etc., I was surprised. We Spanish Brothers were much more used to mixing with the students …'

Arriving in independent Zambia, Brother Juan was not happy to find the prefect system and the use of corporal punishment by the Headmaster, a practice at odds with the teachings of the Founder. Brother Carlos objected to the aggrandisement of some students at the expense of the others, conscious of the scope for abuse:

That whole system of prefects and the whole spirit behind it – a person with a certain status, a lot of abuse of the young fellows – we have this system in Spain, but totally different. To be a prefect is seen to be very much a part of the education of the individual prefect – not so much you are discharging your duties. So the Brother is always with the boys, making sure this relationship is really formative and educative …

The Brothers came to work in a school which took a shape and a structure of student power and hierarchy which militated against what were, for some of them, their most cherished ideals.

The application to establish the school was accepted in principle, subject to the availability of the appropriate grants, by the African Education Advisory Board in July 1957; it 'fitted into the territorial secondary school plan'.[5] The Archbishop and his advisers preferred a boarding school as the best way to provide adequate study facilities for a scattered population. The initial plan, to provide 300 places within the first six years, anticipated being oversubscribed, by at least ten times, by the Catholic Primary Standard Six pupils in the province.[6] The school was to cater for boys from the Catholic population, although it would be open to a proportion of non-Catholics. Brother Jean Pierre recalled early recruiting tours when he would visit Catholic primary schools and interview those boys who had applied to St Antony's. In theory, he was supposed initially to select Catholic boys on the basis of their church membership and their examination performance. He noted that many pupils 'pretended' to be Catholics in the hope of getting a secondary education: 'There was a lot of cheating, but, you see, canon law, the ruling of the church was that the Catholic school was for Catholics only. Soon the rule was dropped – in 1966, I think ...'

A school designed initially only for Catholics would develop a particular theory of continuing conversion. After Independence in Zambia, the mission schools would lose the prerogative to select their own students. Although never officially designated a National School, St Antony's would soon draw many of its students from all the provinces of Zambia. Some 200 acres of Native Trust Land, chosen by the Brothers in conjunction with the Archbishop, were initially granted for the site of the school. Permission to burn bricks on the site was given in March 1958 by the District Commissioner, who enthusiastically supported the project,[7] unlike some of the civil servants with whom the Brothers had dealings during the construction of the school. Brother Jean-Pierre spoke of some of the difficulties encountered in the early days of building the school, each stage of which depended upon government approval of work in progress for the release of funds to continue:

> There was a fellow of the government who was very much against the missionaries. Oh yes, it was remarkable. It was LEA [local education authority] schools in those days and anything not government – well, they were afraid that the missionaries would influence the Africans – you see. The British in general are nice people, but those who were there in those days were very sophisticated people. And they would come – I was there – whenever a foundation was put down, and they would never come to measure the foundation to find out if it was longer than the prescribed plan. But if it had been one inch shorter, they would have cut the grants! They were that way! ... They were very much against us ... you see the suspicion was we might influence the African people to revolt. You see, if you educate an African, you educate the future of Zambia. And at that time – I'm talking about 1961, the revolution had already started – the Kaundas, the Kapwepwes, the Harry Nkumbulas, they had started and this is what worried the Federal government in those days. That's why they were worried and

so it took a long time for us to be accepted as educators – really only after Federation, after Independence, that's when more mission schools started shooting up …

In accordance with procedures for other grant-aided schools, the government was to contribute 75 per cent of the capital expenses and the Brothers were to contribute 25 per cent from incomes in their home province in Quebec. Much of the Brothers' contribution was actually in kind – they did the building, electrical work, plumbing and decorating themselves, together with a small team of local workers. In their recollections about the early days of the school, the pioneer Brothers revealed how their sense of belonging, attachment and possession was developed through the inscription of themselves upon the material fabric of the school. Their physical involvement in its construction gave them a strong feeling of belonging, of being intimately of the place.

These first Brothers were vividly recalled, in interviews with me, by some of the builders who had worked on the first phases of construction and had retired to farms close to the school. The builders explained that they themselves were already experienced in various trades. Mr Kapandula, for example, had been employed at a Catholic mission and had worked as a builder on the Copperbelt. Mr Chimasa had done plumbing, in addition to being employed as an underground train driver in the Copperbelt mines. They had come to the site, having heard in the nearby town about plans to build 'a school for Africans'. There were very few people living in the area and plenty of animals: kudus, impalas, hyenas, leopards and even a toothless lion, named after a local stream.

In the builders' accounts, there is a noticeable blend of proximity and distance in their first encounter with the Brothers. Although they worked side by side, the workers remained 'distant companions' (Hansen 1989). Unlike the workers, who lived in huts nearby, Brother Pierre, the school's French-Canadian founder, slept in a tree for the first few months, although it was not clear to the workers why he had chosen to do this. In the cold season, he fell out of the tree during an attack of malaria and had to be taken to hospital. After that, a small mud-brick shed was constructed for him. He had his own cook and ate apart from the others. His diet consisted mostly of meat and rice and, as Mr Kapundula explained, being a white man, Brother Pierre was unable to eat the local staple, *nshima* (a thick maize porridge): 'It was too strong and took a long time by the stomach.'

Brother Pierre, the workers recalled, was a very strong man. A hard but fair taskmaster, he was 'straight' in his dealings with them and, they explained, 'He didn't like to make things cockeye.' He spoke no local language and they knew little English, but they managed to understand what he wanted them to do, as he would mime actions and say, 'Do this, do this.' Despite being their foreman and the buyer of materials, he, like the other

Brothers who came to join him, worked side by side with them. They particularly recalled how the Brothers gave them leave-pay, mealie-meal and clothes for themselves and, later, their children, in addition to their wages. The workmen assumed that Brother Pierre was a rich man because the school was 'his business'.

Permission to assemble the first students on 15 August 1960 (the feast of the Assumption of the Virgin Mary) and to begin classes the following day was granted by the Provincial Education Officer in June 1960. The Brothers were given the freedom to organise the school and the school calendar as they wished, although a forty-period week (eight times forty minutes each day) was suggested.[8] They were requested to submit copies of the school timetable and reminded that all teaching appointments had to be first approved by the Secretary for African Education, a requirement that the Brothers did not always meet at the appropriate time. Brother Jean-Pierre used himself as an example of this:

> I remember myself – not being approved on the day I got there as a teacher and, all of a sudden, the Education Officer comes, and I was told to go and hide in the toilet so that he didn't see me. Oh, yes, they could have closed the school.

The initial freedom in the day-to-day running of the school granted to the French-Canadian pioneer Brothers was transitory. The visit of school inspectors in May 1964 and their subsequent report and recommendations acted as a foundational event that defined the structure and organisation of the school very much along the lines of an English public school, complete with houses and prefects.

TESTING AUTHORITY: THE RISE OF THE PREFECTS

The immediate cause of the 1964 visit was student unrest. It was the second serious incident in the school's short existence. According to the pioneer Brothers, the time before Independence (October 1964) was a period of unease when it became something of a fashion for students throughout the country to organise strikes. There was more to it than that, however, and in the school files, I found quite a number of such incidents. The point is that the order and discipline achieved at the school was rather fragile; it was susceptible to 'unrest', periodic assaults from within the student body. Carmody (1990) reports similar disturbances at the Jesuit school at Chikuni. The only written records now surviving of the early incidents of unrest at St Antony's are copies in the school administration files of the reports submitted to the Provincial Education Officer at the time by the Brother Headmaster and the subsequent correspondence. From these, and from my interviews with some pioneer Brothers, I have reconstructed the events although I recognise that they form a one-sided account.

The first incident, which occurred in August 1962, concerned a perennial theme in Zambian and other boarding schools: the initiation or 'mockery' of newcomers by other members of the school body. As described in the Head-master's account, the initiation took the form of a parody of the baptismal rite. It is early evidence of Zambian students' gift for parody, and their pleasure in satirising figures of authority. In this example, a new boy was 'christened' by a group of Form Two boys, who drenched him with two buckets of water while the majority of the Form Two students looked on, cheering in approval.

The Headmaster, acting in concert with his staff (mostly comprised of the Brothers of his own Community), decided upon what they considered to be 'a severe though not excessive punishment', according to the Head-master's report: the Form Two boys were to go without supper that night. Although they appeared to accept their punishment, quietly attending even-ing prayers in chapel as usual, the Form Two boys proceeded to boycott the evening study and instead organised a sit-in on the dormitory veranda, refusing to speak to any member of staff. Seven 'trouble-makers', five of whom had already received written warnings about their conduct, were identified as the ringleaders, who had intimidatd the other students into complying with their direction of the boycott.[9] The seven boys were expelled from school, their school fees and deposits paid for school uniform were returned to them, and they were escorted by three staff members to the nearest railway station. The Headmaster argued, in his explanation to the Provincial Education Officer, 'there could be no remission unless we aban-doned the government of the school to the students themselves to do as they pleased.'

In this test of cultural and political strength, the students demonstrated that, despite appearing to accept the Catholic regime of the mission school, which sought to fashion a particular form of subjectivity, they retained a space in which to hold up this regime to ridicule. In this, they offered an early demonstration of the contested nature of subjectivity and the fragile nature of school discipline. Both parties, students and missionaries, demon-strated the limits of their tolerance. The Brothers also indicated the lengths they were prepared to go to regain the upper hand and restore order and discipline. Events were to prove that they had achieved no more than an uneasy truce.

'Insubordination' was at the heart of the more serious disturbances in March 1964 (some seven months before Independence), after which all the Form Five pupils, the first cohort of Form Fives to pass through the school, were expelled along with thirteen boys from other classes. According to the Headmaster's report, the staff considered the Form Fives to be very weak academically. A number of them had been rejected by, or expelled from, other mission schools or minor seminaries.[10]

The Headmaster identified the root of the problem in the fact that, from the very beginning of their final year, 'the Form Five students showed that they wanted to be treated in a special way'. Indeed, I would judge that they wanted to be treated with deference, like *gentlemen*, as a mark of their distinction, and this is evident from their actions and their demands. Among other things, they directed the students of lower grades to dish out their food for them because 'they had no time to do it for themselves' (Headmaster's report). They had requested 'a ballroom dance club', asked to be allowed to study after the other students had gone to bed, and were regularly arriving late for meals and for sports in which they exhibited an increasing reluctance to participate. It is ironic that the inspectors would recommend some of the very markers of distinction and hierarchy that the Form Five rebellion was designed to achieve, for example they would get, among other things, their own 'ballroom dance club'. According to the club's first constitution, eligibility for membership was 'by subscription', and depended upon 'attire – the possession of a jacket, ability to dance and good behaviour' (School administration files 1965).

Matters came to a head when some of the students started dodging classes, among them Religious Education. In reaction to the corporal and other punishment administered by the Headmaster (corporal punishment, of course, contradicted one of the Founder's cherished ideals), the Form Five students staged a demonstration in front of his office, later delivering to him a letter which asked for their grievances to be resolved 'or else something very serious will happen'. Later that evening, the whole school demonstrated in front of the Headmaster's office, shouting him down when he attempted to address them. On one blackboard someone had written 'We want no school'; on another 'Massaka ... Death!'

The Headmaster decided to call the police. Discovering the telephone wires had been cut, he dispatched a Brother to town to summon the police who arrived around midnight, and their presence persuaded the students to retire for the night. After a series of other incidents the following day, the Headmaster expelled the Form Fives and the thirteen others, all of whom were taken away in the school lorry under police escort. All except two students were readmitted only two days later, having submitted written apologies and signed undertakings of future good behaviour.

The upshot of the disturbance was the visit of the inspectors at the request of the Permanent Secretary for Education. They were to investigate whether the causes of the trouble in March 1964 still existed and to recommend whatever changes they considered necessary to forestall a further outbreak. They were requested to report on the relationships between staff and students and to assess the ability of the teaching staff, as some student demands had called this into question (Inspectors' report, May 1964).

While 'considerably impressed' by much of what they saw, the inspectors did report witnessing 'some rather lifeless teaching' and, more importantly, noted 'serious organizational weaknesses' in the way the school was run. They described the Brothers as 'a cheerful, warm-hearted, intelligent lot', supported by three 'keen' expatriate lay volunteers and one 'loyal and capable' African teacher 'who should go far'. However, the inspectors noted: 'The boys do not seem to take much pride in the school or their own appearance'. At the heart of the organisational weaknesses pinpointed by the inspectors was the absence of a house system and a body of prefects 'with real authority'.[11]

The school was described as 'too much of a one-man band', with all power resting in the hands of the Headmaster. It was this, in the opinion of the inspectors, that had created resentment among the older students who were not delegated any authority, unlike their counterparts in other secondary schools in Northern Rhodesia. One comment is partially deleted and initialled in ink. It seems to reveal a certain underlying tension between some civil servants and missionaries: 'There is no place these days for the paternalistic, omnipotent, missionary-in-charge Principal, so common a few years ago.' In a direct assault on the Brothers' monopoly on school administration, they recommended that the African teacher be promoted to the post of Deputy Principal. In addition, a house and prefect system should be introduced immediately. Senior boys were to be given concessions in exchange for accepting posts of responsibility in the running of the school. In brief, the school was to imitate the structure of English public schools that had been judged so successful in instilling the qualities of leadership and producing rulers for the empire (Wilkinson 1964), and in producing *gentlemen* who were committed to service and who knew their place (Williams 1958: 329).

The inspectors more or less deliberately made recommendations to transform the school into an efficient mechanism for the 'civilising mission' towards the African students. The inspectors turned their attention to the physical environment and implicitly revealed their constructions of the African adolescent. They highlighted the need for a more 'gentle' atmosphere, noting on several occasions the absence of any vases of flowers in either the dormitories or the dining hall. They recommended the introduction of a high table for prefects, who should enforce strict rules about students' personal appearance. The presentation of self was evidently considered a key aspect of the character-building necessary to achieve discipline, the prerequisite of the production of academic success and, perhaps more importantly, responsible citizens. The French-Canadian administration of the school responded by placing a great deal of emphasis on the need for the students to behave in a 'gentlemanly' manner at all times and in all places. Canadian headmasters repeatedly reminded students at assemblies, 'A gentleman is always a gentleman' (School administration files). Their behaviour both in and out of school was to be the clearest expression of the pride students took in their school. They were to know their place, never give up in the face of adversity, and recognise the bond that existed between all St Antony's students, good 'chaps' one and all. In the words of the 1960s school song:

Wherever we are, we are proud of our famous school,
The smile on our lips and in our hearts are ever true.
Our road may lead to any land,
Together we will always stand,
And the St Antony's chaps
Will ever be proud and gay.

We march with a step that knows no fear,
We are so bold!
We study and play, we work and pray,
As we are told. [my emphasis]
One mind, one heart, and hand in hand,
Together we will always stand,
And the St Antony's chaps
Will ever be proud and gay.

Whatever our lives may hold for us,
We will pull through,
For nothing can halt the chaps of our famous school.
And one and all, a joyous band,
Together we will always stand,
And the St Antony's chaps
Will ever be proud and gay!

That education 'civilises' was a very common notion among students. Inscribed in many school rules, the theme was often repeated by the Zambian headmaster, although less enthusiastically endorsed by the Spanish Brothers as they wrestled with the problem of how to serve those most in need. The documents emanating from the Ministry of Education at the time of the inspectors' visit explicitly repeated the theme of the 'civilising mission'. Here, for example, is an extract from a 1966 circular from the expatriate Chief Inspector of Schools to all secondary headmasters concerning the roles of the headmaster and the housemaster, positions '*in loco parentis*'. It is interesting to note how much the sentiments expressed echo the teachings of the Brothers' Founder with regard to the value of 'presence':

One of the most effective, and least costly, ways of being constantly on duty, whether for Head or assistant, is that they move about the grounds and buildings, frequently and freely, and speak *civilising words* [my emphasis] to their young people, as they do so ... There is a very definite effect of peace and calm and friendliness which can be generated when all parties feel at ease and at leisure; such moments may come when they have just come from the dining-room, in the interval before the next set engagement, or as the housemaster walks through the dormitory as the boys are getting ready for bed and says a word to this one and that.

(School administration files 1966)

The house system, where each house was 'a family', would do much to foster 'a spirit of pride' through various competitions in sports and cleanliness. The inspectors were shocked to discover that tidiness in the dormitories was not maintained by the students themselves, commenting in their report: 'This must be the only school in Northern Rhodesia where the dormitories are swept by labourers.' The citizens being fashioned at St Antony's were evidently already gentlemen who, as members of an elite, had workers to clean up after them in the dormitories. It was the same in the classrooms, as I discovered in my interviews with school workers.

Turning their attention to the general timetable, the inspectors noted that the school day was 'far too long' and, 'with far too many study periods, there is not nearly enough time for recreation and leisure'. Indeed the school timetable resembled and, in some respects continued to resemble, the daily routine of a monastic house.[12] The Brothers' Founder had expressed a great fear of the opportunities given to the Devil when the Brothers or the children were insufficiently occupied. Accordingly, the days were divided into periods of different types of activity and this constant activity remained a feature of the Brothers' lives.

The inspectors were against the offering of such religious orientations to work and study as part of the school regime. Instead, they recommended that the daily pre-breakfast study period should be cut altogether and that this time be given over to students 'tending their flower gardens etc.'. Similarly, the daily pre-supper half-hour study period 'should be given up to leisure activities'. The formal longer study periods on Saturdays and Sundays should also be abolished.

The nine consecutive forty-minute teaching periods each weekday, with only one hour for lunch, were judged to be 'heavy-going'. The inspectors queried the amount of time devoted to teaching Religious Education. This was one of the subjects that appeared to be at issue during the disturbances, but was for some, if not all, Brothers, following the instructions of the Founder, the most important subject of all. However, the inspectors commented, 'We think that five periods of religion is excessive and would like to see a reduction to two or three.'

The teaching of Latin and English received extensive comment. The pioneer Brothers considered their educational work to be the preparation of future leaders for the Catholic church in Zambia. Latin, included in several mission schools, was judged to be essential for those students who would go on to be seminarians and priests or religious.[13] The inspectors urged that Latin should only be taken by the most able students and an alternative, possibly biology, be offered to the others. The inspectors recommended that Latin would need to be taught in a way that was 'vigorous, resourceful and gay', if it was to recommend itself to African adolescents.

The Brothers had introduced a rule – it was said, at the urging of the students – that English was the only language to be spoken in the school. The justification was that this would help the students with their studies, all of which were conducted in English. In general, the rule appeared to have been accepted by the student body. Brother François is generally credited with the success of the implementation of the English-only rule. In interviews, he recalled only minor resistance around the time of Independence itself. However, English was singled out by the inspectors as:

> Probably the weakest subject in the school ... The boys have to cope with a confusing variety of accents – and it is therefore all the more important that they should have plenty of opportunity of listening to the received pronunciation of such broadcasts as the BBC news.

Books in the school library and those texts chosen for the School Certificate Examination were criticised for showing 'an unreflecting attachment to the so-called English "classics". There is certainly no place for an unabridged edition of such a pinchbeck piece of rubbish as *King Solomon's Mines*'. Brother Roberto, commenting upon his lack of preparedness for departure for the African missions, recalled to me that his sole preparation was to have located and read *King Solomon's Mines*.

The French-Canadian missionaries apparently had much to learn in their own appropriation of the culture of an English-style boarding school in Northern Rhodesia. The covering letter from the Provincial Education Officer that accompanied the report instructed that its recommendations should be implemented as soon as possible.

The Headmaster and staff were generally positive in their response to the report, but two issues continued to be contentious. The first concerned the depiction of the Headmaster's role in school administration as a 'one-man band'. This was considered to be 'in slightly bad taste', especially when 'a strong personality' was judged to be necessary in the early stages of establishing a school. The second point concerned the abolition of various study periods. The opinion of the Brothers-dominated staff was that the students were incapable of constructively organising large amounts of free time. The Catholic Education Secretary, a Polish Jesuit priest, gave his support to the staff in a revealing manner:

> The stress on leisure in Africa rather amuses me, especially when one goes through the locations. I thought a fair amount of 'nose to the

grindstone' is a very healthy antidote to the '*dolce far niente*' and if we can inculcate into our students during their secondary school course habits of sustained systematic work, we shall have achieved a lot.[14]

The expatriate Provincial Education Officer refused to back down on either point, suggesting that the inspectors' comments had been misinterpreted. Invoking a high moral tone, he commented, 'One of the society's greatest needs ... is to learn how to enjoy one's leisure decently so that people are less prone to pursue only various vices when not actually "working".' He thus seemed to share the Brothers' view that 'the Devil finds work for idle hands'. Where he differed was in how to combat the problem.

On the more substantive issues, action was taken promptly. The only Zambian on the staff was promoted to the post of Deputy Principal, and a house and prefect system was introduced, together with some privileges for all Form Five students. The Deputy worked with the prefects on all aspects of boarding school life. It was up to the prefects to decide upon how the food budget should be allocated, and there are copies in the school files of interminable meetings to decide upon the details of diet, dress code and other matters of discipline. Here is an extract from a 1964 report of the Zambian Deputy to the prefects on the food committee regarding the diet:

> You have put too much *nshima* [maize porridge] and too many beans in your suggested timetable. I warn you this may be very unpopular with the majority of boys. Your duty is to avoid every situation of this kind. Remember that *nshima* should balance with rice as they are both starchy foods and that meat should balance with beans as they are both protein foods. I welcome your idea of cutting down on bread. I have always considered one-third of a loaf of bread a bit too much for any one meal. A quarter of a loaf of bread with a bit of rice and meat, crowned with a cup of hot tea, as you suggest, makes a good and palatable meal. This is a sound idea. It shows clear thinking in the right direction.

Records of prefects' meetings kept on school files give evidence of their growing influence in the school and the extraordinary detail with which they went into matters of discipline. From time to time, they also sought to introduce further markers of distinction for themselves, for example, requesting one year that all prefects should wear pink shirts, a suggestion turned down by the school authorities. It was the prefects who insisted that all students should wear a tie, except in the hot season, and there were endless debates about whether to allow shirts with a straight edge to be worn outside the trousers and not tucked inside like other shirts. Although the matter came up repeatedly, it appears always to have been decided in favour of all shirts being worn inside the trousers.

Prefects also acted as language police. During the 1960s and early 1970s there were concerted attempts to prevent the 'Zambianising' of English words and terms. One prefects' meeting minute reads: 'The only Zambian word recognised in this school is *mwana*'. (*Mwana* is still employed in student talk as a term of address, somewhat similar to 'friend'; it derives from the Bemba *umwana*, a child.) 'No slang is allowed,' the minute continues, 'nor is the formation of words that do not exist.'

Because of the role the prefects came to play in running the school, an enormous amount of time and effort continued to be devoted to prefect selection. Former headmasters privately acknowledged that prefects had become indispensable, especially when the staff became dominated by laymen, not all of whom were prepared for the type of total commitment of time and energy demanded of a Brother by the 'greedy institution' (Coser 1974). Conscious of the responsibility, freedom and the concomitant scope for abuse that the position of prefect entailed, a detailed and extended scrutiny of all potential candidates became the yearly norm. All members of the school were acutely conscious of this scrutiny which thus played a significant role in the development of student subjectivity. Many students eagerly sought this mark of distinction and the privileges that went with it, although if they exhibited their desire too openly, by behaving in the eyes of their peers as model students, they were condemned by their class-mates for 'applying'. Performances and productions of self were monitored by students, enmeshed at least to some degree within the mission discourse of subjectivity. Students, with greater local knowledge than their teachers, engaged even more keenly than staff in their unofficial sifting of candidates. In the weeks immediately preceding the announcement of new prefects, the atmosphere in the school was particularly volatile. Small incidents got blown out of all proportion because of the general state of apprehension and excitement.

On the appointed day in October, a special assembly was held in the school hall. The outgoing prefects, seated with the Headmaster on the stage, rose individually to greet their successor as his name was announced. The outgoing prefect pinned upon his successor his badge of office. Sometimes other items – flowers, sunglasses, ties – were also exchanged. The students in the body of the hall expressed their reaction to each appointment in an uninhibited fashion, cheering when they considered a choice was correct, and groaning and murmuring when they did not. Each year, some wags in the audience raised posters or banners. On some of these the word 'Wounded' was painted, to draw attention to candidates who had been considered, by others or themselves as certain choices. Other banners, inscribed with the words 'Red Cross', were facetiously hoisted, requesting assistance for those 'wounded' in the 'October War'. Those on the stage strove to maintain their dignity and to appear oblivious to the reactions of the students below.

At the end of the proceedings, the Headmaster invariably addressed some remarks to the outgoing prefects, reminding them that they were *still* prefects and therefore should continue to exhibit model behaviour, or else everyone would know that their conduct in office was nothing more than a pretence. In the words of one Headmaster: 'Outgoing prefects, your good example, your excellent behaviour and leadership are still needed. We, staff and fellow companions, must not say of you that it was only a light coat of varnish, an artificial facade.'

On official occasions and at school assemblies, the prefects were singled out by successive headmasters; they were 'the leaders of tomorrow', 'the early rewards of our efforts to train worthy citizens of Zambia', 'our best products'. Time after time, prefects were reminded that theirs was a respon-sibility of service. They were chosen after a lengthy process of consultation among students within houses, between prefects and the headmaster, between housemasters and house prefects, and among staff members. It was not unusual to find reports in school files of consecutive 'selection meetings' between outgoing prefects and the headmaster of five, six and seven hours' duration. During these meetings every facet of a candidate's character and personality was carefully sifted by prefects who had intimate knowledge of the students in their house and who acted as supporters or opponents when names were proposed. It was just one of several moments in a student's school career when reputations were won or lost, and the most striking example of the degree of collaboration that could be achieved between student leaders and teachers. These were some of the comments made during a 1970 meeting which, according to the minutes, lasted seven hours and twenty minutes. Among 'positive qualities' noted were: 'cool; easily encourages others; com-manding voice; reasons well; active; respects himself; serious; hardworking, even won a prize in flower caretaking; doesn't lose his temper; understand-ing; not influenced by others; steady; constant; a gentleman; associates with everybody; clean; obedient; a stone [sic] character; stable; can control boys'.

A similar list of positive qualities appeared year after year when, from each cohort of seventy Grade Twelve students, twenty-one were selected for the various prefectorial positions. Indeed, what was striking, from my scrutiny of school files and my own involvement in such meetings as a housemaster, was how invariable, and thus predictable, were the qualities judged to be necessary for a student to be a prefect. Clearly, students rated verbal skills, persuasive rhetoric, matched with strength of body and character, to be ideal qualities for a student leader. Such qualities were often associated with Seventh-Day Adventist preachers. These preachers came to occupy a second chain of command, but acted in their capacity as student authorities in accordance with their own set of values and beliefs. In their contribution towards the creation of student subjectivity, their inventions demonstrated at times selective appropriation of the school's official and unofficial dis-courses. However, Seventh-Day Adventists were also often strikingly at odds with the official *Catholic* discourse of the school. Ironically, then, St

Antony's 'best products' were often non-Catholic, and indeed anti-Catholic, in their ethos and world view.

'Negative qualities' recorded at the same selection meeting also focused upon the power of persuasive speech and the negative assessment of those who could not speak for themselves in front of others: 'low voice; has language problem – cannot express himself well – as a captain, he ought to be able to speak in good English; vernacular speaker' Like the 'positive' qualities, they offered ample evidence of how, in prefect discourse, the self and subjectivity were fashioned within a particular dialectic of successful and unsuccessful productions of self, of those who presented, in this case, a rebellious self. Ideally, the 'good' man had nothing to hide – his life was open to inspection – but there were those who were said to be 'private' and ' hypocritical'.

Among others who were ruled out of consideration in the prefects' stakes were the following: 'power-hungry; a smoker; always out-of-bounds; no interest in his house; anti-authority; has a record for stealing; weak character; easily bribed; short-tempered; too proud; recognises only those higher than himself; 'hammers' small boys; bad health, though he probably pretends; lazy; childish; cannot control boys; rude; bad-tempered; very limited thinking; gives up easily; a weakling; rebellious; complains when there is little sugar in the tea; he is a "rag", only good at taking orders; not clean; cannot co-operate'. But such students did not go away. Rather, by word and deed, they embodied yet one more student discourse.

Identification with one's house was consistently promoted, especially through sport which was judged by school authorities to be an important opportunity for character-building and for the revelation of an individual's character and personality.[15] The discipline of sport was not only considered important in producing good manners; it was also judged to be good for the health of the body and the soul, building muscles and overcoming sin. It played an equally important part in the life of the Brothers, especially those in Formation. While the result was *said* to be less important than 'playing the game', competition was intense. Students and former students talked about 'dying for the house'. 'Team spirit' was built in several ways: each house in the school had its own colours, banners and songs designed to induce 'moralo' (morale). Morale songs, normally improvised for each occasion, were often quite difficult for an outsider to follow. They normally consisted of a series of boasts about members of the team, and taunts towards opponents. The lyrics were composed in a mixture of vernacular slang and school argot.

A high value was placed by students and staff on sports success in inter-school competitions. One could judge the result of an away match long before the returning team arrived back at school, by the songs of the players on the school transport as they were approaching. If they had won, they sang the refrain, *'cipolopolo oyee'* ('bullet') to announce their success. Inter-house competitiveness could reach such a peak that the two days dedicated to the school athletics were sometimes marred by disturbances arising from disputes over the results of individual events or accusations of judges' bias or inattentiveness. Sometimes a whole house would boycott the competition or stage a sit-down protest on the running track, preventing events from taking place. On at least one occasion, students of one house marched to the nearest town to stage their protest outside the local ministry of education offices.

THE FORMATION OF FUTURE LEADERS: CITIZENS AND GENTLEMEN

Student numbers in the school rapidly increased as a result of its success. The Brothers managed to fend off an early attempt to encourage all schools in Zambia to increase dramatically student numbers. Their argument was that numbers in excess of 400 would make it impossible for the Brothers to carry out their primary aims, which they identified in 1968 as giving 'education to boys to work for the Church in helping the formation of Christians and getting recruits to perpetuate the Church in Zambia'. Alone of all mission secondary schools in Zambia,[16] the Brothers refused to consider any substantial increase in the school roll, stating that they would prefer to withdraw from the school rather than accept such measures. Their arguments drew together several of the themes that continued to appear in various public statements concerning their role as 'educators':

> A boarding secondary school containing over 400 boys can turn out boys with certificates perhaps, but not educated men. It is no longer *a house of formation* [my emphasis] where the young people under our care should learn to become reliable citizens, real **MEN** [emphasis in the original] and good Christians. At the moment Zambia needs men on whom we can rely and people who will be trained properly.[17]

The Brothers thus argued that relatively small numbers were essential, if they were to achieve their stated aim. In this way, they inevitably ministered to a very select elite. In 1974, the Spanish Brothers officially took over control of the school from their French-Canadian counterparts. The school continued to be successful, both on the sports field and in the examination room, which added to the pressure on enrolment, especially from better-off Zambians, and created a great gap between the school and local people, very few of whose children were admitted as students.[18] It was only in 1986 that the school was finally opened up to pupils from local primary schools, for them to attend as day scholars.[19]

Two ideal figures – the citizen and the gentleman – need to be kept in mind. The production of the responsible citizen was a prominent theme in the Founder's instructions to his Brothers. The Founder stressed that the education of children involved 'instructing them in their duty', so as 'to give them a Christian spirit and Christian attitudes and to form them to religious habits and the virtues possessed by a good Christian and a good citizen' (Marian Brothers 1989: 535). Even beyond that, not merely the good citizen but the God-fearing Christian gentleman was the ideal that emerged most strongly immediately before and in the early aftermath of Independence. The goal was the formation of 'future leaders' for the task of 'building the nation'. This remained a prominent theme, on the one hand, in the French-Canadian Brothers' public statements and in their rules for the running of the school and, on the other hand, in the rhetoric of the Ministry of Education, especially following Kenneth Kaunda's development of the philosophy of Zambian Humanism. Self-discipline was the key to the development of the individual and the nation.[20]

At the official opening of the school hall in 1966, in the presence of the Minister of Education, the Brother Principal expressed himself in very similar terms:

> I say to you students, if your education is to be of real value to yourselves and to your country, this education must be welcomed and not suffered. Discipline must be considered a need, not a refined means of oppression. Nobody can educate you if you are not willing to educate yourselves. We are not interested in offering the society people who are merely presentable. We want to provide our nation with people of character, people ready to serve, people ready to give. We want to form, or rather, we want you to form yourselves, into responsible and dedicated citizens. We also want you to be dedicated Christians. Our school is a home. Zambia is your homeland; but there is another homeland referred to in the National Prayer, the other home which our good Father has prepared for all of us in heaven ... Honourable Minister, dear Guests, we are all united in this gigantic task of providing this country with people of good will and generous determination ...

The School Captain in his reply (author unknown!) promised:

> In the name of all my companions, I can assure Brother Principal and the staff that we shall always co-operate with them for the betterment of St Antony's and for the fulfilment of our education so that we become true citizens of this country.

The school was given the crucial role of the development of the habits appropriate to the achievement of that aim. The gentlemanly habits of the responsible citizen were, of course, the ones required in the civil administration and the labour market. Young African men who submitted themselves to the school regime did so with the more particular aim of securing employment in Independent Zambia, (see Carmody 1988; 1990). The early growth of the school coincided with the opening of a field of opportunity. In those days, before 'qualification inflation' (Dore 1976), a School-leaving

Certificate could open many doors for the fortunate few. In November 1969, the Headmaster reported to the Chief Education Officer regarding the whereabouts of the thirty-seven 1968 school leavers. Apart from one former student who was recorded as having no job, and one other for whom no information could be found, the statistics showed that one-third of them were in further education, either at the university or at colleges in Lusaka, the Copperbelt or Russia; all the other students had found employment, or training leading to employment, in various fields including the mines, the banks, the railways, journalism and the Game and Fisheries Department (School administration files 1969). Brother Jean-Pierre, who was the principal during this period, explained to me the values he had tried to instil into the students: 'discipline, hard work and a sense of responsibility'. He reminded them repeatedly how these values could be turned to socio-economic advantage because of the 'rewards' available to the students:

> I used to tell my students, 'You guys would be a bunch of stupid individuals if you don't succeed in life. We've just got Independence and we are trying to Zambianise the railways, the army; there's going to be a new airforce, the banks, the mines … If none of you can find yourself a future, don't come and complain to me!' And they just went – that's why we have got so many students in pretty high positions.

St Antony's motto, *labor omnia vincit* or 'work conquers all', appeared to ring true. Catholicism and capitalism went hand in hand for the pioneer Brothers and their students, who enjoyed a good diet, sound teaching, and examination success in a disciplined environment.

The missionaries worked within the newly created nation, which rapidly adopted the system of 'one-party, participatory democracy'. It could be argued that the Brothers, while providing an education that was eagerly sought after, neglected to offer any radical critique of a political climate that brooked no contradiction, or of a system of education with the declared aim of producing leaders, an endeavour which inevitably enhanced the position of a very select few while ignoring the poorest of the poor. The flourishing debating society was not allowed to debate either political or religious topics. On the sensitive issue of politics, there were several reminders to the staff, for most of the early period either entirely or largely expatriate, of the necessity to be guarded in the expression of any opinion. A Headmaster's note of a confidential staff briefing given in response to an anonymous student complaint to the Chief Education Officer in May 1972 is typical of the period:

> Politics: Let us be very careful (especially when we lose our temper) with words on politics; comparisons between different governments (particularly between the western type of governments and the African type); the African governments are running their countries the way

they think is best and they are free to do so ... I think it would be unwise on our part, as teachers, to make any statements, for or against one-party democracy. In particular, let us try to hide our feelings from the boys; they are simply not mature enough to understand.

In this, the Brothers were in danger of losing sight of the vision of their Founder, and of being deaf to his call to assist 'those most in need'.[21] It is the classic paradox, noted by Weber, of the monk whose 'rational ascetism itself has created the very wealth it rejected' (Weber 1978: 332). As the school achieved prominence in the educational field and as successful mission old boys and girls, assimilated into the dominant culture by a process of '*embourgeoisement*' (Bourdieu 1977), sought places for their own children in turn, the school was in danger of becoming primarily a site of secular reproduction and not of religious transformation.

We still need to ask what this reproduction consisted of. Yes, St Antony's equipped its successful students with the means to achieve certification which could then be converted into employment in the labour market or entry into higher education. But was the secular reproduction as thoroughgoing, as deterministic and unchanging as '*embourgeoisement*' and 'disenchantment' might seem to suggest?

The school attempted to inscribe an ethos of discipline, order and obedience, proper to the citizen and the gentleman. Students selectively appropriated, whether consciously or unconsciously, the dispositions that the Catholic mission school had, ideally, wished to instil in its students. They acknowledged their 'need' to be 'educated' and 'civilised', and saw their achievement of distinction as earned by right through the 'suffering' they had endured at school. However, they retained, and attempted to inscribe upon newcomers, their own ethos and a world view which was often at odds with the official discourse of St Antony's.

In Bourdieu's terms, we may wish to say the students became enmeshed within a particular type of habitus through their experience of mission education.[22] Bourdieu argues that the school, in providing the skills required by the capitalist economic and symbolic markets, is an important site of social reproduction – reproduction that is achieved through the employment of 'symbolic violence' (Bourdieu and Passeron 1990). The imposition of this 'symbolic violence' upon groups or classes legitimates systems of symbolism and meaning:

> Even when [the school] does not manage to provide the opportunity for appropriating the dominant culture, it can at least inculcate recognition of the legitimacy of the culture of those who have the means of appropriating it. Symbolic domination accompanies and redoubles economic domination.
> (Bourdieu and Boltanski 1978: 217)

Through such a socialising process – interestingly Bourdieu avoids the use of the term 'socialisation' (see Tonkin 1992: 106) – a 'misrecognition', a 'mystification' of the true nature of the taught culture may well arise. There was some evidence of this in St Antony's where the meritocratic myth was wholeheartedly endorsed by successful students who considered they had 'sweated' and 'suffered' in their studies, and so were entitled to the rewards available in the money economy. Whether the overwhelming majority of those who had 'failed' to make the grade, the 'drop-outs' in towns and villages, were persuaded of such legitimacy was another question; rising insecurity, especially in urban areas, gave expression to a discontent which would suggest they were not.

The Spanish Brothers, among others, tried to address these issues. In the early days of St Antony's, Livingstone's project of the three Cs – Christianity, Commerce and Civilisation (Livingstone 1857; Holmes 1994) – seemed to be well in hand. Yet life in Zambia would lead one to ponder the relevance of such a trinity. The Brothers' mission priorities altered through changing circumstances in their own Congregation and the Spanish Catholic church, and in the context of living and working in Zambia.

CONCLUSION

Order and discipline at St Antony's were fragile entities, constantly liable to disruption and subversion, and largely dependent upon the collusion of students and staff. Whatever the appearances, it was a negotiated order. Conformism was not the only possible outcome. Students retained a sense of agency, which was not all illusory; they demonstrated their power to subvert school discourse. They might well eagerly adopt certain habits of Christian gentlemen, and they might assent to the adage 'Manners maketh the man', or at least the 'gentleman', but their presentation of self might also be mannered, a production of art and artifice. They were constantly monitoring what was offered to them and making their own evaluations. The power of words was not all in one direction. They listened to the words of school authorities, accepted some of them and rejected others. Or they took these words and played with them, appropriating them in parody and irony, for their own purposes.

4

SPACE AND COMMUNITY

For our house is our corner of the world. As has often been said, it is
our first universe, a real cosmos in every sense of the word.
Gaston Bachelard, *The Poetics of Space*

The mission is a very closed and small world.
Brother Francisco

The school compound had within it the Brothers' Residence, the students'
hostels, the teachers' houses and the houses of the workers' compound;
immediately beyond the boundaries of the school compound were the
village homesteads of the local people, the convent of the local Catholic
Sisters, and the homes of those who worked in the health centre. My focus
here is upon the Brothers' domestic space and their movements within and
beyond it. The way we treat our bodies and organise our houses, both
'containers' and 'contained' (cf. Stilgoe 1994: viii), is symbolic of our social
lives. This is not merely a reflection of the relations between the self and
others, but also an active force in the construction of those relationships and
the production and reproduction of sociality.

Zambians and Brothers perceived one another as they went about their
everyday activities; orientation and movement in physical space were, I
argue, read in an interpretative manner, as orientation and movement in
moral space, by all those involved. Such reading was a process; the
Zambians who came into day-to-day contact with the Brothers were
engaged in a largely unspoken, yet profound, moral argument with them.
Moral evaluations of the Brothers' actions were hardly ever addressed to
them directly, although they were hotly debated among students, teachers
and local people.

While there was also some debate within the Community about the
purpose and aim of the Brothers' presence, and how these could be best
expressed, the general local Zambian assumption was that the Brothers, like
other missionaries, had come 'to help'. For students and neighbours the
issue was, did these Brothers 'really' care for them? Were they ready to
engage in relationships with them which would demonstrate this care, and
in which some kind of exchange was possible?

One major index of the Brothers' willingness or unwillingness to fill this role was in large part judged by students, teachers and others, by the Brothers' 'availability' to them and by their willingness to share what they, the Brothers, had. A good Brother was one who was seen to take pleasure in being physically close to them, spending time with them, someone who communicated warmth and openness. For Zambian students especially, it was important that others should 'feel free' in his presence. Ideally there should be nothing hidden, and there should be little reserve beyond that which was deemed appropriate for their age or status. For many, these missionaries were the first 'white men' with whom they had come into anything approaching 'close contact'. Being physically close to others was regarded by students and teachers as the primary way in which one discovered what a person was 'really' like. When they were asked to comment upon someone's character, a frequent reply was, 'I haven't stayed with him, and so I don't know what he is like'. 'Stay' was used here in the sense of 'lived with'. The issue, then, was what kind of relatedness were the Brothers prepared to engage in. Physical orientation and degree of proximity both expressed and provided a commentary upon relatedness.

Postcolonial missionaries in Zambia, as elsewhere, could not throw off entirely their association with the colonial world out of which they emerged. It was in this world, whether they liked it or not, that their origin and roots were to be found; they were thus deeply implicated both in those origins and in the postcolonial state. Recent Catholic thinking on the question of missionaries has stressed the notion of 'inculturation', a major theme that developed out of the Second Vatican Council in such documents as *Ad Gentes* and in Pope Paul VI's letter, *Africae Terrarum* (see Shorter 1988: 206). Yet the extent to which the Catholic church in Zambia could identify with Zambians and Zambian aspirations remained problematic. The Catholic church was still dominated by expatriate missionaries, and there was at times a palpable lack of trust on both sides, perhaps particularly at the level of the 'professional religious', the priests, nuns and Brothers. Distance between expatriate missionaries and indigenous religious and clergy promoted distrust. In an analysis of Catholic missionary activity in the Sepik region of Papua New Guinea, Huber (1988) raises this issue. She writes of the contradictions of a group of people who have come to 'help' and yet who simultaneously maintain a considerable degree of social distance, thus emphasising their origins in a 'different world'. Huber observes, 'because missionaries never completely left their own world, native people sometimes concluded that missionaries had dealt with them in bad faith' (Huber 1988: 108).

The Brothers at St Antony's, with only one or two notable exceptions, showed little evidence of having 'left their own world'. One source of evidence of this parochial closure was their everyday lived experience which was centred upon their life in common, 'in Community', according to their

Rule, behind the screen of their temporary home in Zambia. Bachelard quotes Baudelaire to the effect that in a palace 'there is no place for intimacy', but the building itself should not of necessity rule out all intimate expression. While the Brothers' domestic space was by no means a palace, it was still strikingly more splendid and more comfortable than the nearby homesteads, and built on a much grander scale than the accommodation provided for teachers and workers.

The Brothers' house retained a certain ambiguity about it, having, as it did, the quality of the religious institution from which it never really escaped, however hard the occupants might try to rescue some sense of the 'homely' and the familial. Their dwelling place, the building in and around which they spent the overwhelming majority of their 'free' time, was never referred to as 'home' either by the Brothers themselves or by the school and local community. Known by all as the 'Brothers' Residence', its name signalled a degree of formality which in itself created a sense of distance and apartness. The pioneer Brothers, together with local workers, built St Antony's and fashioned their own dwelling place in the African bush. Yet Heidegger (1971: 146) reminds us, 'To build is itself already to dwell'. Houses have unfinished life-histories too (Blier 1987: 2). The Brothers followed a design that they had used before in other parts of Africa, in particular in Southern Rhodesia. Their building situated and oriented them in a specific way in relation to their neighbours, and spoke powerfully of the nature of that relation. The manner of their building, of their taking root (Bachelard 1994: 4) in an alien world, was an expression of their already being in a dwelt-in world (Ingold 1991: 15; 1995: 76). Their established material presence spoke of the inequalities of the mission encounter.[1]

At St Antony's, the compound of the mission school was composed not of one house-type, but of a variety of different lived-in structures. Each provided different spaces to live in 'with all the partiality of the imagination' (Bachelard 1994: xxxvi), prototypes for, and possibilities of, action and socialisation through their very different sets of spatial configuration and objects. There were quite different sets of actions available for imitation, although some were valued higher than others. Typical of expressions of the colonial and capitalist world, each person was allocated 'his' or 'her' particular structure, sited in a particular place. He or she was expected to remain in the allocated place. Everyone must know their place. Different 'orders' of persons were clearly separated, and marked off from one another. Where one found oneself told the individual and those who encountered him where his place was, not only in physical terms, but also in terms of 'worth' or 'value'. The dwelling places differed markedly in such considerations as the material used to construct them, the amount of living space within them, the distance that separated them from other structures, and the degrees of comfort.

More importantly, they also differed in their degrees of transparency or opacity. It was much easier to peer into some lives than into others. For example, the dormitory existence of the students was, in many ways, the one most obviously open to inspection by others, both formally and informally. The Residence of the Brothers and the 'life' that went on there were not so easy to inspect. Because of this, they held a certain mystery and mystique for outsiders such as students and teachers who speculated constantly about what went on in the Brothers' Community. However, some members of the school community were much more mobile than others and therefore had greater access to the differing perspectives that movements in space could offer. In the case of the Brothers' domestic world, some members of the school were in a position to gain more knowledge of what was 'really' going on there.

Two spatial processes need to be distinguished: negotiation and interaction. A number of questions follow: How was space negotiated? How did space and place, the built environment, act upon the Brothers and other members of the school community who inhabited this space, and, reciprocally, how did they act upon it? The built environment did not determine all the types of interaction that took place within it. Individual Brothers and outsiders acted creatively within it. Space can be both constraining and enabling.

The Brothers' Residence was designed in such a way as to facilitate the Community life to which the Brothers believed themselves to be called. It was a life which, while being a call of service to others, required at the same time a boundary to be maintained between the 'world' and the Community. The needs of the Brothers for prayer, meditation and relaxation had also to be met. Thus contacts with those beyond the Community had to be both limited in frequency and constrained in the type of interaction, out of consideration for what the Community decided was appropriate for a celibate male religious. The Residence of the Brothers was the place where Community spirit was to be forged, nurtured and maintained. The spiritual dimension of Catholic religious life demanded that the body be constrained in a number of particular ways, and thus brought under control. The Brothers' life was ruled by a particular discipline, learnt in childhood, that required Brothers to seek help throughout life from the Virgin Mary, their Founder and other spiritual resources, but also from the encouragement and example of one's Brothers in Community.

In the Brothers' own accounts, I noted a paradox. They told me of the 'freedom' which they said being in Africa gave them. Yet their everyday routine practices demonstrated little evidence of the exercise of this 'freedom' in relation to others, such as the 'outsiders' beyond the Community of Brothers. Running through the accounts was an identification in space of the authentic with the exotic. 'Africa' or 'Zambia' was portrayed as a space in which a Brother claimed to have 'found himself', a place in which one could at last be 'true to oneself'. In contrast to the large, rather anonymous, constraining Communities in Spain, Brothers recounted how in Zambia there was much more scope for self-expression. Thus the depiction of the experience of exotic space was central to the Brothers' construction and presentation of the self.

Many Brothers had left the domesticity of their family home at a very early age. They had been introduced into religious educational institutions set up by the Brothers for the purpose of educating children, but also in order to gain recruits and discern vocations. In such institutions they were socialised into the male religious family to which they now belonged, a family modelled on that of the Holy Family of Jesus, Mary and Joseph. In many of the Brothers' schools in Spain, the Community's dwelling-place was situated in the middle of, or directly adjoining, the school premises. This siting of the Brothers' dwelling was a powerful expression of the 'greedy institution' which demanded total commitment. Such spatial arrangements implied that there should be no distinction between the life of the Brothers and the life of the school. Arbuckle (1991) has suggested that close identification with their educational institutions is a particular feature of Brothers' Congregations, at times making them unable to see more urgent pastoral needs, a point also made in circulars from the Brothers' Superior General, the superior of all the Brothers of the Congregation.

Brothers had been enculturated from an early age within a particular kind of 'religious' built environment, in spaces and under regimes designed to create a 'docile' body (Foucault 1977). They had grown up in the large spaces of religious residences – so unlike their contemporaries, growing up at home in the village or the provincial town – under the surveillance of older Brothers who monitored their progress, in an atmosphere in which not all were to be chosen. There was, in the Brothers' phrase, a regular 'shaking of the tree', and those deemed 'unsuitable' were sent away or elected to leave at various stages along the way.

This special education of the mind and body (although the formulation of two separate entities is of course misleading) was acted out upon a wider canvas than the purely domestic. This must have had far-reaching consequences for the Brothers' perception of the world and their place in it, shaping all subsequent knowledge of other spaces (cf. Stilgoe 1994: viii). Such an experience of being-in-the-world must have had a profound impact upon their emotional lives.

Spanish Brothers' accounts often recalled the distress felt at the separation from parents and home life. The suffering seemed to form an important part in the making of the Brother's vocation, for the Spaniards. In some of the narratives shared with me, the experience of adolescent pain was recalled with a measure of resentment and a sense of loss. Brother Francisco was not the only one to recall the 'abnormality' of his childhood, robbed, he considered, of many experiences that he now judged to be part of the ordinary course of 'growing up': having friends, both boys and girls, going to parties, learning how to dance. At the age of ten, he had left home to attend the Brothers' school. Although the school was only three kilometres from his parents' home, he rarely saw his family, although his brother would bring fresh laundry every week, and he would be allowed home only once every couple of months for Sunday lunch. Now, in adulthood, he told of a gnawing homesickness, a nostalgia for a lost childhood.

The Spanish Brothers had been 'brought up' in institutions that had always placed a premium upon control and self-control. They had been 'set apart', 'called' to follow a special life trajectory, in places in which the familial had given place to the institutional, whatever the idea of 'family life' that was imported into discussions of religious life. The Brothers had received a particular kind of 'religious formation' in accordance with an orthodox discourse that gave a particular twist to notions of privacy and individualism. Religious life had set them in opposition to the 'world' beyond the boundaries of Community, a world that harboured dangers even within the domestic spaces that they returned to for holidays. Brother Carlos recalled his visit home, at the age of fifteen, just before the start of his novitiate:

> We had so many stories, you know, about being careful! I remember my whole family going to the circus – it was considered a wonderful show, but I never went, I wasn't allowed to. And I remember a cousin – a girl – coming to visit at home. And again I had to be careful, even to embrace her …

He went on to describe a dramatic instance when the harsh reality of the 'break' with home was vividly brought to his awareness, when the loss of family was felt painfully in embodied practice:

> I was living in the same town as my mother and father and I was passing within twenty metres of our home and I wasn't visiting them, just passing. So, well, I felt it, but not as very painful … But I remember my father and my mother and my family visited me. It was my birthday, they had brought me some cakes. My father gave me a cake and I started eating and then I saw one of the Brothers coming and I hid the cake in my pocket, all the cream! And I remember my brothers and my mother saying 'What's happening?' And, you know, you feel – it is something that marks you. So these details remain with you because, well, they have gone totally against you. You realise that you are in a system that makes you do things that are – you can't even rationalise that … You know, you are sweating and you feel you are caught in something wrong, but you don't know well – and you see your family. They see that you feel that you are doing something

wrong, but you don't know why! Well, I could continue until late, but the origins of vocation are there ...

THE BROTHERS' RESIDENCE

The Brothers' Residence was an imposing building, when compared with the huts of the villages around. It was in a part of the school campus where other buildings associated with the sacred, or, rather, associated with official Catholic 'religious' matters and activities, were located: the church, the Brothers' chapel, the chaplain's house, the novitiate or Juniorate where trainee Brothers (the postulants) lived with two finally professed Brothers who were charged with their care and initial instruction in the life of the Brothers.

The house was built in the shape of three sides of a rectangle, and the first impression was one of size and space. There were rooms for twelve people. For most of the period of my fieldwork, the Brothers of the school Community numbered only five; two others were attached to the postulancy, and three more formed the Community on the Copperbelt. At earlier periods, the Community had been somewhat larger. Each room opened out onto a veranda along which were trained vines from Spain, a 'touch of home'. The general plan resembled similar residences constructed by the Canadian Brothers in Zimbabwe. As with other such community residences in Zimbabwe, the building was situated quite apart from other buildings, far from the usual disturbances of neighbours. The rooms were all of equal size and simply furnished by European and North American Brothers' standards, although not by the standards of many of the teachers' homes, and certainly not by the standards of the homesteads of those who lived around the school.

The air of privacy that seemed to surround so much of the Brothers' domestic life was interpreted by some Zambians as an example of the 'European's' liking for 'being alone'. It revealed to critics the basic selfishness of the *musungu* (the white man) and of the Community who were accused at times of 'being Brothers to themselves only'. This assessment ran directly counter to the Zambian students' self-professed enjoyment of being together with others.

A frequent debate among Zambians surrounded the topic of whether the expatriate Brothers could live 'like Zambians in a village'. The issue was one of physical strength in the face of hardship, an important value among male students and teachers. The general opinion was that, with only one exception, the Brothers were too weak – like some of the students, often young men from urban areas, who were branded 'broilers' in student argot – to survive such a hard existence.[2] The Brothers were expected to keep their rooms neat and clean. The general rule, with one or two notable exceptions, was that they tended to keep their rooms and their work materials in a state of great order and tidiness. This attention to, and desire for, order extended to aspects like their handwriting, the style of which most of them were taught when they were training to be Brothers. Their handwriting thus tended to be extremely similar, and was another example of how the discipline of training in religious life might lead to a common, and in this sense anonymous, expression, relieved of individual style. This is not to suggest, however, that in their manner of living and self-presentation, there was great uniformity. Indeed each Brother exhibited great distinctiveness in his style of being-in-the-world. There was a constant tension between an individual Brother's personal aims and wishes and the demands of Community living.

The common spaces in the Brothers' home – the veranda, toilets and showers, sitting-room and dining-room – were looked after by a female domestic worker, Mrs Chanda. The Brothers employed two other workers: Mr Mwanza, their cook, prepared their meals and kept the kitchen and dining-room clean, while Mr Bwalya tended the Brothers' garden, the poultry and the pigs. Mrs Chanda and Mr Mwanza, while still 'distant companions' of the Brothers, offered a running commentary to certain outsiders, selected on the basis of friendship, on the life of the Brothers and on day-to-day events inside the house and beyond. They noted, in particular, the 'moods' of the Brothers and offered moral evaluations of them as individuals. They often emphasised each Brother's aloneness and apartness, even from the other Brothers in the Community, describing them as each living 'alone in his own house', that is, his own room.

In the sitting-room, which was not used a great deal for Community socialising except in the cold season when a fire was set in the hearth, there were a number of armchairs with small sidetables arranged in a circle. On a big table next to the French windows was a selection of reading matter – Spanish newspapers, *Time* and *Newsweek*, the *Guardian Weekly*, *National Geographic*, the *Tablet* and so on – and a noticeboard where communications from the Provincial House and other mail to the Community was posted. This was where the Brothers' incoming mail was also normally left.

Beyond the French windows on the veranda, there was a row of garden chairs, in various states of disrepair, in front of a long heavy table built by a Brother. This was the preferred gathering place for most of the year when the weather allowed. It was here that timetabled 'Community gatherings' most often took place, particularly important of which was the weekly 'get-together' (this was also known in the Community as the 'press conference' because if someone had recently returned from a trip, he was expected to give a full and, if possible, entertaining account). This was also the place for post-lunch relaxation during term-time, when there was insufficient time to take a siesta.

Behind the sitting room were the kitchen; the visitors' parlour, which was very rarely used; and an office-cum-storeroom with a typewriter, duplicator, writing materials and stamps, and photocopier. The end of the building also housed the office of the school bursar who in the past always used to be a Brother, but this had changed in recent years and the post was held by a succession of Zambian teachers. The foodstore and the deep-freezer were kept locked by the Brother in charge of the food, and he issued the food for each meal to the cook. Everything was controlled.

The dining-room was next to the kitchen and it was here that a great deal of the 'socialising' at Community level took place over meals. There was one long table with places set along both sides and, at one end, the position occupied during the period of my fieldwork by the Superior, a Chinese member of the Community. The food was set out by the Brothers' cook on another table and the Brothers, having been summoned by a bell, assembled. Once the blessing had been pronounced by the Superior or, in his absence, by another Brother, the Brothers helped themselves buffet-style.

There was a marked contrast here to the eating 'traditions' of the Zambians. The Spanish Brothers took the meal very much as a 'social occasion'. Here one could measure the general mood and 'take the temperature' of the Brothers' Community, and of individual Brothers. If a Brother was quiet or withdrawn, he would not normally be challenged during the meal, but his mood would be noted and discussed by other members of the Community later. If such a mood persisted, he would be approached privately by some of the others.

The meal was an occasion to talk about the events of the day. Normally, this meant the life of the school. Brothers commented about how things were going, about various students and events in the classroom, about teachers and the performance of their tasks. Someone might report teachers' talk in the staffroom, gossip concerning the school community and the neighbours around the school. During all this talk, the Community's nicknames for various protagonists in the tales were used, and observations and moral evaluations of various school characters were made. These exchanges, usually in English, were very difficult for any outsider to follow, because of the accents and intonation patterns of the Brothers, and because of the content of the subject matter and the references to past events that made up one 'history' of St Antony's. For example, one female member of the school community noted, among other things, for her smart clothes was variously described as 'Mrs Marcos', 'Imelda', 'Our Lady', and 'Our Lady of Rosario'. The atmosphere could become rather claustrophobic at times, at least to the observer. However, during the period of my fieldwork, the state of the economy, the progress of the first multi-party elections, and the attendant possibility of unrest and violence were also common table topics.

Meals were also occasions to thrash out disagreements, to talk about the goings-on in the 'next-door Community', the house for the postulants, still called the 'novitiate' because of its former use. Here also was the place to tease others, to joke and, for the more extrovert members, to 'perform'; it was perhaps the most striking context in which 'Community' was constructed, maintained, threatened and repaired, at the affective level. Continuing jokes were endlessly retold, and stories were told about, and sometimes against, another Brother, often one who was not present. Certain catchphrases, imitations of others' modes of speech or favourite expressions were repeated day after day. The meals, like the Catholic Mass and the prayers, were evidently considered to be the most important of the 'Community exercises'. Absence at any of them led to considerable, sometimes *apparently* jocular, comment. The eating habits of all were known and commented upon, as was the habit of those who regularly came late to meals or prayers.

The Zambians generally did not speak while eating. The Brothers did not normally eat with Zambians outside the Community, and did so infrequently within the Community, for example when a Zambian guest or visiting priest was present or when the Zambian aspirants, the postulants, joined them for a special celebration (however, the two Brothers who lived with the postulants did eat with them daily). The situation I observed had clear parallels with that observed by Burke (1990) in her ethnography of Zairean and expatriate nuns in Lower Zaire. Burke observes that for the Zaireans the table was 'not the place for social intercourse'. She also describes how important the presence of all Community members at meals, recreation, prayers and Mass was considered (Burke 1990: 178).

On the school side, the premises of the Brothers' Residence were shielded from view by a tall mulberry hedge, which was invaded by children and students when the bushes were in fruit. A recent addition was two dog kennels, situated at either end of the property, in which at certain times the Community's dogs were chained or tied at night. The dogs were seen by the Brothers as necessary to frighten away, or to alert the Community to the presence of, thieves during the night. The incidence of thefts on the Brothers' property was considered by some members of the Community to be a reliable barometer of relations between the Community and the local people. Relations were good, they argued, when the Community was seen to be taking an interest in and providing employment to others on selected projects; then the problem of thefts almost disappeared.

The Brothers' house looked onto a large, well-established garden in which, depending on the season, one could find a variety of vegetables and up to twenty different kinds of fruit. Excess vegetables were sold to teachers and villagers, but the fruit was not sold and this was a source of tension, at times, between the Brothers and the teachers and students. Below the house were also situated the poultry shed and the piggery.

Above the vegetable and fruit garden was the Brothers' chapel, planned by a former Brother according to a circular 'African' design. It was mostly made out of concrete but had a thatched roof which needed yearly repair. The chapel was decorated in a mixture of styles. There were examples of

African carvings in statues, door panels and the altar itself, as well as paint-
ings produced by the Brother responsible for its construction.

In the Brothers' everyday routines around the mission, their movements
were tightly circumscribed. Most Brothers rarely went beyond the rather
narrow limits set by the location of their prescribed activities: prayer, work,
teaching, eating and study. Manual work, in particular, appeared to set the
Brothers apart from others, in at least two ways. First, it physically isolated
them, for it often involved a Brother working alone or with other Brothers.
Secondly, most Zambians saw manual work as, at best, an unavoidable
necessity. Students at St Antony's associated manual work with punishment
for transgressing school rules, and they certainly saw it as something that, in
later life, should be avoided by those 'educated' enough to be able to obtain
a white-collar job. Yet love of manual work was said to be one of the Brothers'
defining characteristics. In the Brothers' Rule, the notion of family was
closely tied to that of work; indeed, it was seen as a way of building the
family. The Brothers' place was very much a place of work, of almost constant activity. It was noticeable how their days were taken up with industry,
either intellectual work in the school or manual work within or around their
house, and this left little time or opportunity for social visiting. This industry
accorded well with the example and the instructions of their Founder. The
Brothers took great pleasure and pride in manual labour, and the accomplishment of manual work carried with it a moral evaluation of the person.
Since the educational reforms of the mid-1970s, manual work, timetabled
as 'Production Unit', had formed a part of the school curriculum. On the
whole, it was difficult to persuade either the students or the Zambian teachers
of the value of this exercise. Brothers who, like the other teachers, were
required to supervise this work found the task a particularly frustrating
experience and they often had to contend with great reluctance on the part
of the students.

The Brothers saw themselves as men of action, rather than of words.
There was a particular irony here in the Zambian context, where words
counted in a special way. Facility with words carried a high value and silence
was often read as a sign of anger. Willingness to join in any common work
on the part of young Zambian Brothers was seen as a willingness to join the
Brothers' family. It was very positively valued and openly commented upon
by the Brothers. Any reluctance to 'join in' raised serious doubts in the
Brothers' minds about a young Brother's or aspirant's suitability. Work thus
became one way in which outsiders were excluded.

Most Brothers did not normally stray as far as the teachers' or workers'
houses or the surrounding homesteads. As a result, they were often perceived by their neighbours, villagers, teachers, students and others to be
very self-enclosed, a tightly-knit group, closed-in upon themselves, not open
to either neighbours or strangers, and forming a community clearly set apart

from others. The villagers and teachers often remarked 'the Brothers do not come to our funerals'. In the moral economy of the local community, their absence vividly expressed their detachment from their neighbours. The argument went beyond the perceived lack of any fraternal relations to the idea of the Brothers as ontologically 'different', apparently not 'touched' by the death of another in the way that the local people required themselves to be. Many Brothers appeared awkward at the prospect of attending funerals, feeling themselves to be 'out-of-place'. They doubted, at times, the sincerity of demonstrations of grief and questioned the readiness and frequency with which staff asked for time off work in order to attend funerals.

The Rule stressed the need for prudence in encounters with outsiders. Visitors' reception was affected by the layout of the Residence itself and the negotiation of the space in which these encounters took place. Built forms not only expressed but directed and, in part, shaped social processes concerned with sociability and sociality; they played a role in controlling behaviour in host-guest or insider-outsider relations.

The rear of the building was quite open and, as a result, it was possible to gain uninterrupted access to the various parts of the house without alerting the inhabitants to one's presence in advance. How individuals approached the Brothers' Residence was, of course, dictated by the quality of the relationship that they enjoyed with the Brothers. It was not generally considered an easy house to approach; former students spoke of going to the Brothers' Residence as a stressful experience. In the past, for a time, there had been a bell near the sitting room, and students were told to ring this and wait until someone came to attend to them. One former student, Peter, said he would start 'shivering' when he walked towards the building. David, another former student, now a university professor, recalled:

> I don't remember ever having gone to the residence of the Brothers at any time. I thought the Brothers were a closed society. They knew almost everything about us but we knew very little about them. We were not able to look into their lives.

A visitor had a number of options for making contact with a Brother. The actual strategies used depended upon the quality of the visitor's relationship with the Community or with an individual Brother. What might be described as 'purely social' visits from teachers or local people were more or less unknown. Hence actual encounters were assumed to be for business and had a businesslike tone. Teachers came to buy eggs, to request a lift to town or Lusaka, or to borrow money for some emergency, such as a funeral. The latter requests were normally addressed first to the Superior who, if the amount requested was substantial, then brought the request to a Community meeting. Thus charity was dispensed in a measured way and only after due consideration of all relevant factors, not least of which was the petitioner's track record in repaying loans. The option of an immediate personal response was removed, and refusal on the grounds of insufficient funds was not an option open to the Community. Instead, the would-be borrower's worth was put in the balance and weighed.

Student visitors also fell into a pattern. They sought extra help with their studies, transport money or assistance with school fees. They came to borrow balls for basketball or volleyball, or, sometimes, simply to spend time with a favourite Brother.

One way of gaining access to the Brothers was through Mrs Chanda or Mr Mwanza, who were often found together in the kitchen. One of them would go to call the Brother from his room while the visitor or visitors waited, either by the kitchen or on the veranda in front of the sitting-room.

Those who had established a close relationship with the Community, or with a member of it, simply went straight to an individual Brother's door. Again, the quality of the relationship with the visitor could be further publicised by whether the ensuing interaction took place out on the veranda, in full view of others, or whether the visitor was received in the Brother's room. Female visitors were always entertained on the veranda but if there was a need for privacy, they were invited into the sitting-room, where the French windows ensured that the interaction could be seen, although not necessarily overheard, by anyone in the vicinity.

The trainee Brothers, the postulants, were also expected to keep strictly to their house, and all reported feeling 'locked in', 'cut off' from 'ordinary life', unable to see everyday life going on around them. However, the reactions of the postulants were occasionally ambiguous. Although they reported that the experience of enclosure made them 'more anxious' about sex, they also spoke of the dangers in going out for a walk alone, for they thought that one might easily have sex with someone one met on the way. The world beyond the house was thought to be full of temptations. A constant anxiety among Zambian Brothers throughout their training was that they would be cut off from their families, literally and figuratively. This anxiety about separation was expressed in their feeling that, if they lived in the same house as expatriate Brothers, they would not be free to have members of their family to stay.

The etiquette of the reception of visitors was dropped when the Brothers received the visits of relatives and friends from Spain. It was similar to occasions when the Community received visits from Brothers from the Copperbelt who had originally been part of the Community at St Antony's. At these times, the tempo inside the house changed noticeably, and indeed was remarked upon by Zambian Brothers and others who had the opportunity to witness it. Such visitors transformed the sense of place and, consequently, a Brother's sense of being a foreigner and outsider. They highlighted the paradox whereby many of the Brothers felt, on the one hand, distant from the African contexts in which they lived and yet, on the other hand, close to the place that was physically remote. Brother Tomas described the visit of one of his relatives from Spain thus: 'It was like a month's holiday in Spain; imagine, and she is only a niece!' The annual Christmas visit of the Brother Provincial was also a moment when a sense of being in Spain was brought into the house by the many gifts of the *turron* (nougat), *churros* (fritters), cocoa, wine, brandy and other food and alcohol sent by the Brothers' families. The smells and tastes of home transformed the Brothers' Residence. They might, like Proust's *madeleine*, have recaptured a lost childhood, conjuring up what was beyond description (see Bachelard 1994: 13, on 'the odour of raisins').

PERSONAL SPACE AND THE PROBLEM OF BEING ALONE

Issues of personal space highlighted the conflicting attitudes of missionaries and Zambians. Basic, in the Brothers' life, was the obligation to live in common. It was in the Community that the Brother was called to a life of grace. It was also in the Community that he would receive the assistance to persevere in his vocation, bolstered by the mutual encouragement of his Brothers: they stood before him as examples to emulate, and, for them, he had also to be a source of edification. The Brothers recognised, however, that Community living was not easy, for it carried with it many trials and tribulations. In one of his talks, the priest who came to lead the Brothers' Good Friday recollection day commented, 'We live in Community, and so we hurt each other every day.'

The Brothers were not all the same. Each had his own personal style, expressed in dress, in posture, in his ways of relating to others. Despite the call to 'live as one', they had their own ways of doing things, of approaching problems, of working out the way in which they wanted to be accessible to or, in their Founder's instruction, 'present to' Zambians. Seen in terms of pressure, in the push and pull of everyday life, beyond the communal pull, there was a personal push towards individuation, which followed the logic of Christian conversion and, in particular, the call to the religious life: in the Brothers' manuals, the orthodox discourse described 'the *ongoing* process' of conversion. The Brother, as person, became an individual. Each Brother was himself responsible for the fate of his soul. Each played out the religious drama on the same stage: the Community. And yet, the response to God's call was the discernment of a vocation, in other words, a response inescapably individual in nature. In the Catholic setting of St Antony's, this individuality was given an added visible expression in the requirement of the celibate life. Further, the Christian notion of personhood, some would argue, the modern 'Western' notion, is also one that has developed as if it were a movement from the exterior to the interior. One has an interior life, whether it be the life of the soul or of the psyche. The move to inwardness, which Taylor (1989: 127f.) charts from Augustine, through Descartes and Montaigne, has made 'autonomy' its central feature.

The Brothers' orientation in physical space was read by Zambians as indicative of their orientation in moral space.[3] The Brothers read Zambians in a similar fashion. Being able to stand alone, albeit alongside one's Brothers, was a key value of the Brothers' religious life: detachment from persons, places and things. For Zambians, being alone, or standing alone, was much more problematic.

Being alone and 'moving alone' were generally interpreted by students, teachers and local people as lamentable and dangerous states. My own preference for taking a stroll alone was viewed by students as a custom to be pitied. They told me that if I spent a long time alone, I would 'think too much', and that the result would be that I became sick and would have to go home to England. For students, and indeed postulants, being alone was considered threatening in a moral sense; alone, one was thought to be much more likely to do 'something bad'. Most threatening of all was moving alone at night, because this was the time when one was most likely to encounter a ghost, or to be attacked by 'witchcraft', especially if one went beyond the boundary of the school. In this, as in other ways, there was the opposition between the school compound as a place of order and predictability and the surrounding bush as a place filled with the potential for disorder and the unknown.

The ideal of adolescent friendship among Zambians was one in which you always 'moved together with your friend', eating together, showering together, sleeping together. There was a sense in which one should always be in contact with others. This degree of physical proximity, evidenced, for example, in students of the same sex walking hand in hand, was often re-marked upon by Brothers, especially new arrivals. At times, it was seen in a positive light, a sign of mutual care; at others it might be cited as a demonstration of moral weakness, of 'lack of moral fibre' in the students and, by implication, the Zambians. It was taken to be proof of an inability to stand up alone for what one believed in, to stand out from the crowd, 'to think for oneself', to adopt a stance different from the common opinion.

For some Brothers, individualism was a matter of 'human dignity'. An example of this attitude was reflected in the response of Brother Miguel, the postulant master, who discovered two of the Zambian postulants sharing a single bed. While he did not suggest that the two young men had any sexual attraction for one another, it was, according to him, a sign that they had 'no sense of human dignity'. Brother Miguel commented that, in his day as a young Brother in Spain, the discovery alone would have been sufficient reason to expel the young Brothers. 'Particular friendships' were considered a great evil in religious life, dangerous both to the individuals engaged in the friendship and to the Community itself.

In my room at the Brothers' Residence, there was a spare single bed, and whenever students first came to my room, they invariably asked who shared the room with me. 'Love' was read very much in terms of *close* physical presence to others, 'feeling free' with them, making journeys to visit them when they were away. The relationships within the Brothers' Community were read by outsiders in terms of who 'moved' with whom. According to the general view of the students and teachers, two Brothers, often seen together, were said to 'love one another very much'.

It would be wrong to suggest that the Brothers were unaware of the irony marking the distance that separated them from the people they had chosen to live among. In the memories pioneers shared with me, this trend towards separateness was evident; it was perhaps a function both of the Brothers' way of life in the particular historical circumstances, and of their perceived place in the world. It may well be that the architecture of the house soon combined with a certain tradition of relating to others in the immediate vicinity and that this was taken up by the new Brothers when they joined the Community. However, the Spaniards thought the Canadian pioneers had 'kept their distance' from students and local people, and the Spaniards initially saw themselves as 'warmer' people who found it easier to be 'close to' others.

The accounts of the first group of Canadian Brothers disclose a Community that was self-supporting and self-enclosed. In it, Brothers – either individually or in groups – rarely ventured beyond the school compound. Brother Jean-Paul, a Canadian who arrived at the school in 1963, having spent the previous ten years at the Brothers' missions in Southern Rhodesia, recalled that, from the beginning, the Brothers rarely ventured beyond the mission except to escort a school football team, collect maize or recruit children for catechism classes. He attributed this sense of separation both to the Brothers' religious tradition and to the influence of the colonial system.

In the early days, when the school was small, there seem to have been few other teachers to visit. The school was mainly staffed by Brothers. Then, as the school grew, the other members of staff were either European or Asian. This division led to other patterns of interaction, based on perceived or felt 'understandings' of one another, the shared 'Catholic' identity being a readily identifiable axis along which to 'connect'. But now there was an almost exclusively Zambian staff, several of them not Catholic.

In the opinion of some Brothers, it was a bad thing for a Brother to spend much time beyond the Community with teachers or local people – although not with students – either individually or in the company of another Brother. Such absence from the Brothers' Community was read as a sign that a Brother might well be 'on the way out'. Brother Francis recalled that a member of the Community in the 1970s who, unusually, liked to visit the teachers in their homes, was challenged by members of the Community with the remark, 'Why don't you just marry?' The Brother himself tried to be discrete about his own contact with teachers to whom he was giving practical assistance. But far from it being a secret from the rest of the Community, the Brothers were well aware of it and commented upon it among themselves.

When the Brothers left the school grounds, they usually did so in the company of at least one other Brother. They either shopped in the nearest town or went further afield. If they went to Lusaka on a shopping expedition, they often stayed there overnight in their own house. Longer trips were usually to Zimbabwe where they stayed with Brothers of the same Congregation. Thus, when they travelled, they usually kept to their own hermetically sealed world, in the comfort of their own transport. In common with many other expatriate missionaries, few of them ever travelled on public transport within the country. They appeared to be, and portrayed themselves to be, a self-contained group of self-contained individuals. Even within the Community itself, this could sometimes be seen in the way that individual Brothers attempted to hide the fact they were ill.

The Spanish Brothers were conscious that they had no-one whom they could truly call 'neighbour'. In part, it was because of the physical distance that cut the Brothers off and set them apart from others. In part also, and perhaps most importantly, it was because of the barrier that existed for all but one of them, because of their inability to speak a local language with any fluency. But the distance was also, as they were keenly aware, related to wealth and lifestyle.

Some of the Brothers had had the experience of living both at the school and at the Brothers' training centre on the Copperbelt, which was situated in the middle of a miners' compound. These Brothers were the most alive to the spatial expression of contradictions in life at the school. Brother Francisco, who regretted that his early life in Spain had been 'a very enclosed kind of life', in which he had moved 'from one enclosed world to another', commented to me about the situation in the school: 'Here there is no community whatsoever, it's a very artificial situation. Community here cuts us off.'

Brother Francisco described the way in which new Spanish Brothers were readily incorporated into the Community, where all their needs were taken care of. They found themselves among Brothers with whom they had either lived already in Spain or who, at least, shared a common experience and understanding of Marian Community living. Brother Francisco observed, 'You build your own world here ... You can be here twenty years and know very little outside. OK you know something of the experience of the kids, but it is a very closed world, a very closed and small world.'

Brother Francisco also told me of his own dream, a dream that he knew would never be realised in Zambia: to live 'an ordinary life' in 'an ordinary house', to go out to work and come home again, sharing the everyday life of those around him in the village or the urban compound.

One caught glimpses of the desire for something more familial among the Brothers at, for example, the Sunday evening supper, the only meal not prepared by the Brothers' cook. This took place in the kitchen, if numbers allowed, and consisted of fried eggs and eaten with *churros* or chips. For the Brothers, this was the most enjoyable meal of the week because, they said, 'we can take what we like'. The formality of the dining-room gave way to the informality and warmth of the kitchen.

Just as there was a need for a sense of order about the house, and in the rooms of the Brothers, things and people in their correct place, so there was also order in the employment and management of time. The Brothers lived according to the precisely defined rhythms of timetables, both of the Community and of the school. Their daily routine, which varied little from month to month and year to year, was formally agreed at a Community meeting. One could know precisely what the Brothers would be engaged upon at any particular moment. The students' time was similarly apportioned both in and out of class. Following the practice in many other religious Communities, the Brothers' day was split up, in a regular and orderly way. This division of time mirrored the order of the Brothers' way of working which was often commented upon favourably by the students, teachers and local people, although the approbation was not without a degree of ambivalence. The schedule was thought to explain the Brothers' efficiency, which was a quality very much associated with 'white men' (*musungus, basungu*). Yet it was perhaps this same perceived quality that was at the heart of so much for which the Brothers were also criticised as being 'unnatural'. It was a way of life that, both for Brothers and at least for some Zambians, provided a strong contrast with life beyond the enclosed world of the school; 'real life' in Zambia did not allow for such order.

Adherence to their routine seemed to make some Brothers unwilling to be disturbed by unexpected, unscheduled events, or delays to an expected event. Some Brothers were critical of what they perceived to be 'Zambian' ways of doing things, either within the school or in their brushes with Zambian bureaucracy in the wider society. Their construction of 'Zambian life', beyond the confines of their Community and the school, denied the possibility that native culture might have its own set of ordering principles (cf. Huber 1988: 87). The Brothers perceived this sense of a lack of order in everyday life in the builders who seemed unable to build a 'straight' wall or lay tiles in a 'sensible' manner, or in Mrs Chanda's supposed inability to arrange furniture in an 'orderly' and 'neat' fashion.

The perception of the Brothers as 'withdrawn' and 'set apart' had a particular irony. The Brothers' Founder stressed the value of 'presence', that is, living in close proximity to the students as the key element in the process of education. But apparently contradicting this, his pedagogy also stressed that a Brother should never touch a child.

The complaint of both teachers and boys that, 'The Brothers don't visit us,' carried with it a special moral weighting in a place where greetings and visiting were crucial to the construction, maintenance and expression of sociality. The religious value of 'detachment' was also often read by Zambians as a sign of indifference, or worse. Coupled with other aspects of the Brothers' life, it seemed to make relationships of reciprocity between them and those outside the Community extremely difficult. The Brothers constructed their presence as one of 'service' to others, in which the value of exchange appeared to be absent. In the privacy of the Community, however, they often spoke of how much they had received, and learned, from their mission experience in Zambia. Nevertheless, at times, they also expressed fears that they were being taken advantage of. The Brothers' position within, and restricted movement around, the exotic space of the Zambian bush acted as a metaphor for the relationships that were embodied in quotidian practice. Spatial relations were read by the local community as signs that while the Brothers might be incorporated, however uncomfortably and partially, within their physical universe, it did not seem possible to truly incorporate them in their moral universe. 'Space spoke' (Hall 1959: 187) about the things that the protagonists could not find words for.[4]

A great deal of ambiguity surrounded the relationships that did exist. The Brothers had skills and access to resources that appeared to place them in a position of power in the Zambian context (cf. Burridge 1978: 27). They might, in some senses, be said to have been in control. The missionaries built the school. They said, 'This is our school.' As 'white men' who continued to be held by many to possess a certain mystique, they held the economic power, even in postcolonial Zambia. And yet it was possible to read the situation in quite another way.

The Brothers and Zambians might have spoken as if the missionaries were 'at the centre' and 'in control'. However, in many ways, one could read the encounter as one in which the Brothers were on the periphery, excluded – often, perhaps, out of their own choice – from the life of the African community, or communities, that was going on all around them. The distance was created as much, if not more, by the local people themselves, who might dress it up as the kind of social distance, the 'respect', due to 'religious people'. Strickland (1995) offers a subtle and insightful analysis of the giving of respect in contemporary Kunda society. He demonstrates that regularised gestures are 'a form of knowing' which entails 'a certain masking' (ibid.: 210). There were those who were quite happy to have the situation thus: to keep the Brothers at arm's length, to have them 'imprisoned', trapped within a confined space, so that they could go about their lives in an uninterrupted fashion. With movement there was knowledge, and with knowledge there was power. Because the Brothers did not move, at least in some ways, they did not 'belong'. There were many things that they did not know, many ways of relating that they denied to themselves. They did not normally meet or engage with the Zambian teachers, students or villagers as they went about the many ordinary ways in which sociality was maintained. Nor did they meet those male teachers and students who went out 'hunting for women', or returned home drunk from a beer party. There was a great deal they did not share with the people among whom they had chosen to live.[5]

The school had come to appear to some of the Brothers like a prison, a burden they would rather do without, especially in the wake of the 1990 strike when, they said, it was the students who had been 'closest' to them who turned against them. The Brothers, individually and collectively, questioned the reason for their working in Zambia and being involved in the kind of work that the school offered. Whatever face the Community gave to outsiders, there was a continuing debate among the Brothers and much dissension as to the way forward.

Pioneer Canadian Brothers stressed to me their strong identification with St Antony's through their physical involvement in its construction 'out of nothing'. Some of the Spanish Brothers who arrived later felt that they had been sent simply to 'fill a hole'. It was among them that there was the greatest feeling of displacement, although this was a theme that could be picked up in one form or another in all the Brothers' accounts that I collected. From the distance of Spain the mission project should have been a straightforward pastoral and catechetical one. The experience of life within the particular space of the school had undoubtedly had a profound effect on the Brothers who went to Zambia; they debated what the mission project should be, and how it might be accomplished. Huber (1988) details the manner in which missionaries in the Sepik region had to adjust their projects and how, in the process, 'the mission church established acquired special inflections in function and form', and she comments, 'If one can examine "literary encounters with the exotic" for a "poetics of displacement" (Clifford 1984: 683), one can examine the history of these encounters for a sociology of displacement too' (1988: 200).

Through an examination of spatial relations within the built environment of the school, it is possible to read how the experience of displacement was worked out in the routine practices of the Brothers, not only in the ways they interacted with one another and with local people, but also in the gaps in the interaction, in withdrawal, in avoidance and in non-involvement with the other. The Brothers, of course, were not alone in their experience of the displacement inherent in the postcolonial condition. They had created and maintained an institution, a mission school, which was a place of transformation for all who passed through it. Teachers and workers were displaced in varying degrees. They had moved, or more often been transferred, to the school from home, or other areas, to work in a very distinctive place, which made new and different demands and offered diverse opportunities. Those at the sharp end of this transformative process were the students who came to live in a place, in an 'ambience of advantage' (Burridge 1990: 103), which, at its best, seemed to be in 'another country', to follow regimes often quite unlike the ones they had been accustomed to in the domestic spaces they had left behind.

Despite their vow of poverty, the Brothers acted as a reference group for elite behaviour. They were aware that they lived in an island of plenty, but when they tried to act 'simply', they aroused grave suspicions on the part of most local people, who wondered at their motives for 'pretending to be poor'. There was always a tension and a contradiction in the missionaries' attempts to find a way of being that would not be a scandal to those they had come to serve, and would also bear witness to the religious values they proclaimed. Much of their ethos surrounded success, despite their desire to be, like the Virgin Mary, 'hidden and unknown'. Whatever they did appeared successful, whether it was running a school or raising pigs and chickens. Their approach to their classroom duties produced similar results. They demanded, and usually received, an appropriate response from their students. In such circumstances one could almost be persuaded of the truth of the school motto, *Labor omnia vincit*, 'Work conquers all'.

CONCLUSION

The Brothers' Residence was strikingly different from all the other domestic spaces the students had known: a house, which was not quite a home, in and around which the Brothers were seen to move and relate to people in particular ways, ways which approximated more or less to their Rule of Life. Their ways of acting out relatedness at times appeared unnatural or impenetrable to the Zambians who encountered them. The celibate life, in the absence of marriage, affected not only the ways of life within the Community, but also the way in which its members were perceived by the people with whom the Brothers worked. In the eyes of the teachers, the Brothers, being unmarried and childless, were at times more judgemental and less forgiving than they would have been, had they had children of their own.

Yet the Brothers' socialisation into religious life led to routine practices which rarely appeared to give them cause for reflection. Their education was one in which how one related to others came out of a particular notion of personhood and individuality. It was one in which there was, through the process of detachment, a high degree of individuation, the logical end of the call to Christian religious life, albeit one lived in a Community of Brothers. It was also one which stressed the interior life, the life of the soul. Zambian postulants were told that they must first look inward to discover whether God's call was true. They had to find out about themselves. And yet, like other Zambians, they asked, 'How can we know about ourselves? How can we see within ourselves?' A Bemba proverb says: *Munda ya muntu tamwa ingilwa*, 'You cannot enter inside a person.' In contrast, the Brothers, ambiguous figures who might be read now one way and now another, at times drew apart and turned inward to discern God's will; but, in doing so, they made themselves vulnerable to tacit accusations that they were turning their backs on the very people among whom they had come to live.

5

EVERYDAY STUDENT REGIMENTATION

Like the routine practices of the Brothers, the students' quotidian activities were regimented within particular requirements of mission time and space. Members of the school acted to discipline and constrain, and thus to form, the students who passed through it. The student body was acted upon at St Antony's, organised in its bodily movement and controlled in expression and posture. The consequences of real and apparent power were revealed as a relation that penetrated the body through knowledge. For Foucault, the body is the site upon which, in Dreyfus and Rabinow's phrase, 'the most minute and local social practices are linked up with the large-scale organisation of power' (Dreyfus and Rabinow 1982: xxii). In *Discipline and Punish* (1977), Foucault, in his 'defamiliarising the past' (Merquior 1991: 72), offers us a history of repression in which the school is allocated a role isomorphic to that of the barracks, the hospital and the prison – these are all institutions, he argues, which act with precision, through 'technologies of the self' (Foucault and Sennett 1982: 10), upon individual subjects in order to effect their transformation. A key technique was the establishment of panopticism, the inescapable gaze inscribed in social space, 'power through transparency, subjection by illumination' (Foucault, in Gordon et al. 1980: 154) proposed by Bentham and others to ensure a surveillance 'both global and individualising' (ibid.: 146). Foucault explains:

> In the panopticon each person, depending on his place, is watched by all or certain of the others. You have an apparatus of total and circulating mistrust, because there is no absolute point. The perfected form of surveillance consists in a summation of malveillance.
> (Foucault in Gordon et al. 1980: 158)

In Foucault's scheme, the gaze is linked to interiorisation, the process by which the individual becomes his own overseer, and thus constrains himself. It is a process which Foucault traces through a history of Catholicism, but to what extent might St Antony's approximate to the model of the panopticon?

THE OFFICIAL SPACES OF INSTRUCTION

The bounded space of the school property, although unfenced, was clearly marked by several concrete beacons in the bush and along the paths that circumvented the school. Around the periphery of the school compound there were signs in Bemba, *Tapali nshila*, 'No entry' (literally 'There is no way'). The signs were put up to discourage 'villagers' from crossing the sacrosanct space of the boarding school on their way to their fields or the school grinding-mill, in the process distracting and disturbing the scholars at work in the classrooms. Prohibiting trespassers was also generally considered a necessary security measure to keep out 'outsiders' who might include would-be thieves. The boundary, of course, played an equal, if not more important, role, in keeping the students 'in' the school, aiming to restrict their movements for large periods of their time at school.

The school compound fitted, in important respects, the image of a place of quarantine for creating and maintaining a 'massive, binary division between one set of people and another' (Foucault 1977: 198), not unlike the clausura of a monastic institution. For this school, as for many others, the spatial and temporal setting of formal learning had great significance for the practical embodiment of the nexus between the knowledge transmitted and the society at large (Eickelman 1985: 91).

The establishment of this bounded space, a place of enclosure, was integral to the work of the civilising process carried on in the postcolonial school, no less than the colonial one. Indeed it was a prerequisite for this project, in which students were treated as objects to be moulded and thus 'formed' into 'complete' human beings. The control of space and the control of the body were inextricably intertwined.

It might be argued that a formal orderly grid had been established and that this was effective for both constituting and commanding space. In this argument, individuals were observed, evaluated, transformed, in a word 'educated', through technologies of discipline in which 'Each individual has a place and each place has its individual' (Foucault 1977: 143). It follows further that the space of the school, through its architecture and through the internal organisation of the social space created, ensured the regular distribution of such individuals, generating a 'cogent vision of subject and society' (Comaroff and Comaroff 1991: 33). Yet there are limits to this argument: at St Antony's there were counter-technologies which resisted the technologies of discipline. The spaces in which the 'ritualised transaction' (McLaren 1986: 23) of the transfer of one kind of knowledge took place were the classrooms and the academic block. The other spaces of the school were generally referred to by students and teachers as 'the boarding'. There, so many other lessons of the school, other kinds of 'knowledge', were inscribed onto the bodies of the students by members of the student body. I will focus particularly upon the spatial movements by which students were oriented in everyday life, movements experienced through modes of circulation and confinement within the school. The gaze of authority was ever-present. In the classrooms, it was the direct gaze of the teachers and their 'officers' (Foucault 1977: 175) chosen from the 'best' students – the class monitors who reported to them. Outside class, the indirect gaze was of the prefects who administered so much of the running of the boarding school in the name of the school authorities. The question must be asked whether there was an unofficial gaze, authoritative also, and perhaps even more so, in certain spaces.

School life was lived out in a built environment much larger and grander than that of the villages or urban compounds familiar to the majority of the students, prior to their entry into secondary school (see notes, Tables 1 and 2, for the rural/urban split in the student population). The built environment, and the organisation of space within it, worked upon the students who inhabited and passed through it, transforming their perceptions both of themselves and of the world around them, as they themselves were resituated within the modern state of Zambia. For the vast majority of students, it operated as a means of separating them, in some respects, from their old selves and from their primary school peers who failed to make the grade. They became, I would argue, strangers to themselves. St Antony's thus manufactured distance through the creation of difference and distinction. Several students told me how their experience of mission secondary life had deeply affected the way they saw the lives of their parents, brothers and sisters who had failed to get into school. Indeed, some explained that a visit home became a painful experience, when they saw, as if for the first time, the misery of the lives around them. The message of the school was that their life would be quite different, if they applied themselves. They could climb the ladder out of this misery.

The comportment, dress and orientation demanded in these spaces were different from those required in the village or the urban compound. At this mission school, students learnt the conduct proper to its official spaces: the huge school chapel reminded them of their Christian identity; the academic blocks and dining halls called from them the manners and behaviour proper to educated citizens, 'civilised' gentlemen and ladies. They learnt where deference was expected both in the classroom and in 'the boarding'. Processing large numbers of individuals through the various grades necessarily entailed a shift in scale, but this scale also highlighted the public as opposed to the private nature of school life.

The school blocks, the furniture, and the placement of the furniture were highly standardised. The high degree of regularity and uniformity was national and part of nation-building. It was a pattern of regular grids repeated in other mission and state schools throughout Zambia. The classrooms in each classroom block were rectangular, of equal size, and built in the period 1960–4 according to regulations which carefully specified the amount of space per student. In 1967 the regulations were judged to have been 'overgenerous'.[1] Although classrooms resembled one another, each room became an isolated space, a discrete compartment. The opaque walls at the 'front' and the 'back' cut off pupils of the same grade from one another. A successful school career entailed occupying an almost identical amount of space in regular and regulation-size compartments; the student moved 'up', both physically and metaphorically, from the lower grades at the front of the school to the higher grades at the back.

Visibility was also standardised. Windows along one side of the class-room looked out onto a lawn and to the classrooms of the next block or the school dormitories. Each classroom door opened upon a continuous veranda, the wall on this side of the room completed at the top by a set of louvre windows. Behind the classroom door stood a broom and a waste-paper bin. Once the door was closed, pupils could see out on this side only by standing up. However, they quickly discovered that at night, and sometimes during the day, it was possible for them to detect the presence of someone on the veranda if the louvre windows were open because of the reflection on the glass. The same louvre windows made it possible for someone on the veranda outside to observe, at any time and normally undetected by the occupants, all that went on in the room. Only teachers and ancillary workers had the right to be on the veranda during class times or study periods.

In St Antony's, classes in the junior grades normally had around forty students, while in the senior grades the number was limited to thirty-five. The seniors thus had access to rather more space for academic purposes. Most mission schools managed, despite much external pressure from both the Ministry of Education and parents, to stay within their school enrolment quotas, unlike state schools which tended to suffer from severe over-crowding.

Each student, at each stage in his or her school career, was required to occupy a particular place within these official spaces. Within the classrooms, students were ranged in rows, each with his or her own desk and chair, on which was inscribed a number identifying its proper place. Some competi-tion for places was usual at the beginning of the academic year. Students who arrived 'early', that is on time, chose their preferred places. Younger and smaller male students, and all female students, were normally forced to sit towards the front of the room by older and bigger students. They considered that their rightful place was at the back, dominating the class at a distance from the teacher.[2] The younger students, forced to sit at the front, were often those best equipped to engage in classroom interaction because they had a greater ability to follow the lesson and respond quickly and confidently to the teacher's questions. Often, they were children of elites.

Families of elites exerted constant pressure on the Zambian mission school. Such pressure was subversive in that the school's principal mission was to be a site of conversion and transformation of rural Zambians. The mission school was intended to initiate young people into modern ways and to equip them with the means required to succeed in the modern state. The children of the elites had an initial advantage: they tended to have a much greater facility in English, the language of instruction, and they might also have acquired a certain orientation to language (in Bourdieu's term a 'linguistic habitus'), which could be a distinct asset in competition with rural and non-elite contemporaries (cf. Bernstein 1975) [3] Class teachers might intervene and make changes in the seating order in the class for disciplinary or other reasons but, once the seating plan was established, no student was allowed to change his or her place without the permission of the class teacher. Given the placement, the standardised spacing called for the maintenance of a grid. The responsibility for keeping the desks in neat rows was an aspect of classroom order and cleanliness delegated to the class monitor. A member of the class elected by fellow class members and approved by the class teacher and the deputy headmaster, the monitor normally dealt with day-to-day matters of discipline. It was the monitor's duty to ensure that the daily class rota, posted on the wall at the back of the class, was followed for the sweeping and the cleaning of the room by the class members. The class monitor was also responsible for keeping order and silence during the night study periods and in the hiatus between class periods, when one subject teacher left and another arrived. Students who failed to keep the rules were reported to the class teacher or the deputy headmaster.

The teacher's furniture consisted of a much larger desk than that of a student and normally a more comfortable chair. It was situated at the 'front' of the room, in front of or slightly to the side of the blackboard, in an area which, in some respects, became a space of authority. The notion of the 'front of the class' and the accepted authoritarian mode of delivering 'knowledge', received from above, to students who were 'below', went together (Kohl 1970). However, the teacher's knowledge was only one kind of knowledge, derived from one type of authority. Subordinated and constricted within the classroom, students had inscribed upon them one type of orientation – dictated from the front – to the physical environment of the school, and through this an understanding of its social organisation and their position within it (cf. Willis 1977: 67). Yet, from the back of the room, there was another source of authority, another chain of command, directed by students who distanced themselves from orthodox authority and the authoritarian mode, and who embodied, implicitly or explicitly, the means of resistance and subversion. In the junior grades, older and bigger students played this role. In Grade Twelve, it was normally the prefects who commanded from the rear.

At the top centre of each blackboard hung a crucifix. The crucifix as a piece of classroom furniture was at times made into a focus of contestation.

Either seated or standing, the teacher could normally hold the whole class in view. However, the pupils seated behind the front row had at best only an interrupted view of the teacher if he or she was seated, and apart from their immediate neighbours, saw mostly the back of the heads and the shoulders of those in front of them. The message of the seating arrangement was always to look ahead, but this was again subject to powerful counter-statement by those who commanded the back and thus saw *all* the backs in the whole room, along with some view of the teacher.

The confined space of the classroom and the type and placement of the furniture within it ensured that the students' bodies remained markedly docile during class time; their movements were normally restricted to raising a hand to answer a teacher's question or, occasionally, to seek assistance from the teacher during the performance of written exercises. The further message embodied was clear: learning takes place best in silence, with the body unmoving and virtually immobilised (cf. Delamont and Galton 1986: 119; Bullivant 1978: 120).[4]

In Zambian schools – and the mission school was no exception – students were required to sit in an upright, alert and 'attentive' fashion. They were not allowed to move around the room or to leave it without the teacher's permission. The exercise of daily body functions also fell within the power of the class regime. Students had to obtain permission to leave the room in order to go to the toilet or to blow their noses. Only teachers moved around the school from class to class during the course of the day. The students sat and waited for them to arrive from one period to the next. Even when the teachers failed to appear, order and silence were usually maintained.

But did the students experience this process of highly disciplined educa-tion as a type of enchainment from which they longed to escape? The answer is no, and, in this respect, they differed from some children in British or Canadian schools (Jackson 1971; Willis 1977; McLaren 1986). For the great majority of students, the mission school was a privileged place. It was not a place of confinement, but of honour and pride, a prize much sought after by their contemporaries. The statistics regarding school enrolment testified to their elite status.[5] To have entered secondary school at all was, in the eyes of many students and their parents, to have already achieved a considerable measure of success. One could, of course, take their pride to be evidence of their ensnarement in a dominant discourse, an imprisonment in a 'false consciousness', a misrecognition of the 'true' order of things, and thus the clearest demonstration of the power of Catholic mission discourse. However, the 'subject' is even more paradoxical than Foucault suggested in his early work. While there was evidence of the degree to which students might become enmeshed in orthodox school discourse, such enmeshment fell short of total entrapment. Students acted, both playfully and more seriously, in ways that contradicted the appearance of docility.

CLASSROOM INTERACTION

In the postcolonial mission school, the didactic pedagogic style employed by most teachers was primarily one of 'chalk and talk', in the educationists' phrase, consisting of lecture-style teaching to passive students and the giving of copious notes. The teachers appeared in their privileged speaking role (Bourdieu and Passeron 1990: 131). Authorised and equipped by their 'livery of the Word' (ibid.: 125), they did the overwhelming majority of the talking. Their dominant role was signalled by an authoritative and even, at times, domineering stance and commanding gestures.

The students sustained a deferential silence. In addition to being appropriate to subordination, it was a silence felt to be the most efficient strategy for receiving the teacher's wisdom. Any attempt at the slightest disruption in class by one or more students was most likely to be quickly brought to an end by classmates who rebuked the offenders for 'disturbing' them. Students did not normally speak in class, unless requested or given permission to do so by the teacher. Spoken interaction tended to follow a predictable pattern of teacher's question, then student's response, followed by teacher's evaluation of the response. The students acquired the strategies to obtain the right answer or the approved response, in the manner of what Holt calls 'right-answerism' (1969: 21f.). Implicit in this procedure is the subtext of the lesson: what is to be received is generally ready-made and unchallengeable (cf. Edwards 1976: 172). The high level of formality employed by many teachers reinforced this, causing, as Bloch has observed of another context, the content and the order of the material to be perceived not 'as the result of the acts of anyone in particular, but of a state which has always existed' (Bloch 1975: 16; cf. Eickelman 1985: 94).

In the study of 'secular subjects' little or no resistance was normally encountered. However, this was not true where students' religious views were challenged, for example in the theory of evolution and the study of genetics.[6] Here the students at St Antony's might still not challenge the teacher openly, but might explain simply that they would pretend to accept this information 'for examination purposes only'. They would, however, engage in a lively debate when they felt, as many Seventh-Day Adventist and 'Born-Again' students at times did feel, that the literal truth of the Bible was being called into question. In general, however, where religious sensibilities were not offended, teachers' questions had a rhetorical quality about them, not unlike the 'responses' made by the faithful who take part in a religious service.[7]

Male students, particularly in the junior grades, competed to have the privilege of answering the teacher's question by raising their hands and waving their arms in an energetic fashion. In this way, they sought both to demonstrate their knowledge and 'intelligence' and to win the teacher's approval and regard. Senior students, while very co-operative, did not normally exhibit the same degree of enthusiasm. Girls in all grades were generally more circumspect in choosing when to answer questions, aware that a high profile in this activity would gain them the resentment of the boys, who considered themselves superior in intelligence and in all academic matters. Indeed, at St Antony's, as is also reported to be the case elsewhere in Zambia (Serpell 1993: 181), 'education' was largely considered to be an intrinsically masculine enterprise.

Unlike the Spanish or Zambian Brothers, who normally employed a rather egalitarian mode in classroom interaction, many Zambian lay teachers tended to adopt a condescending manner, an 'artificial aggrandizement'.[8] This approach was inculcated by early missionaries, Serpell argues, as part of their civilising mission. A similar style was evident in Zambian primary schools (Serpell 1993: 93).

The message of the pedagogic style was to place the teacher on another plane, beyond error and beyond challenge. Students had to submit to their teachers. It was a style that would have meshed well with the Catholic church of an earlier era, so sure of its possession of the 'truth' and so secure in its place in the colonial world. Yet, it was also one that sat equally easily within Zambian traditions of wisdom being the prerogative of the elders. A Bemba proverb has it: *Akanwa ka mwefu takabepa*, 'The bearded mouth does not lie'. This is just one example of the hybridisation which was a striking feature of this mission school life. The authority of age met the authority of 'learning' and, *within the classroom* where orthodox authority was vested in the teacher, they would seem to have meshed easily together. When it came to authority within the student order of the boarding school, the coming together of disparate 'traditions' resulted in a more complex relation.

The magisterial discourse acted as a powerful distancing technique. The distance words could create added to the distances inscribed in school space through the placement of teachers and the distribution of students in it. Such distances were also guaranteed by the school's rules and regulations (Bourdieu and Passeron 1990: 110). The teacher-student interaction was one in which the puerility of the students was exaggerated (Serpell 1993: 91; McLaren 1986: 121). In the foreign discourse and space of the classroom, students and teachers were engaged in modes of interaction which would have been considered disturbingly anomalous if such behaviour were displayed by adults in other contexts of everyday living. Serpell observes of the Zambian context:

> known answer questioning; eye-contact interaction with children of the opposite sex; verbal praise for appropriate performance of simple, assigned tasks … Like verbal utterances in a foreign language, each of these culturally exogenous behavioural practices requires a foreign 'grammar' for its interpretation.
> (Serpell 1993: 121–2)

THE LANGUAGE OF THE CLASSROOM AND THE SCHOOL

The language practice, unlike the language policy, of the school was far from simple. As stated in School Rule number twelve, the medium of instruction and the official language of the school, as of Zambia itself, was English. Every student was expected to speak English at all times. There was a clear difference in the way language, especially English, was employed by the Brothers, the students and local people. The Brothers were, almost without exception, men of few public words. As 'men of action', they doubted the sincerity of the eloquent speaker. In this they followed their Founder, who had a great distrust of 'fine phrases' (Marian Brothers 1947: 303) and did not hesitate to remove from class any Brother who expressed himself in complex language or with high-sounding eloquence. This he saw as being contrary to the key virtue of 'simplicity', and thus evidence of the sin of pride: the Brother was 'puffed-up' (ibid.: 304). In contrast, students revelled in complex grammar and abstruse vocabulary; it was evidence, *par excellence*, that one had achieved the competence required in the postcolonial world. Here, then, was evidence of student rejection of the missionaries' attitude to words. Students would decide for themselves; for them, the simplest way of expressing oneself in English was not the best.

There was a perhaps surprising lack of resentment on the part of students to the rule about speaking English, as far as the conduct of the 'academic life' was concerned, although this was less true of school life outside of class. In general, they judged it to be an asset to their studies; it was also a badge of their 'education', a mark of distinction between them and 'villagers'. For the Brothers, especially in the early days when they made up most of the teaching staff, the rule had obvious advantages in terms of discipline and control. It curtailed the use of the vernacular languages, of which most of them had no knowledge and which they had little inclination or encouragement to learn. However, learning at least one local language was recognised by the Brothers in the 1990s as a priority for their work in Zambia.

The result of the rule meant that virtually all members of the school community were expected to conduct all communications in school in a second or a foreign language. During the time of my fieldwork, I was the only native English-speaker in the school compound. All the teachers were either Zambians, from various parts of the country, or African expatriates. The Brothers were Zambian, Spanish and Malay Chinese. The students came from a wide range of Zambian ethnic groups and from various parts of the country (see note 5, Tables 4, 5 and 6). Such ethnic diversity led to a distinctive situation of heteroglossia, officially dominated by one language and unofficially marked by many.

The postcolonial Catholic mission students, like the colonial ones (Carmody 1988; 1992), were powerfully aware of the economic and political weight of English in present-day Zambia. Performative competence in

English, both in the classroom and beyond, was widely admired. The prestige of English could readily be observed in classroom interaction, in casual talk and in more public moments, such as school debates. Debaters vied with opponents to produce the largest number of unfamiliar or unknown English words in their attempt to dazzle the judges and their student audience. Particularly unusual or archaic words, such as 'pellucid', were greeted with loud applause, if not with comprehension, by students who shouted encouragingly, 'Now you are using!'

Beyond the politics of language use in day-to-day school life, it was clear that competence in English was a major determinant, distinguishing those who were enabled through exam success to proceed further up the educational ladder. That the language of 'scholarship' was totally distinct from the first vernacular languages spoken by teachers and students was not an uncommon occurrence (Goody 1977: 125). However, language is crucial in the construction of knowledge (cf. Berger and Luckmann 1971: 85) and the extent to which the categories of understanding are influenced by the preservation of the 'unspoken' language remains uncharted territory (Serpell 1993: 99ff.). At St Antony's an 'educated' person was not supposed to 'stumble' when using the 'white man's language'. English oral transmission, however, was achieved in a context in which the spoken word was dominated by the written word. One had the sense of living in a time warp, a return to an earlier moment of English usage, as a result of the often archaic language the students employed. For example, male students spoke of their girlfriends as their 'darlings'. The sense of time warp was heightened by the degree of formality that tended to colour much interaction involving respect or reserve of some kind. The English teacher received frequent requests from male students wanting to be taught 'expressions', the more 'complex' the better. The students would employ them in displays of sophistication when trying to attract girls or when demonstrating how 'educated' they were to family and friends during the holiday period. Clearly, achieving competence in English, a language both powerful and alien, was construed by students and others as becoming a different kind of person (cf. Serpell 1993: 124). In the school context, I observed how the Brothers, like other members of staff, perceived those who had already achieved a high degree of competence in English within their home environment to be quite different from other less articulate students. This competence might appear to some Brothers to signal a community of interest, a tacit agreement of a common understanding of the world, but this was often a misreading which could lead to a sense of bewilderment or even of betrayal. This was evident in the 'riot' that preceded my return for fieldwork. Among the ringleaders of the student strike were students from influential backgrounds, identified by some Brothers as being among 'those who were closest to us'. In everyday school life, students had little access to printed material in local languages, beyond a few 'story books' that circulated among friends. However, there were hymnbooks in vernacular languages, used by different denominations during their services. Although the school Mass was said in English, the Catholic choir and students would sing in Bemba or Nyanja, as well as in English, during the service. Seventh-Day Adventist students also sang hymns in Bemba, Nyanja and Tonga, in addition to English, as did members of other groups such as the United Church of Zambia and the Born Agains. At Seventh-Day Adventist services students would also preach in a vernacular language. There were two attempts to teach a Zambian language at the school, but both came to nothing.[9]

Students' Zambian languages tended to employ a great deal of slang and to be the language of the town, for example 'town Bemba', rather than that of the village, the 'real Bemba', which students often described as being 'too deep' for them to understand. One consequence of this vernacular illiteracy, or rather creolisation, was that students frequently wrote 'home' to their parents in English. Their parents, in turn, if 'uneducated', often had to find a translator, underscoring the distance thereby created between them.

Students' nicknames for teachers exemplified their play with language and they demonstrated the ludic space students could create for themselves in the face of teachers' control. Within each cohort, there were a number of students who exhibited a particular gift for mimicry and impersonation. They were, like their fellow students, careful observers of mannerisms and displayed an almost uncanny ability to replicate the voices of teachers or student authorities. The impersonations were at times unmistakable because of exaggeration, but at other times they were much more subtle, and one needed considerable local knowledge to be aware of what was being enacted. The subjects of school discipline thus retained a measure of agency against attempts to enforce order. In caricature and mimicry, students domesticated and contained those placed in authority over them.

The nicknames were often English words or expressions connected to the teacher's subject speciality, for example 'Good Will' and 'Ledger' for the two Accounts teachers. Or they might be words frequently used in a teacher's subject, perhaps satirically apt for caricaturing a teacher's personality or appearance: 'Glacier' (Geography teacher), 'Conc.' (abbreviation of 'concentrated', as in concentrated acid, for a Science teacher), and 'Hunter' (History teacher, said to resemble a 'Bushman'). Students changed some of these names, of course, to fit fresh events , and from one cohort of students to another. My own nickname changed at least three times, from 'Jesus' to 'The Walking Dictionary' to 'Chuck Norris', an American 'B' movie actor admired for his ruthlessness and fighting prowess, my alleged resemblance to whom was also remarked upon by *'mishanga* boys' (cigarette sellers) in the nearby town and in Lusaka. The Spanish Brothers' nicknames tended to be examples of words that they habitually mispronounced, highlighting the students' anxiety about the Brothers' competence or frustration at their lack of fluency, for example 'Shabstance' ('substance', for a Chemistry teacher) and 'Jes' ('yes' for a Mathematics teacher). However, when competence in English was not an issue, their nicknames reflected other attitudes, as with the other teachers, for example 'Computer', for a Brother, a Mathematics teacher whose powers of mental arithmetic were judged to be prodigious.

Zambian teachers, often more competent in English than the majority of missionaries, exhibited a certain degree of ambivalence towards the rule regarding the use of English in the school. Their attitude in practice was sometimes an indication of the state of relations between them and the Brothers' Community. Some Zambian teachers rather pointedly interspersed vernacular expressions, for example to check on comprehension – 'Mwaumfwa?' ('Do you understand?', literally, 'Have you heard?', in Bemba) – or for entertainment purposes. This facility to switch codes – and to make a meta-statement about the capacity for code-switching, 'introducing a fresh message about the making of messages' (Werbner 1989: 224), denied to all but one of the Brothers – could have the result of creating a marker between 'us' (Zambians) and 'them' (non-Zambians), in which the Zambians, *pace* other appearances to the contrary, retained the upper hand. Thus Zambian teachers and students would lay down markers that demonstrated the extent to which they had not been 'captured', or exclusively entrained, in the foreign language of mission discourse, while at the same time demonstrating their facility to 'deal' in it and with it. In the staffroom, at break and other times, it was not uncommon to hear more than one vernacular language spoken, although there could be a great deal of code-switching during such interaction, depending upon subject matter, context and audience (or those thought likely to eavesdrop).

The mutual monitoring of everyday spoken utterances was mirrored in students' evaluation of classroom knowledge and its presentation. Students constantly checked the material they were given in class against that given in other classes in the same grade. Prescribed knowledge is normally said to be of high status (Young 1971: 37) and 'expert', and thus contrasted to 'commonsense' (Keddie 1971: 155). Other knowledge is often said to be devalued as a consequence, as Giroux, in his comments on Bourdieu, has observed:

> By linking power and culture, Bourdieu provides a number of insights into how the hegemonic curriculum works in schools, pointing to political interests underlying the selection and distribution of those bodies of knowledge that are given top priority. These bodies of knowledge not only legitimate the interests and values of the dominant classes, they also have the effect of marginalizing and disconfirming other kinds of knowledge.
> (Giroux 1983: 268)

What happened at St Antony's was rather more complex than what is suggested by Giroux and Bourdieu. Yes, students held the knowledge stored in syllabi and textbooks to be generally 'true' and of high status, the rightful property of the educated gentleman. However, this was not true of *all* such knowledge. For example, students might consider that techniques studied in Agricultural Science were much better than the 'traditional village' knowledge of such matters, but this perceived superiority of 'the white man's' knowledge did not apply across the board. Other knowledge was not necessarily marginalised. Students were conscious of the powerful 'African science' of witchcraft, of the activities of sorcerers, and also of a variety of spirits, despite the disclaimers encountered in their study of science and religion. Indeed, in religious matters especially, the 'truth' was hotly contested, albeit within Christian frames of reference.

The systematisation of the institution's 'knowledge' about the students was considerable and so too was the ordering and rationing of academic knowledge for transmission to students. The curriculum was narrowly tailored to the requirements of the public examinations of Grade Nine and Grade Twelve.

Each taught course or subject had its own syllabus within which, according to term and grade, each week was allotted a certain amount of knowledge to be transmitted to the students.[10] Teachers were required to make a plan and keep a record of each term's work. In theory, plans of each lesson in their 'Schemes of Work' and 'Records of Work' were supposed to be submitted to department heads and the headmaster, for checking and approval, at regular intervals. Kept on file, the plans were open to scrutiny when external subject inspectors, authorised by the Ministry of Education, visited the school and evaluated the performance of both students and teachers.

It is important for the analysis of discipline and its theoretical implications to note that monitoring was an extremely anxious activity within subjectivity. The subjects themselves, the students, monitored the process of making them subjects, in the specifics of teaching and learning. Students were acutely conscious of the allocation of knowledge as 'bits and pieces'. They inspected the way in which 'knowledge' of each taught course was divided up and distributed to them, according to their level and status within the educational hierarchy. They monitored the information given by different teachers in the same grade. They did so by exchanging evaluations with friends in other classes of the same grade, both in their own school and in others, and they ranked teachers accordingly. Students immediately expressed anxiety, if they suspected that their teacher might be straying in any way from the approved syllabus.[11] Implicit was the notion of contract which both parties had to honour.

The transmission of appropriate knowledge was largely achieved through the giving of notes. Normally, these were dictated or written on the board by the teacher, or copied on the board by a student, usually the class monitor, to whom the teacher made his or her notes available. Students complained about a teacher who refused to give notes or who suggested that the students would gain more from making notes of their own. They often preferred to have Brothers as subject teachers because the Brothers tended to be far more consistent in their appearances in class, unlike some of their Zambian colleagues who had a high rate of absenteeism. The Brothers' Community had its own supply of paper, often a scarce commodity, and their own means of duplicating material. The Brothers' popularity, especially in Grades Eight and Nine, was at least in part because they produced extensive printed notes for the students to copy. Students placed great faith in notes as the key to success. They inherited the notes of friends on higher rungs of the ladder or who had already completed their secondary education. It was not uncommon to see circulating among a group of close friends the notes of a particularly successful student of five or ten years past. Such notes came with the *imprimatur* of an exemplary biography recorded in the academic history of the school in recognition of outstanding achievement in the public examinations of Grade Nine or Grade Twelve. The inalienable aura of success was still attached to his notes, which acted both as a talisman and a source of knowledge. The transmission of knowledge as a social exchange of notes, before and after examinations, was thus productive of personal biography, no less than subjectivity. Once the notes had been copied, the next stage was the lengthy process of committing them to memory, thus taking 'possession' of the knowledge (cf. Eickelman 1985: 167), following a method of rote learning instilled in students from their earliest days in primary school.

The collusive nature of the process must be stressed. Students and teachers colluded in the construction of students as 'empty vessels' (Freire 1972: 45; Fanon 1972: 169) who had to be filled by the teachers with the relevant knowledge required to pass the exam. Although they generally interacted with the teacher energetically in the classroom, they saw their role as essentially passive. In this temporary and partial surrender to teacher authority, students played the part of accepting subordination. They clearly judged this to be the most effective way of achieving their aim: success in exams. It would, of course, be a mistake to read into their behaviour a total acceptance of the school authority vested in teachers. Their 'submission' was strategic and situational and not to be read as evidence of their 'capture' within some all-embracing discourse of power. In the Foucauldian scheme, the exam is the site where the techniques of hierarchical observation and normalising judgement combine.[12] The exam is said not only to test the knowledge of the students, but also to provide teachers with further information about the students (Foucault 1977: 185). Yet, it should, of course, be noted that some students cheated in exams. Indeed, it was in this way that a number of students in Zambia gained entry into secondary schools. Rather than being a revelation of the 'truth' of the student's ability, the exam might instead be a site of student resistance, of a calculated revolt from the gaze. This information, whether 'true' or 'untrue', played a vital role in the construction of the individual student's school biography in terms of his reputation for academic ability, and contributed in large measure to the production of a student's 'social essence' (Bourdieu 1990: x), his worth in the education or labour market.

Given the fact that the transmission of knowledge was tied to examination requirements, it could be argued that much of school life, both inside and outside the classroom, was fixated upon examinations. The culmination at the end of the academic year was what Bullivant terms 'examinamania' (1978: 124). Success in exams provided the passport to the higher echelons of education, to the top of the educational pyramid. It would be difficult to exaggerate the degree of anxiety that surrounded exams for the vast majority of students. They went to elaborate lengths to prepare themselves by cramming through the day and most of the night (known in the language of the school as 'going for nocturnos'), in contravention of school rules (Simpson 1990: 110). End-of-term reports, detailing and commenting upon both academic performance and behaviour in class and in the house, were sent to parents and guardians three times a year.

Student records, inevitably important for my own account, informed the making of students' subjectivity, no less than the systematisation of knowledge about them. Students were aware of these permanent moral accounts whose existence was persistently recalled by the Headmaster at school assemblies, by teachers in class and by preachers in the school chapel. I examined the whole archive, some of it prey to white ants, from the beginning of school enrolment in 1960.

A close record was kept of lateness or absence and the individual was called to account regularly for any shortcomings. Students' presence in class was marked by the subject teacher on a class register at three transitional moments in the course of the day: at the beginning of the day's first class, at the beginning of the first period after morning break, and at the recommencement of classes after the lunch break. At staff meetings, the Headmaster or Deputy repeatedly reminded teachers of the importance of a careful and accurate record of attendance. In addition to the class rolls, house monitors conducted roll-calls in the 'boarding'.[13]

A school secretary collected and collated the class-attendance information daily and checked absentees against other registers. These recorded permission to remain in bed or to leave the school compound. This information, a small part of the record of student progress, was kept on file together with other documents for which each student was assigned a file number on admission to school. A personalised dossier, containing the student's photo-graph and sometimes quite detailed observations of the minutiae of every-day life, was built up. It fitted within the disciplinary regime in which the 'ordinary' displaces the 'heroic' (Foucault 1977: 190), at least for all but the most exceptional students. The dossier was the primary means for the school's construction of an individual's official school biography.

In the students' case, the moral account was not merely what Foucault calls a 'penal accountancy' (Foucault 1977: 181). Beyond that, each moral account also recorded students' 'gifts' and 'talents', evaluations of their suitability for boarding-school life and for promotion to posts of responsi-bility within the school. All of that was used, although on occasion quite selectively, in character references issued by the school to institutions of higher education and prospective employers. Here then was the 'cooked' or processed data for a particular presentation of the self; it was a one-sided construction of a biography largely beyond the control and the direct know-ledge of the individual student. The students knew that a dossier was kept, but not necessarily what went into it.

Also kept in the dossier were demographic details of a student's family, home address, parents' levels of education and occupations, the number and gender of siblings, birth order, and religious affiliation. This personal information was all provided by the student, who gave these details on a printed form completed soon after arrival. Accompanying him or her to the mission school was the student's academic record from the beginning of primary school and the primary school headmaster's recommendation and moral evaluation of the student's character and abilities, together with an assessment of the individual's 'potential' in academic and other areas, particularly sport. Each term's internal exam results and grades achieved in all public exams taken were also recorded here, as were reports of any disciplinary cases, letters from parents or guardians and copies of any letters sent from the school regarding the student. Students were not given the right to consult these 'confidential' files, and access to them was normally restricted to the headmaster and deputy, the secretaries and the careers teacher. Personal files were also kept on all teachers and school workers. These were updated annually with comments on performance by the head-master or assessments of school inspectors and were seen only by the headmaster, his deputy and the secretaries.

It is striking how much power and influence can reside with those who hold the post of secretary.[14] One school secretary at St Antony's, Mr Chisenga, achieved an influence, in the eyes of both students and staff, quite disproportionate to his nominal status in the school hierarchy. He was known by the teachers as 'the Eyes and Ears' because, until the announce-ment of multiparty elections, he was a local UNIP party activist; in addition to his other duties, he was a special constable. However, two other aspects lay behind his influence: first, his unrestricted access to school records and thus biographical information concerning teachers and students; second, his role as a Seventh-Day Adventist preacher.

The world of this mission school, with its myriad rules and mass of micro-penalties, created extensive space for the commission of 'crimes', or 'offences' in the school phrase. Constant attention to the detail of presentation and performance was required of each student. The monitored self had to learn to be *self-monitoring* in the particular areas of life deemed to be of importance for the civilised, Christian gentleman; it was a secular mode of being which, especially in its attention to the minutest detail, had its parallel in the daily examination of conscience conducted by at least some religious Brothers.

The daily timetable was a most accurate instrument for the control of subjectivity, drawing together with time, as it did, the regulation and codification of space, motion and placement. It was proclaimed in a manner which punctuated each day, strictly dividing it into various periods to which adhered a range of qualities at different points in the day or week. The actions and movements of individual students were placed within a system of 'normalizing judgement' in which there was what Foucault calls 'a whole micro-penalty of time (lateness, absences, interruptions of tasks), of activity (inattention, negligence, lack of zeal), of behaviour (impoliteness, disobedience), of speech (idle chatter, insolence), of sexuality (impurity, indecency)' (Foucault 1977: 181).

The number of periods allocated to each subject and the length of each period were fixed by the Ministry of Education.[15] Behind the timetable, the key to the daily operation of the school and the movement and placement of bodies around it was an official notion of time. This official notion had it that time could be measured with precision and, as a commodity, like money, should not be squandered (Bullivant 1978: 55; Willis 1977: 67; Comaroff and Comaroff 1991: 64). Efficient time usage and speed and accuracy in the performance of classroom tasks were the signs of the 'good' student whose efforts were expected to be rewarded in the end-of-year exams.

The beginning and end of each period was marked by the school bell, rung by a junior student assigned this special responsibility by the Headmaster. Being a distinction in handling a very prominent instrument of public control, it was a much sought-after post; certain qualities of 'modernity', such as smartness in personal attire and punctuality in the performance of all duties, were considered obvious prerequisites by students and teachers alike. The bell ringer had to be, in the student idiom, 'jacked-up'. The class bells, like those of the monastery, were but one part of the regular sequence of mission school bells and sirens calling students to attend to their tasks, or signalling some measure of respite.

Within the school compound, the day was divided by a further sequence of bells. Huge lorry wheel-rims, struck by a thick iron bar, produced a distinctive sound, more sonorous and penetrating than the bell of the academic block. In addition to these bells, there was the dining-hall bell, as well as the school siren which called the students to class, three times a day, and to evening study. The siren also signalled the beginning and the end of other activities, such as housework and sports or club meetings. Following the custom of religious houses, the Brothers' daily routines, whether sacred or secular, were signalled by the ringing of a bell. Obedience and commitment were demonstrated by the promptness with which the Brother responded. Similarly, students were expected to respond immediately to the summons of the bells. Especially urgent were those that signalled the beginning and the end of the day and required students to be found in a particular place at a precise moment. For example, by the end of the morning rising bell, every student was required to be out of bed, his two feet planted firmly on the ground. A few seconds late, and the student would be booked by prefects for 'oversleeping'. Such failure to respond promptly normally resulted in punishment in the form of manual work, an appearance at 'manpower'.

The student's most urgent task in the first class of each term was to copy the timetable. The message was that the first, and perhaps most important lesson, concerned punctuality and the proper use of time. Students, conscious of the importance timetables had for their day-to-day existence, carried copies around with them and also posted them on the inside of their lockers, or on the wall for those who had the privilege of their own private personal space. The temporal axis received as much attention as the spatial (Comaroff and Comaroff 1991: 236). The intent in the work of transformation was clear. Standardised mission practice linked neatly here with nation-building. Yet, as elsewhere at St Antony's, it would be wrong to think that mission discourse had it all its own way.

The timetable, in common with schedules found in other mission and government schools, outlined the division of time and of 'knowledge', each portion of which was contained in a syllabus to be completed according to a strict schedule. Expressed in ways and in terminology which were new and exotic to a Grade Eight student, it encouraged him to think of himself as a different person. He had to deal with specialisms quite unlike the subjects he had studied at primary school. The programme of studies was more complex; the whole day was sub-divided into more and more precise units of time, both in the academic block and in 'the boarding'.

There were those, however, who refused, guardedly or more openly, to play the game. In this way, and in contrast to those who made a prestigious name for themselves as models and leaders, some students became notorious in the annals of the school as 'trouble-makers', their names regularly entered into the prefects' 'delinquents' book'. Their punishment was highly visible, seen by both students and teachers, at the weekly punishment session of 'manpower'. There were few markers of distinction separating Grade Twelve 'Commoners' from students of junior grades and so some of them appeared to choose another route to prominence. Some Grade Twelve 'Commoners', 'wounded' in the prefects' stakes, and some of the academically weakest students in other grades, were normally said by prefects and teachers to be the most recalcitrant.

THE SCHOOL UNIFORM AND THE CELEBRATION OF THE PERSONAL

The school uniform could be read as a normalising technique that also acted to restrict the body and to regiment the students into docility. However, students of St Antony's also regarded it as an emblem of their elite status and wore it with pride on extra-curricular outings to other schools. The uniform spoke of their difference, their distinction, their civilised, educated, gentlemanly selves.

Fine distinctions could also be made in the uniform, with individual students making personal statements in their dress. Most obviously, office-holders, prefects and monitors had their badges of office pinned to their shirt pockets or on their ties. Care and attention to one's uniform, or the blatant disregard for such care, was a good indicator of the wearer's place in, and submission to, the school hierarchy.

Prefects had to be smart, but so too had all 'Commoners'. The carefully turned-out uniformed self indicated a willingness to identify with the school. Tight shirts and frayed, faded trousers might be an indication of poverty, but deliberate neglect might also be a silent expression of the distance a student felt, or wished to create, between himself and the institution's authority. In day-to-day life, when added to other regimes of the class, the uniform lent to academic activity both a drilled and a processed quality. It operated to create in the classroom setting a business-like, formal air to the task of learning.

There were two versions of the school uniform: the weekday and the Sunday uniform. The weekday uniform consisted of black shoes, black socks, black trousers (a black skirt for the girls), a blue shirt and a plain black tie. Grey pullovers were worn by those who could afford them in the cold season. In the hot season, permission was granted for students to forego wearing the tie. The Sunday uniform differed in that the blue shirt was replaced by a white one. Frequent collective and individual inspections were conducted to ensure that all conformed to the student dress code. Negligent students were punished, and not having the correct uniform in good condition was a sufficient reason to be sent away from school. Students' hair was subject to careful scrutiny and monitoring. Long hair was forbidden, and any student judged by teachers or prefects to have unkempt, unruly hair would be ordered to have it cut. There were a number of student barbers who provided this service free-of-charge. The ubiquitous school secretary, Mr Chisenga, was the most popular student choice; students said he gave a really 'smart' look. Never short of customers, Mr Chisenga charged a few *kwacha* for a cut, and he did not cut hair on Saturday, in accordance with the Seventh-Day Adventist rule forbidding work on the Sabbath. Students were not allowed to wear beards, and facial hair became a site of contest, with senior students especially eager to manifest their manhood in this way. School authorities, on the other hand, insisting upon their construction of puerile students, strove to remove the contradictory evidence from the faces of those in their charge.

Although teachers' styles of dress varied, many Zambian teachers wore suits or jackets, shirts and ties. The expatriate Brothers, however, were noticeable in their casual style, and they often eschewed formality in favour of an open-neck shirt, blue jeans and sandals. At times this was commented upon disapprovingly by some students. In their attire, the Spanish Brothers differed from their French-Canadian predecessors. In the early days of the school, the French-Canadian Brothers wore religious habits. When, in the 1960s, it was decided to forego the habit, the French-Canadians wore trousers, shirts and ties and, on occasion, jackets. In contrast, the Spanish Brothers' style of dress made a statement, consciously or unconsciously, which was at odds with the value attached to appearing like a gentleman. In this way they were at odds with both the earlier Brothers' practice and that maintained by the Zambian administration.

The Spaniards wished to appear 'ordinary' and to construct the academic exercise into a type of 'work'. In their dislike and distrust of any type of show or the desire to cut a dash, they situated themselves close to the Founder's wishes. Humility and simplicity should have no truck with the fine things of this world. At least, such was their intention. However, while the Brothers wished to stake a claim for the 'ordinary' and the 'everyday', their dress, ironically, was judged by some students to be the height of 'cool' fashion.[16]

Against the constraint in formality emerged a striking contrast in body posture and movement in the student body, during certain periods of weekends and holidays. It was marked when students were given permission to wear their 'personal' clothes and the rule against speaking vernacular was suspended. I observed how public holidays, such as Africa Freedom Day and Youth Day, were celebrated in students' attire, signalling release from formal control. Students would don caps, hats, and dark sunglasses (called 'goggles' by the students and considered a particular mark of being 'cool', normally worn by the better-off).[17] Many students also wore belts and carried sticks.[18] The uniform, ornamented and no longer standard, spoke of indivi-duality, of being one's 'cool' self. I read a sense of release from constraint, also, in the way in which the individual body was 'extended' by these additions and the escape from surveillance attempted through the 'hiding' of the eyes, seeing and not being seen. School gatherings at these moments tended to be much noisier than usual, and I often noted that social inter-action among students had a rougher quality about it, illustrated both in their language and their comportment. Order and discipline were revealed at such times to be extremely fragile constructions. It was an atmosphere in which one sensed that things might easily get 'out-of-hand'. Few teachers, if any, were present on these occasions. The student body, consciously or unconsciously, reclaimed a larger share of the common spaces of the institution, at times creating an ambivalent arena for any teachers who might venture there.

Such holidays also tended to produce the more serious disciplinary cases. Some students, dressed 'like villagers', went out-of-bounds to attend local beer parties in surrounding homesteads and were either spotted by teachers and prefects, or came back to school in a 'drunken' condition, perhaps merely 'smelling of beer'. In the regimented and somewhat confined space of the boarding school, the gaze was augmented by a distinctive smell. Students who smoked, for example, were easily identifiable, because one could smell on their breath, at inappropriate moments in the day, the tooth-paste used in their attempt to mask the odour of tobacco or marijuana.

Outside class and study periods students spent the great majority of their time in or around the dormitories, the school library, the sports fields and the bush that immediately surrounded the school and fell within the school boundary. All boarding students were required to remain within school bounds and they normally needed permission to go beyond the school boundary, although there were certain times at weekends and on Wednesday afternoons when all students were allowed to go 'out-of-bounds'. At such times, students often took the opportunity to 'move together' with their friends.

The release depended upon access to the uncontrolled space of the African bush. Such 'moving together' into another space freed students to relax completely. Like the wilderness of the English garden in Jane Austen's novels, the bush often became the site for activity forbidden within the ordered confines of the school. Students needed special permission to go beyond a reasonable walking distance from the school: they were not, for example, allowed to travel as far as the nearest town, some thirty kilometres away. Within the compound, teachers' houses were normally considered 'out-of-bounds'. The variation in the observance of this rule was considerable, with teachers differing in their desire to protect their privacy. The Brothers' Residence fell into a somewhat anomalous position, not being regarded by students and teachers as a 'home' and therefore unlike the houses of other staff. This was perhaps a consequence of the nature of the building itself and perhaps also of the absence of the 'normal' family structure of a teacher's wife, children and other relatives.

LIFE IN THE 'BOARDING'

The space within and around the dormitories took on different qualities at various times in the course of the day and on different days of the week. At some times, a relaxed atmosphere prevailed, for example, immediately after class and study periods and for much of the weekend. In the absence of staff, students could be found at these moments relaxing together in varying degrees of physical intimacy on the beds in each dormitory wing, with groups of friends of the same sex often piled together on a single bed, chatting, going over the day's events, exchanging stories, solving homework problems, or merely resting quietly. It was a tightly gendered space; no female students were allowed in or around the dormitories.

Students were put into houses by the school administration at the beginning of Grade Eight on a purely random basis. However, when, by chance, a house seemed to gain a larger-than-average number of good footballers or athletes, suspicions of deliberate manipulation and favour-itism were aroused. No house wanted too many 'mosquitoes' (very small boys) because of the importance attached to inter-house sports competi-tions. Each student was normally allocated a bed and a locker for his possessions by the resident house prefect of his assigned house, although a shortage of beds and lockers meant that some junior students had to share.[19]

A student could not change his allotted place without the house prefects' permission. The space where he slept and kept his belongings came to be known as his 'place', and it was the first port of call for anyone trying to locate him. If he was not 'at his place', other wing members would normally be able to tell the enquirer where he was to be found. An individual's habitual movements during the day and the friends he moved with were generally well known by his neighbours.

Boarding-school life was on the whole a very public life. It was conducted in the unpartitioned dormitories and other spaces of the school, where an individual's moral character, strengths, weaknesses and slightest habits were open to inspection and evaluation by some, if not all, of his peers. His wealth or poverty was also there for all to see. A student from an affluent home could be identified by the fact that he possessed a bedspread and a pillow. The quality and number of his sheets and blankets would furnish additional information. Communal showers and washing facilities, common in schools of this type, added further to the denial of privacy (cf. Wakeford 1969: 66 on British public schools). Grade Twelve students, however, were an exception as they had their own communal showers, which other grades were forbidden to enter.

The place allocated to the student on arrival in the dormitory depended mostly on his grade, although other factors might later come into play. Grade Eight newcomers, *kwiyos*, were allocated what were considered by the students to be the lowest places in the wing. These were either the beds situated in the middle of the wing or close to the doors that opened onto the veranda, practically on the threshold of the dormitory (from this latter position the new boys became known as 'wind-breakers' in the cold season). Their allocated place physically demonstrated their marginal condition of being 'betwixt and between' (Turner 1974), as they began their initiation into boarding-school life. If there were low internal dividing walls in the dormitory, spaces against these walls were normally reserved for Grade Ten or Eleven students. The most coveted spaces were the corners of the dormitory. Usually reserved for senior students, they were sometimes won by students of lower grades who had achieved prominence as 'post-holders' within the house, being wing monitors, house treasurers, florists, or members of the food or sports committee. 'To be given a corner' was to be declared a man of influence, and might well indicate suitability for the post of prefect in years to come. However, as 'Commoners' in student parlance, all students (with the exception of prefects, monitors and some favoured Grade Twelve 'Commoners'), were required to live out their school days 'on the surface' of the dormitories.

Each dormitory wing had at least two cubicles, commonly called 'cubes', reserved for Grade Twelve monitors and other Grade Twelve 'Commoners'. Such students, while not having 'won' the post of prefect, either enjoyed a good relationship with their house prefects or were known to be 'humble', unlikely to challenge the prefects' authority. The cubicle walls, seven or eight feet in height, did not reach the ceiling, had no door, and could thus normally be entered easily at any time. Students often used sticks or iron bars to wedge their open locker doors against the cubicle entrance, thus hindering unwanted intrusions, although this was strictly against the rules. Each cubicle normally had two bunk beds, and prefects deliberated at length about who should be assigned such a privileged position. Even the partial screening from the rest of the dormitory, which removed the occupants from the uninterrupted gaze, afforded them the greater possibility to engage in activities contrary to the school rules.

The prefects' status and authority were marked by the achievement of privacy not granted to any other students. Each prefect was entitled to a 'room' of his own, in most houses the storeroom at the end of each dormitory block. It was barely enough space for a bed, a desk and a chair, and usually the chair had to be moved around to permit entry and exit. A prefect had a key to his room, although the school authorities held master-keys and thus reserved the ability to intrude upon his private living-space at any time. The electrical system gave him access to power, when all the other dormitory lights were switched off. A prefect, therefore, had the opportunity to study at any time, a considerable advantage over his fellow Grade Twelve students, the 'Commoners', and at times a source of tension with them.

The prefect was allowed to personalise his living space in a way denied to others. 'Commoners' often placed pictures on the inside of their locker doors (see Wakeford 1969: 78 for similar customs in English public schools). But a prefect was allowed even more: to buy curtains for his window, and to put up pictures and posters. On a prefect's walls were normally the school timetables, together with the occupant's personal class and study timetable. The most popular pictures, photographs cut from magazines, tended to fall into two types: pictures of black, especially Afro-American, sportsmen, or pictures of consumer goods and expensive cars. Also displayed were photographs of the occupant, normally dressed in school uniform with his prefect's badge prominently displayed, together with rather demure photographs of girlfriends. Students were normally eager to have their photograph taken. Several members of staff and one or two students had a profitable line in amateur photography. The better-off students 'sponsored' snaps for their friends to join in. The staged settings, the clothes worn, the props employed and the poses adopted for this particular presentation of the self deserve a study of their own. Some soft pornographic pictures of women, normally white women, circulated among students in the dormitories, but the school administration was quick to confiscate any pictures deemed unsuitable. A school rule required the approval of the school authorities for any publication brought into the school. While one could find some pornographic novels circulating among the students, novels by African writers were widely read. Even more in demand were James Hadley Chase and, rather surprisingly, Mills and Boon romances.

Various maxims or slogans, written in the prefect's own hand and prominently placed, acted as a means of self-exhortation: for example, 'No sweet without sweat', or, for students active in groups such as Seventh-Day Adventists or Born Agains, verses from the Bible or short prayers. Also prominent, printed with indelible markers, was the list of prefects who had occupied the room in previous years. This memorial situated the prefect within a school tradition and legitimated his presence there. The occupant added his own name at the end of the year, permanently recording his prominent place in the school hierarchy.

Before class each morning, the dormitories were swept by the junior students of the dormitory, according to a rota organised and checked by the wing monitor. Each student made his own bed; the sweepers aligned all beds and lockers in their proper place. During weekdays, the locker was placed facing towards the head of the bed. Teachers made weekly spot checks for order and cleanliness in the dormitories, the adjoining ablution block and the surrounding area. Marks were allocated for each wing and totals given for each house, the scores being added to those awarded at the Sunday inspections described below. At the end of the year, a trophy was awarded to the cleanest house. During class time the dormitories were normally considered to be out-of-bounds, except for sick students who had obtained the requisite permission to remain in bed.

In addition to the weekday checks by members of staff, the Sunday inspection was the more individuating scrutiny of place and person. It was conducted before the Catholic Mass or alternative religious service held simultaneously in the school hall, at one of which all students were expected to be present. This inspection, carried out by the Headmaster and House-masters together with the prefect body, had changed little in its format since the earliest days of the school. For most students, preparations for the inspection began on Saturday with housework. This general cleaning and tidying in and around the dormitories was supervised by wing monitors. Originally, all students had been required to take part, but by the 1990s Grade Twelve students had established a 'tradition' of exempting them-selves – they were 'too busy' with their studies to have time to engage in such activities.

'Education' was generally considered by all students to be the escape route from manual labour, the only kind of labour to which they gave the term 'work'. It was accepted that rising up the academic echelons relieved one of such menial tasks. Some students went to the extent of growing and keeping one or two finger nails extremely long, as if to signal their refusal to engage in such work. This attitude directly contradicted the enormous educative and spiritual value that the Brothers' Founder placed upon manual work. However, many other students stressed the fact that they assisted in agricultural work during school holidays. A common response to questions about students' plans for the holidays was 'I will go home and help my parents on the farm.' Around the dormitories at housework times, it was mostly the junior students who were engaged in preparations for inspec-tions. The Grade Eights were expected to do most work because, in the opinion of students in other grades, they were 'the least educated'.

A recent development in the school was the exemption of all Seventh-Day Adventist students from Saturday work. This concession allowed them to keep their Sabbath holy by attending their religious service and meetings and by abstaining from unnecessary servile work. They did housework and washed their uniforms and other clothes on Fridays, after class or early on Sunday mornings. In this way, as in others, Seventh-Day Adventist students set themselves apart from the rest of the student body, proving both their difference and their influence. In keeping the Sabbath on Saturday, they also pointed once more to what they judged to be the serious errors of the Catholics and others who persisted in 'praying on the wrong day' and thus failed to keep the Commandments of God (Exodus 20: 8–11). All students were required to 'stand for' Sunday inspection in their Sunday uniform and, in general, took this exercise very seriously. At the approach of the inspec-tion team, wing monitors shouted 'Enter' and 'Stand properly' to the students who were normally milling around on the veranda of the dormitory, putting the final touches to their personal appearance and checking that of their friends. Each student stood silently to attention at the foot of his bed, hands by his sides, staring directly in front of him and avoiding any eye-contact with those carrying out the inspection. The Headmaster or Housemaster, preceded by the school or house prefects, moved solemnly through the wing. The prefects, pen and paper in hand, made copious notes while they inspected in turn each student, bed, locker, window, and window sill before passing on to the ablution blocks and the areas around the dormitories.

The moment was tense, and no one wanted the embarrassment of being singled out for having failed in this presentation of self. No one wanted to incur individual shame and, in the process, let the house down by causing it to lose vital points in inter-house competitions. Nor did anyone want to suffer the punishment for failure: manual work supervised by the house prefects. It was not only the student who came under careful scrutiny. His locker was placed at the foot of his bed, with the door open to allow for the inspection of all his possessions and also of the manner in which they were kept. Everything in the locker had to be kept neatly in order and fall within permitted items in the school. At St Antony's, it was not only God who saw everything. There was little of a student's life that was not open to regular inspection and evaluation.

Once the inspection team had passed through the dormitory and was out of earshot, a great sigh of relief usually came from the members of the dormitory, accompanied by loud comments and laughter as lockers were closed and noisily returned to their normal position. The results of the inspection were usually read out in each dormitory by the prefects before the last bell. If many points had been lost, recriminations and punishments followed. If the surroundings or the ablution blocks failed the inspection, a whole dormitory might be given additional manual work in punishment. The house judged the 'cleanest' received a trophy. Although this cup did not carry the same kudos as those awarded for athletics and other sports, it was still proudly displayed on the prefects' table during the annual house party.

The party, organised by the prefects and monitors of the house, was the occasion towards the end of the year when each house celebrated its triumphs in various fields of endeavour. The house which had secured some of the major trophies for inter-house competitions in football, athletics and other sports had much to celebrate. Such trophies were seen by students and teachers alike to be indicators of the morale of the house; the ability to hold a successful celebration was yet one more pointer. The house members who had little or nothing to show from their participation in the various inter-house competitions would be mocked by the others.

House parties were conducted with an extreme degree of formality. These were the celebrations of cultured gentlemen, although, behind the scenes, there might well be much arm-twisting of those 'Commoners' who showed reluctance to attend and to pay the agreed amount for the purchase of provisions. Representatives were invited from the other houses, together with a few specially favoured members of staff. Each guest received a typed or handwritten invitation, at the bottom of which, instead of RSVP, were printed the words 'Regrets Only'. 'Distinguished guests' and the house-master, the 'father of the house', received a precisely detailed programme of events, with each event scheduled for an exact time (in my experience, this was never adhered to). Each hour of the programme was usually broken down into five-minute, or even shorter, slots. Here is the beginning of one such programme:

> 19.00hrs, National Anthem;
> 19.01hrs, Opening Prayer;
> 19.02hrs, Welcoming speech by the Housemaster;
> 19.08hrs, Toast;
> 19.10hrs, Biscuits;
> 19.15hrs, Speech by Outgoing House Captain;
> 19.20hrs, Dance by Housemaster and Outgoing Prefects;
> 19.25hrs, Speech by Incoming House Captain;

And so the evening proceeded. Speeches were punctuated by music and dancing, by the whole house together or by grade or office. There were numerous toasts which were concluded by the invitation to repeat the name of the house together with the refrain 'Oyez'. All prefects made speeches, recalling their school careers from their first days at St Antony's. The out-going prefects invariably asked forgiveness from anyone they might have inadvertently hurt, and offered advice to those they were about to leave behind. The food appeared, in dribs and drabs, throughout the long evening, often served by house-members who were unable to raise sufficient funds to attend as guests; each 'course' was served at long intervals. Reports later stressed the number and variety of courses enjoyed and the quality and loudness of the music.

Houses vied with one another to go on the longest and the latest into the night. There was a tension between order and disorder which belied the precision of the programme, the planned sequence of events, and the formality of the speeches. These all suggested a sincere effort to hold what students, especially prefects, judged to be a cultured and civilised event worthy of modern, educated gentlemen who knew how to behave in such circumstances, and had the *savoir-faire* to pull it off. Yet there were other forces at work that constantly threatened such civil society. There was the possible disgruntlement of house members who often complained that they had not received their money's worth and suspected that some of the funds had been siphoned off for other purposes. There were also those few students who, despite all efforts to persuade or coerce them, refused to attend. They were often Grade Twelve 'Commoners' who had clashed with the prefects in the past or who simply suspected that the party was, first and foremost, a celebration and demonstration of prefect power by new and old incumbents.

THE DINING-HALLS

Just as each student had his place in the dormitory, so too did he have a place allocated to him in the house dining-halls. Tables were set out in rows in each hall, with separate tables for house prefects and, in one hall, a high table for 'the Big Five': the School Captain, Vice-School Captain, Sports Captain, Vice-Sports Captain and Boarding Captain (formerly called the Chief Kitchen Prefect). Prefects demonstrated their superior position by choosing to eat after the majority of students had completed their meal, the kitchen prefects eating from a common dish out of sight in the kitchen. The prefects' rationale was that they were often too busy 'solving cases' such as arguments among students, discipline matters to keep to the mealtime schedule. For this activity they sometimes used the term *milandu* in Bemba, drawing an explicit parallel with the work of a village headman or a chief at a local court. In this way, they underlined their superior status, for they had no need to rush for food like the 'common man'. Their 'share' remained secure, not something that an ordinary student, particularly one in Grade Eight, could be sure of. Students were grouped six to a table with the junior grades of one house mixed together.

Discipline and order were imposed on the students by the prefects. At the signal of the kitchen bell, the students, already milling around the verandas of their dormitories, plates in hand, proceeded to the dining halls, dressed in school uniform. Late arrival, after the doors had been closed, or incorrect dress, such as shorts or an open shirt, resulted in the student's being refused entry and being 'booked' for punishment. The act of eating had to be performed in a *civilised* manner. 'Nakedness' was considered to show a lack of respect.[20] All meals began with a perfunctory grace, intoned by one of the kitchen prefects, the most common formula being 'God Bless Our Food', to which the students replied 'Amen'.

Students were not allowed to help themselves to the food presented on each table in two large dishes, one containing *nshima* (mealie-meal porridge) and the other containing a relish, normally vegetables, rather than the meat (called 'World Cup') that students often craved. Order and measure had once more to prevail. Before the kitchen bell rang, Grade Ten members of the house food committee, known in the school as 'shunters', moved around the tables in a procedure known as 'balancing', making often very minor adjustments to the amounts of relish put into each dish by the school cooks and waiters some two hours earlier. 'Shunters' explained that the school workers, being 'villagers', did not know how to 'balance properly' and that 'fairness should prevail'. The kitchen prefects checked the work of the 'shunters' and made their own further adjustments before the meal bell was rung.

The position of 'shunter', whose appointment was the prerogative of the kitchen prefects, was much sought after. The acquisition of this post was normally a good indicator of the holder's future prospects in the prefects' stakes, two years ahead, if he was judged to have performed well. It was generally agreed to be a difficult job. A 'shunter' was expected to be of good character and 'active', that is someone who participated and demonstrated talent in sports, for example, a good footballer. He had to be someone who could handle problems and troublemakers. 'Lazy' students were ruled out of consideration; it was thought that they would only go to the kitchen to eat and use the position to their own and their friends' advantage. There were one or two perks, however, like a regular supply of *chikwangwa*, the crisp *nshima* scraped from the bottom of the cooking pots. On each table, there was also a 'sharer', the student who was judged by the members of the table to be the one best qualified to divide the food into equal shares. Students ate in the 'traditional' way with their hands, although from separate plates that contained their share.

Meals were occasions for general announcements from house or school prefects and times when the mail was distributed. Students were instructed, 'Listen to your letter', and then the names of those who had 'received' were read out. Reputations were won or lost according to the amount and type of mail received. Wednesday lunch was also the moment when the names of the previous week's 'offenders' were announced. This was said to be necessary to remind students to present themselves at that afternoon's 'manpower', manual labour punishment, although it was obviously another moment in which public judgements of individual character were broadcast.

SCHOOL ASSEMBLIES

At certain moments during the week the school met. This happened on three weekday mornings for school prayers in the chapel, and, most formally, every Monday morning for school assembly. The Headmaster, Mr Mwila, held a regular school assembly, that keystone ritual of the school institution which attempted to set a frame for the coming week (cf. Willis 1977: 67). The assembly, held before the first period, was normally the one moment in the week when all students came together. Serving a number of functions, such as the opportunity to give a homily and to communicate information concerning current events, it also acted as a manifestation of authority. Attendance by staff was expected in theory, although in reality few of them apart from the Brothers normally put in an appearance. Teachers' presence or absence at assembly was usually a good barometer of the Headmaster's authority.

The assembled students stood outdoors, in front of the administration buildings, under the gaze of the 'Big Five'. All students were dressed in their weekday uniforms and held their books and other things required for class. The 'Big Five' stood on the top of the steps at the main entrance to the school and looked out over the assembled students. When a bell tolled the time for assembly, the Headmaster, dressed smartly in suit and tie, emerged from his office. When he reached his accustomed place on the edge of the veranda steps, a respectful silence fell among the students, and the prefects flanking him immediately relieved him of any books or papers he carried. The assembly followed a regular format. The Headmaster began by reading from the Bible or another religious text which he then paraphrased and commented upon. The general tone of his sermon was normally 'uncontroversial', tending to deal with Christian themes at a high level of generality.

Mr Mwila indicated the end of his exposition with the words 'Let us pray', at which all heads were devoutly bowed.[21] He then uttered a short prayer, at the end of which the students replied 'Amen'. This was invariably followed by a period of coughing and clearing of throats and shuffling of feet, while students relaxed after this solemn moment.

The Headmaster then made various announcements and drew attention to forthcoming events. Certain exhortations appeared with regularity. One involved the encouragement to 'suffer now' through an acceptance of discipline and hard work in often difficult situations, especially with regard to the worsening school diet, so that one could 'enjoy later'. The message was thus future-orientated. Endurance would reap its own reward. However, the Headmaster frequently reminded students that this future to which they all aspired was simply a further stage of the journey, often linked to the notion of Christian pilgrimage, upon which they were already embarked. The detailed itinerary of that journey was daily being added to, as the students' exam performance and all aspects of their behaviour were constantly being recorded. It was this school biography, he reminded them, that would follow students out beyond the confines of the school after they had completed their education, as future employers and others consulted the school authorities for such details. It was therefore in the students' interests to be meticulous in keeping the school rules.

Another constantly expressed theme, despite the presence of a small number of female day students in the school, was the need to act, always, like *gentlemen*. The transformation of students into gentlemen had been a recurrent theme in exhortations to students since the beginning of the school. The current formulation stressed by the Headmaster concerned body care and becoming conduct. A gentleman was, above all, courteous in his dealings with others, teachers and fellow students alike. Knowing his station in life, a gentleman was never rowdy, would never mock others, nor use harsh words, and took pride in himself and in his personal appearance. When young, he did not smoke, drink or engage in other such 'adult' behaviour. As the Headmaster reminded the students repeatedly in assembly after assembly, drawing as was his custom upon his full store of Zambian proverbs, 'A gentleman does not wish to be like the cock who broke his wing while still young.' The use of proverbs by Mr Mwila, a Bemba, was one example of the hybridity of 'traditional' and 'modern' in the school. Bemba wisdom was transmitted through the employment of riddles and proverbs. Proverbs, *milumbe* for men, *inshimi* for women, were taught by elders. Young men were expected to display such knowledge in public speaking (cf. Frost 1963; Garvey 1974: 348). Regularly citing the expression 'a gentleman and a scholar', Mr Mwila thus drew together two dominant aims of schooling at St Antony's.

Mr Mwila himself was generally judged to be a gentleman by both Zambian staff and students for several reasons. He was immaculately turned out in suit and tie on all formal occasions. Thought to be 'understanding', he was not known to speak harshly or lose his temper. On more than one occasion, I heard teachers and school workers commenting of him: 'He drinks at home, like a gentleman.' This seemed to imply, first, that he did not frequent the local bars, some of which had a reputation for drunken brawls and the availability of women, and second that, should he get drunk, he would not provide a spectacle unbefitting his status. Students normally listened to the Headmaster attentively and respectfully. On certain topics, however, their response turned to annoyance or only partially veiled challenge. This happened especially with money matters, such as a Parent-Teachers Association (PTA) Committee decision to increase school fees, or introduce an additional charge of some kind.[22] The power to increase some of the fees resided in the hands of those elected to the PTA Committee at the annual general meeting to which all parents were invited. In practice, few parents attended and the committee was usually dominated by wealthy articulate parents who were unrepresentative of the majority of the students' parents. Students also responded ambivalently when they were warned on the perennial problem of the mockery of newcomers. Except in the most extreme cases, when the school faced a crisis because of a student demonstration or class boycott, they normally restricted their expressions of disagreement to collective bouts of laughter or nasal groans of disapproval.

The Headmaster brought the assembly to an end, after various announcements, by instructing the students to prepare for the singing of the national anthem, with the words 'At Attention'. The students duly adopted the appropriate stance. The Headmaster or a school choir member intoned the first line, 'Stand and sing of Zambia, proud and free', after which all students joined in. The school assembly was framed within a public discourse, resonating with religious and national images and themes, pointing a lesson for each student about both the religious and the civil nature of the educational institution. The first public moment of each week thus recalled the students to a sense of purpose, above all as Christian gentlemen and citizens. The student body, dressed alike and adopting a posture of respect and conformity, which could be read as an acknowledgement of its place within the institution, might seem to reaffirm a common identity in a common endeavour.

It would, however, be a mistake to interpret such moments as the 'achievement of common meaning' (Lonergan 1972: 79) in any simple sense. The school assembly was an arena in which the Headmaster could articulate the orthodox discourse of the Catholic mission school. But at St Antony's there were multiple discourses at play, countering the orthodox. Each discourse worked off the others, in the process marking out the boundaries of distinct moral communities. This contest was embodied and enacted in a variety of contexts.

PREFECT POWER AND 'MANPOWER'

One indication of a reluctance to conform readily was to be found in students' responses to the many school rules. Failure to keep school regulations rendered the culprits liable to various sanctions, among them manual work or, in the students' phrase, 'manpower'. Much of the burden of maintaining control of the student body fell to the prefects. However, their part in the schooling of character was a complex one. They often acted to achieve purposes at odds with the intentions and values enshrined in orthodox school discourse in an attempt to create yet another variety of student subjectivity. There was both the officially sanctioned means of correction, and also an unofficial discipline, rooted in Seventh-Day Adventist teaching, and thus antithetical to orthodox Catholic conduct.

The numbers of those punished varied from week to week. Some students made regular appearances, almost every week. In some weeks, the names of many, if not most, students were entered into the prefects' penal account. Such were the moments when prefects decided to have a 'clean-up campaign' – a term borrowed from the activities of the Zambian police force – especially at the beginning of their period of office. Other students appreciated that the 'new brooms' were eager to give concrete expression of their authority.

Offences fell into two categories. Category A offences were lesser ones meriting one and a half hours of manual work, while Category B offences were the more serious, meriting three hours. Table 5.1 is an example taken from the prefects' register of offences.

The types of offences collated from each prefect's lists of offenders and then entered into the School Captain's register, called the 'Delinquents'

Table 5.1 Prefects' Register of Offences (excluding smoking and drinking), 14 October 1991 to 6 November 1991

Offence	Number of bookings
(A) TIMETABLE	
Late for meals	200
Late for prayers	166
Out of bed/late for bed	110
Insolence	104
Missing prayers	64
Oversleeping	51
Missing roll-call	25
Late for roll-call	23
Sub-total	743
(B) SPACE TRANSGRESSIONS	
Out-of-bounds	85
Trespassing (walking on flower beds)	58
Taking share out of dining hall	28
Sub total	171
(C) OTHER	
'Blasting' (using vernacular)	247
No toilet paper	92
Incorrect uniform	89
Making noise in dormitory	48
Sleeping carelessly (not covered with a blanket)	02
Fighting	02
Urinating on flower beds	01
Sub-total	481
Total Offences in this three-week period	1395

Book', offered an insight into the strategic placement of the prefect in discipline. The school authorities required the prefect to police the space of the mission school *beyond* the classroom, disciplining and punishing anyone who contravened school rules.

The period covered by the bookings listed shows an extremely high total, averaging about one bookable offence a week for each student in Grades Eight to Eleven. The outgoing prefects and 'Commoners' of Grade Twelve no longer considered themselves students, once the examination period had begun. This meant all their disciplinary matters were dealt with directly by the Headmaster, Deputy or Housemasters. It often proved a difficult period for the school authorities; some students flaunted the fact that, as 'school leavers', they no longer considered themselves bound by school rules. The school administration arranged transport for Grade Twelves to leave within minutes of their last exam, in acknowledgement of the threat that these students posed to the school authority. The following three-week periods were closer to the average number of bookings throughout the year, with 401 bookings in the period 6 November to 27 November 1991, and 864 in the period 24 January to 15 February 1992. Compared with prefects' booking figures in the 1970s (School administration files), these numbers were still extremely high. It would appear that booking offenders was a technology of discipline that had increased dramatically in the frequency of its use.

The totals listed above excluded smokers. Many students in the school smoked ordinary cigarettes and a substantial number smoked marijuana, known locally as 'dagga'. The first students at St Antony's, who were often in their early twenties, had been given permission to smoke by the pioneer Brothers, many of whom were heavy smokers. This privilege was withdrawn at the insistence of the Ministry of Education. The policy of the school, in line with Ministry of Education directives, was that all smokers were to be reported to the Deputy Headmaster or the Housemaster. However, in dealing with this matter and with students caught drinking or stealing, the prefects demonstrated how they could also act *ultra vires* (see Wakeford 1969: 111 for similar prefectorial activity in British public schools). The School Captain and his Deputy decided to deal with smokers separately and without the knowledge of, or recourse to, the school administration. Both being Seventh-Day Adventists, they were opposed on religious grounds to an activity defiling the body, the temple of the Spirit. Including the Chief Kitchen Prefect, more than a third of the prefects were Seventh-Day Adventists, who were overrepresented among prefects for a number of likely reasons. One of the most important possible causes was that in their role as preachers, some of them gained early reputations for being articulate and forceful speakers. A facility with words and the ability to speak in front of large gatherings without 'shivering' were considered important qualities in a 'leader', and above all in a prefect. In their attempt to enforce a discipline more in keeping with their own faith, the Seventh-Day Adventist prefects singled out activities widely known to be indulged in by at least some of the Catholic missionaries and some of the other teachers. In so doing, they made a political statement in a moral discourse. Embodied, rather than spoken, it was thus all the more forceful in their continuing campaign of voiced criticism of the Catholic authorities and students whom they considered to indulge in activity no 'true Christian' should condone.

Senior students caught smoking were taken after 'lights out' to the sports storeroom. There, placed within a circle of prefects, they were instructed to remove their shirts and bend forward. The light was switched off and a torch was shone onto the offenders, who were then slapped hard on the back by the prefects, using the lower palm of the hand. After this, the culprits were made to parade through all the dormitories, carrying with them their 'Peters' (cigarettes, from the brand name Peter Stuyvesant), as a warning to the other students. Some senior students resented the fact that the prefects took the law into their own hands. Others preferred not to have the matter reported to the school administration. However, a sense of injustice was widely expressed, for it was known that some prefects, not Seventh-Day Adventists, smoked with impunity. The same treatment was meted out to students caught drinking beer, an offence liable to harsh official punishment and thus one for which the prefects' punishment was less resented. Under official punishment, students were suspended from school while the regional Ministry of Education officers deliberated whether to sentence them to a further period of suspension, corporal punishment, manual work or, in extreme cases, expulsion from school. The frequency in the use of corporal punishment, officially reserved to the Headmaster and his Deputy, had varied considerably over the years depending upon the views of the holders of those posts. Many students came from primary schools where corporal punishment had been liberally employed and so, on the whole, showed little resentment about it, provided that it was administered privately and not as a spectacle to be observed by the whole school. A variety of items were employed, including belts, sandals and rubber hoses.

The prefects dealt with thieves in a similar manner, although with greater emphasis placed upon the aspect of shame. After being 'beaten', the thief was painted with the white lime used to mark the running track, before being paraded through the dormitories. While smoking and drinking were not viewed by all students to be wrong, as in Zambian society in general, expressions of loathing for thieves were universal. For the one branded in this way, school existence was often made very difficult. He was ostracised and immediately fell under suspicion whenever any property was reported missing. It was not uncommon for such students to escape by transferring to other schools.[23]

The prefects, led by a core of Seventh-Day Adventist students, thus imposed a discipline upon students that was more in line with the religious tenets of Seventh-Day Adventism than those of the Catholic missionaries officially in charge of the school. Elected and approved by the school staff, they established and maintained a counter-authority from within. They seized the moral high ground, and created a distance between themselves and the school regime. They demonstrated their ability to fashion another variety of Christian subjectivity, in their rejection of the one intended by the Catholic mission school, which they judged to be in serious error. Orthodox Catholic discourse had no power over them. They were not ensnared, in any early Foucauldian sense, within a total or institutionally imposed discourse through which they were persuaded of the nature of their 'true' selves. On the contrary, they worked with, and within, a competing part-discourse and sought to discipline all students in accordance with it.

CONCLUSION

Control of the body in all its detail was crucial when students were required to submit themselves to education as a civilising process for gentlemen and citizens, for an elite in the making. Awake or asleep, no area of activity or body function was left out of consideration. Even failing to be in possession of a reasonable supply of toilet paper was a sufficient cause to be labelled deviant or 'delinquent'.[24] The requirement of the punctual presentation of self, dressed and groomed in conformity with all other students, was a key technique of discipline, and was the area of most bookings by prefects. Self-control was expected at all times. Within the dormitories, talking was subdued and, at certain moments, forbidden altogether. After the last bell at night, students were required to observe silence; one is reminded of the 'Grand Silence' observed in monastic houses. The school dormitory did not physically contain individuals within isolated compartments, as in the Ecole Militaire described by Foucault (Foucault 1977), but dormitory silence performed the same function, of isolating and individuating each student.

One could, of course, read this in another way. The penal accountancy revealed, and was one measure of, student resistance. For example, no objection was raised against the imposition of the rule for speaking English within the classroom. The revolt against it came when the rule was to govern all spoken interactions at school; significantly, 'Commoners' often noted that this was one of the rules most commonly flouted by the prefects themselves. Similarly, some students were not enthusiastic about attendance at the daily prayer in the school chapel. Breaches of discipline in smoking, drinking and sexual activity, much of which went undetected as bodily engagement, demonstrated that apparent conformity in some areas should not be read as total submission.

My description of social and personal spaces, timetabling and regimentation discloses the schooling of an uneasy, transitional subjectivity in the everyday life of St Antony's. The analysis deconstructs the pervasive inscription of discipline upon the student body. One avowed aim, at least for some staff, was the civilising mission of education for elites in the making, transforming them into Christian gentlemen (and now Christian ladies too) as citizens. Staff appeared to dominate the discourse which the discipline embodied. But divided among themselves, most obviously along ethnic and denominational lines, staff hardly had it all their own way, no more than did the students who, as prefects, became increasingly authoritative within the school hierarchy. If, at the start of the school, Brothers as teachers initially minimised the stature, autonomy and force of prefects, they had to yield; elitism in the boarding tradition prevailed. With the development of prefect authority came a growth in fundamentalism, especially Seventh-Day Adventism – indeed, each trend fostered the other, within a single process. What was evident was that the prefects, upon whom the staff increasingly had to depend for policing the boarding spaces, took the bit between their teeth and seized the moral high ground. As Seventh-Day Adventists, secure in their popular reputations as articulate preachers, they came to play their part in the schooling of subjectivity with pious aggression openly, if somewhat guardedly, directed against Catholics, Catholic teaching and Catholic practice.

The regime of discipline itself, so total, finely discriminating and seemingly inseparable, was actually in many ways fragile. It was politicised, negotiated, covertly contested, submitted to with open gestures of resistance, and suborned for unofficial purposes contrary to the official.

6

THE STUDENTS' ORDER OF THINGS

Separated from their home lives in the village or the town, students of St Antony's lived in a segregated milieu, somewhat apart from other Zambians. The school, remote in the countryside, was implicitly cordoned off, in various ways, from nearby village life. Student movements, both licit and illicit, went back and forth into the world beyond the school, but the rhythm of their lives and the myriad requirements of the school established their sense of difference. They felt themselves set apart both from those who lived around them and from the majority of young Zambians, labelled 'drop-outs'. The majority of Zambians, unable to find a place in a secondary school, were expelled from the formal education process through the mechanism of the Grade Seven leaving examination. The students, despite other differences among themselves, shared and proudly acknowledged a common prestigious identity as members of an elite school.[1] This chapter considers how this identity was constructed and maintained in student discourse and practice, and a major concern is the unofficial formation process known as 'mockery' that all new students experienced, especially when they first arrived at the school.

Foucault made us recognise we are constructed in discourse, but the notion needs rethinking for mission school life. Here multiple part-discourses were at work, not all of them in the control of school authorities, and not all of them dominantly Catholic in attitudes and assumptions. Students not only moved in and out of part-discourses, but also played active roles in their construction, maintenance, disjunction and development. The very disjunction between the part-discourses – the fact that they did not add up to one single encompassing or total discourse – was an accomplishment, and one in which student effort at compartmentalisation often subverted what might otherwise have made for more of a unitary discourse.

Many students positively embraced their experience of mission education. It was part of the civilising process which they considered created a positive distinction and a distance between them and 'villagers'; it mitigated certain aspects of being 'African' which many of them often evaluated in a negative manner. It is noteworthy that they normally described themselves as 'African', rather than 'Zambian'; they constructed, or acknowledged, a sense of identity that had much more to do with notions of 'race', and supposed innate characteristics, than of 'nation'. An 'African' essence was thought to transcend local boundaries. In everyday talk, its elaboration had obvious resonances with the colonial discourse of many earlier administrators and missionaries, traces of which could still be observed in some missionary constructions of 'Africans' and vice versa. Of course, local boundaries, marking ethnic group, religious affiliation and class membership, did have a salience for students at other moments in the different contexts of school life.

Education equipped students with the necessary credentials for entry into the higher echelons of the sociocultural pyramid. Even more, students, like their teachers, believed in the transformative power of education, for it 'modernised' and 'civilised' them. The point I want to stress, however, is that it also created in them an ambivalence towards, or even a rejection of, their Africanness. Caught within a moral discourse of failure, students judged Zambia and Zambians to be inferior in the modern world. In many ways, 'these black men want[ed] to be white' (Fanon 1972: 9; 1986). In everyday interaction and talk, especially when relaxing around the dormitories, students revealed a predominantly negative evaluation of people and things 'African'. The term 'African', of course, acquired value and meaning only in relation to other terms (de Saussure 1949: 153ff). For the students, it often formed, explicitly or implicitly, one side of the oppositional pair, *umuntu*: *umusungu*, 'African', 'black man': 'European', 'white man'. Some students cited biblical authority in Genesis 9: 22–9 for the inferior status they accorded to black skin tone. Highlighting a perceived break between 'black' and 'white', students often remarked that when God made black men, 'God was very unfair'.

Dormitory talk offered many examples of this discourse. No student wished to be described as 'black', and the lighter one was, or could be made to appear through the application of 'skin-lightening' cream, the better. The 'best-looking' student in a class, or house, in the opinion of the students, was invariably the one with the lightest skin. This was mirrored by the many pictures of Afro-Americans, such as Carl Lewis and Mike Tyson, found on the walls of prefects' rooms. The 'lighter' they appeared, the more they were described as being 'handsome'.

The adjective 'African' was often employed by students in a pejorative sense: an 'African promise' was one that was not kept, an 'African friend' was a fairweather friend, arriving 'like a pure African' was arriving well after the time arranged for meeting. 'Africans' were said to be greedy and heartless, a deceased's relatives arriving at a funeral only to 'grab' everything and leave the widow 'naked'. 'Africans' were said to be 'naturally jealous' of the success of their fellow Africans, a jealousy often expressed in backbiting and in witchcraft attacks, and when they suffered, they were said to desire company in their suffering. An often-heard student remark was, 'We Africans, we don't love one another.' Students commented upon this alleged character trait, again and again, especially in relation to the AIDS epidemic/pandemic. They said men diagnosed HIV-positive infected as many sexual partners as possible for the sake of 'revenge'. In an inversion of the positive value of always being together with others, a common student reaction was, 'Yes, no one wants to die alone.'

Students maintained that 'Europeans' were 'advanced' in all areas of life: technology, possession of material goods, provision of services. Even in sexual expression, the supposed 'European' orientations of homosexuality and lesbianism, although not condoned, were often cited as evidence of advanced development. 'Kissing' was said to be a European invention and an activity that overexcited young Africans, when they saw it in films, leading them to engage in sexual activity because 'African desire' was greater and less easily controlled than European desire. Europeans were said to be hardworking, whereas Africans were described as lazy. About an alleged racist remark by one of the Brothers, an allegation that was strenuously denied, Bruno, a nineteen-year-old Grade Twelve student, said, discussing it with his friends in the library:

> Brother Pedro said we Africans are lazy, and the boys were angry because they knew it was true. We know that the white man is superior to the black man and that there is no one superior to the white man. But even so, even though it is true, the Brother shouldn't have said what he said.

Here is another example of such discussions from students chatting together on their beds in the dormitories, and it is merely one out of the many I recorded. Gerry, aged eighteen, from Lusaka, the son of an MMD politician, is chatting with five of his fellow Grade Eleven students, among them Robert, also eighteen, from Kabwe, the son of a primary school teacher:

> *Gerry:* Why are blacks behind? Why are we so poor in thinking? Why are all the things invented that side? [i.e. Europe/North America.] Blacks think differently.
> *Robert:* Africans are selfish and that is why we haven't developed. You know, through witchcraft people have made jets and they can fly anywhere they want, but they keep such things secret because they don't want to share with their friends. We are not civilised. We haven't made much progress ...
> *Gerry to me:* 'How do *you* feel, coming from such a developed place? This country – it must look like a village to you. How can you like it?

At moments of tension, this self-denigration could become even more disparaging. The local was consciously perceived within the global, the present explained in terms of a particular reading of events in the wider world and of 'the past'. Accordingly, school problems were cited to be evidence of a wider malaise in Zambian society. In the following example, another Grade Eleven student, Peter, angrily harangued a large group of his housemates on the veranda of his dormitory. His remarks followed a student demonstration about poor food, for which the blame was laid at the door of the Headmaster, Deputy Head and Boarding Master, all Zambians:

> We Africans! There's something missing up here [pointing to the back of his head]. Those Europeans, they are more advanced. I mean, what has an African ever invented? Those *musungus* – they invent everything – here we just pretend. And when they bring their technology here and they explain it to us, 'It's like this and like this,' we don't even have the intelligence to follow their explanation! How are we to progress? Impossible! Impossible! I think this is the limit. Here, where we are now, this is the limit. The only thing we can do is to try and fit into our poor society. Here there are only two groups – the poor and the very poor ... It's no good blaming the past, blaming others – like those colonists. No! Well, why did we let them come and take everything? We did nothing! What's wrong with us? We can't progress ... And then again people are stepping on development, misusing the money other countries give us ...

No one in his audience attempted to contradict him, although they laughed occasionally and appeared nervous about his unveiled attack on the school administration.

Closely associated with the notion of 'African' was that of 'villager', in a discourse in which the village was described as the 'natural' home of the 'African'. Discussions of village life frequently surfaced in dormitory talk. The village was often portrayed as the place to escape from, a place where nothing happened, a place deprived of all the amenities of modernity. The term 'villager' was typically associated in student talk with 'ignorance' and a lack of education, physical attractiveness, economic power, civilisation and sophistication. Education not only made people, or more precisely young men, 'intelligent', it also made them attractive to the opposite sex.

Villages and villagers were a constant resource upon which to draw in the opposition between the 'traditional' and the 'modern', the 'uneducated' and the 'educated'. The theme was frequently returned to in student drama club sketches performed for the school on such holidays as Africa Freedom Day and Youth Day. The following are resumés of a couple of the sketches impro-vised for Youth Day celebrations, and performed mostly in Bemba or Nyanja.

SKETCH ONE

The sketch opened with the scene of an old, illiterate villager who wanted to 'propose love' to a young schoolgirl. He engaged the help of a friend who was supposed to be 'educated', but it transpired his English was 'not up-to-date'. Between them they composed a letter, peppered with malapropisms which they sent to the girl. Some time later, the girl's reply arrived, and the villager called his friend to read it for him. Although the letter was a catalogue of insults, it took some time for the full import of it to dawn on either of the two men, both of whom initially believed their advance had been well received. The girl rejected her would-be suitor on three counts, all of which played on the care and the presentation of the body: first, he did not take showers, and was therefore dirty; secondly, he was dressed in rags, so was not attractive; and thirdly he did not use tissue paper when he defecated, and so he smelt. This last bit of body humour was greeted by the audience with loud roars of delight.

SKETCH TWO

Sketch Two also played on the theme of the disadvantaged illiterate villager: A villager wanted to 'hook' a girl and approached a friend, 'a failed form five' student, for advice. The latter instructed the villager to greet the girl, and to 'propose love' to her, in the following fashion: 'Hi, Beauty! I love you! I profound you!' (This met with great hilarity from the audience.) The villager, in his nervousness, got everything mixed up and was rejected by the girl, on whom the 'instructor' began to have designs of his own. Two meetings were arranged, at which all three characters met, the girl sandwiched between the two men whom she had instructed to approach her with their eyes closed. At the last moment, as the men made their moves, the girl escaped, leaving the men to start fondling one another. As a result of their tactile explorations, they realised their error, hastily recoiled in horror and started fighting. This also produced excited cheers in the audience.[2]

The sketches played upon several themes, among them the transformations that 'education' effects. Much of their humour came from satire on those who claimed to be, but who in reality were not, 'educated'. The 'real thing' – 'education' – was highly valued, but any *pretence* of it was ridiculed. These were public moments, when students demonstrated their awareness of the deceptiveness of appearances. Their attitude is expressed in a Chewa proverb: *Cikomekome cankhuyu mkati muli nyerere*, 'From the outside the fig looks very appealing, but inside it is full of ants.' In these sketches students exhibited a flair for the mimicry of affectation and pretentiousness in 'village life'. In other, less public, arenas in the school, they exhibited an equal facility to burlesque figures of authority among both staff and students. The body humour was levelling. Not all transformation processes were in official hands at St Antony's. All newcomers were required to subject themselves to the custom of 'mockery', and it was through this initiation process that each student gained the right to belong to the student body.

MOCKERY

In the practice of mockery, students embodied the 'truly educated' person, his make-up, and their perception of their own role in his definition within a hierarchy. The 'truly educated' person was one who had gone through the ordeal of education, even more, one who disciplined others as he himself had been disciplined. Inequality between the 'truly educated' and the yet-to-be educated was a basic embodied message in student discourse. The yet-to-be educated became 'free', freed to move between different school spaces, 'tamed' at the hands of the more educated – so the incorporation of Grade Eights through mockery moved as a process of informal education immediately under the unofficial control of the students themselves. Becoming 'truly educated' turned out to be an experience of learning the reality of the unofficial in tension with the official, and discovering the intimate hold the unofficial had on one's person and subjectivity. Such learning for adulthood fitted many felt truths of elite life in postcolonial Zambia.

The school's official discourse was realised in classroom talk and at other moments, such as school assemblies, in school rules and in the non-discursive practices, the minutiae of everyday physical interaction between those who represented the school authorities and those who had come to the school to 'receive an education'. The 'secular' project aimed to create docile bodies, malleable enough to be transformed by the education process into responsible hardworking citizens, good Christian gentlemen and ladies, who knew their place. However, the students themselves also acted on their own on the bodies of 'newcomers', in the students' argot, '*kwiyos*'. They worked their own transformations; in turn, they were transformed, as they acted to socialise newcomers in ways which at times reinforced the master narrative of the institution and, at times, expressed values that were at variance with it.

The most palpable manner in which this informal education took place was through the practice of 'mockery'. It was the yearly initiation and incorporation of cohorts of Grade Eight students, who were quickly taught their place within the school hierarchy, being inferior in the moral order. Mockery took place mostly in 'the boarding', especially at night, and out-of-bounds, and thus beyond the gaze of the school authorities. Dimly aware of what they could not see, the authorities issued repeated warnings. Their attempt was to curtail activity which appeared to militate against or subvert the image of the school as the nurturing family.[3] Mockery of new students, a practice found, in a form that was more or less severe, in all secondary boarding schools in Zambia, was said by students to be a 'tradition' of the school.

Past and present students offered vivid and often emotional accounts of their own experience of being mocked, although they were not always so forthcoming about their subsequent mocking of others. In recollections, many focused on their experience of physical pain, homesickness and initial regret at being among the fortunate few who found a place in secondary school. However, mockery was considered by all students beyond Grade Eight to produce certain necessary beneficial effects. Newcomers, especially from rural areas, were said to be 'sleepy', when they first arrived and in need of awakening, of being, in the students' phrase, 'jacked-up'. The term was associated with the ultimate symbol of success and modernity, the motor car. 'Jacked-up' they had to be, if they were going to be able to cope with the demands of secondary-school life and to 'forget' about the life they had left behind at home. 'Forgetting' was thought to be necessary, if the new student was ever going to settle down and concentrate on his studies. This awakening was, then, in part considered a prerequisite for coping with the intellectual demands of school life. Mockery was expected to give new boys insights that would assist them in their life at school and beyond. Novices were expected to return to the social world 'with more alert faculties perhaps and enhanced knowledge of how things work' (Turner 1974: 106).

However, this was only one aspect of the 'modernity' and 'civilisation' that education was universally acknowledged to bring. Being 'jacked-up' described a whole new orientation to the world and a way of being-in-the-world. It was to be read on the surface of the body through new codes of cleanliness and hygiene, in a student's posture, and in the way he spoke, walked, dressed and interacted with others.

These rituals of initiation were purposive and transformational (Kapferer 1979; Heald 1989), working upon the individual to produce and to confirm a new identity, a new sense of self, a new subjectivity.[4] Heald argues that ritual can be seen 'as a formative process in the construction of the self, structuring the psychological field in which the person acts and is made capable of acting. Ritual, then, does not just enact a theatre of forms but engages the person in that theatre, moulding his aspirations and his self-understandings' (Heald 1989: 78).

One lesson of the mockery process was the need for autonomy. The lesson was presented dialectically in phases of thesis, antithesis and synthesis. The Grade Eight had to learn to stand alone. The antithesis of this prescription was acted out in the demands of rituals. The Grade Eight was compelled to acknowledge his surrender of autonomy, even the hint of it, to all other students of higher grades, especially Grade Nines, who were usually the most active. Regularly, they claimed that they needed to 'take revenge' for what had happened to them the year before. The mockery was thus transformative of the mockers, and not merely the mocked. The phase of synthesis, and the accompanying change in a sense of identity, which acknowledged the interplay between the need for autonomy and the need for others, was gradual. It was first signalled in rites of reaggregation, and later experienced in a student's school career.

The mockery had a tripartite form: separation, liminality and reaggregation (van Gennep 1960), and the recurring theme of death and rebirth. In the preliminal phase, new students were separated from home and family. Their liminal status was created through the way in which they were at first roughly treated. The newcomer had to learn to act as if he was of no worth. It was a discourse having non-discursive practices that proclaimed the end of order and a reign of disorder, although the 'disorder' was normally carefully governed by its own rules (see Marsh et al. 1978).

During this period, many Grade Eights exhibited clear signs of fear and distress. In the first stage, denied personhood and treated, in the students' phrase, 'like animals', newcomers were physically and verbally abused; their former status was rejected and all signs of it were stripped away. A second stage, marked by the giving of a 'speech', was actually the construction and narration of a student's 'autobiography' to the members of the house dormitory. The successful accomplishment of that signified a greater degree of public acceptance within the house. A third and final stage, acceptance by the whole body of students, was known by the 'cutting of tails', after which Grade Eights were acknowledged to be fully incorporated. Achieving a degree of acceptance, Grade Eights recovered a changed sense of themselves. This change was proved in their self-presentation, in their talk, facial expressions, posture and movement.

On arrival, newcomers were shepherded together and shielded during the day by house prefects, with whom they spent a great deal of their time. They remained closeted in their rooms or cubicles, surrounded by groups of excited students, especially from Grade Nine, who were never far away and clearly intent upon getting their hands on them. *Kwiyos* were instructed to hand over all their money to the school administration for safekeeping, in acknowledgement of the fact that bullies would endeavour to seek personal gain at their expense.

The early days in the new school were marked by a series of restrictions on expression and movement. On their first night, the first few arrivals often slept in the prefects' rooms. Eventually, when a number of them had arrived, they were placed in the care of the wing monitors and instructed to sleep in the dormitories. Newcomers soon realised how little the official authorities of the school could do to protect them, especially once they were outside the classroom block. At first, they moved in tight groups, with other Grade Eight students, in a small circumscribed area between the dormitories, the classrooms and the dining halls. For them, there were, in van Gennep's phrase, no 'neutral zones', spaces 'where everyone has full rights to travel' (van Gennep 1960: 18). Students controlled the space of 'the boarding' and the incorporation of Grade Eights was embodied spatially in gradual concessions. Grade Eights gradually won access in stages to 'free' movement, first around the classroom blocks, then the boarding area and finally, the whole school compound and beyond.

All students placed great value upon 'feeling free' in the company of others. However, it was a state not given in the nature of things, but achieved in the gift of recognition by more senior others. It was only after their speech that Grade Eights were noticeably more at ease within their house and moved more freely around it, and it was only after the last stage of 'tail-cutting' that students felt free to move around the school. Only then did they dare to make their first tentative forays into the surrounding bush, although such expeditions still entailed an element of risk for them.

Stage one: physical suffering and humiliations

Socially 'invisible', his personal name neither known nor used, a Grade Eight novice was called in student talk, a *kwiyo* or a *zeze*, both being forbidden terms in official discourse. Threats, humiliations and 'beatings' denied him the status of being fully human. In symbolism modelled upon human and animal biological processes, a newcomer was cast in the identity of the new-born (cf. Turner 1967: 96). Several former students who were 'small boys' when they arrived at St Antony's recalled being forced to wear napkins because of their size, although they noted that small boys were generally not mocked as roughly as bigger and older students. The newcomer was said to cry '*kwiyo*' like a young animal, and would be variously told to cry, or be slapped for so doing, when distressed. The term *zeze* was said to be derived from the custom of greeting newcomers with a harsh continuous 'Z' sound, an expression of hostility. Another term of address and reference was *mono*, from the Latin prefix, which, later in their school career, students recalled in such expressions as 'I came as a *mono*. I came alone,' – a proud assertion of independence and survival. Initially, however, it exemplified the lonely and hence precarious nature of the first few weeks of secondary school life, in a kind of 'social limbo' (Turner 1974).

Being a *mono*, the Grade Eight was denied acknowledgement of his relatedness to others. The loss was the sociality, the acceptance of being a part of the whole, which was fundamental to any notion of being and of personhood. Stripped of his former status, the *kwiyo* experienced radical shifts in his moral career (cf. Goffman 1961b). Social relations, which would return to him a sense of meaning and belonging, had to be earned, first through expressions of submission and deference, and later through claims of moral worth.

The liminality of mockery rites was highly structured. Hierarchy had to be maintained by putting newcomers in their place, as inferiors. Students generally agreed that failure to impose that would only create problems from students, who were above themselves, too proud and 'pompous'. Students and former students often remarked upon this need for mockery so that the newcomer would know his place and not get ideas above his station. As Stephen, a former student, commented, 'To be "pompous" meant that you were not co-operative. You wanted to have your own way. You see, it was about being tamed. For students mockery was not interesting with tamed ones ... Students were always interested in the negative side.'

Kwiyos were said to be 'slaves', at the beck and call of others, sent on errands by senior students and given tasks for superiors, such as carrying their plates and washing their clothes. Contrary to official school policy, they were instructed to address the prefects as 'Sir', and to refer to them by the title 'Mr'. In yet another order of school life, bullies demanded the same terms of reference and address. Newcomers would be instructed to follow other students around the school compound or would be told to stand in one place and wave until the mockers were out of sight. Grade Eights were intimidated into responding, in the students' phrase, more like 'robots'. This was a term generally used both for traffic lights and other machines which, while not 'human', appeared to behave as if they were, when controlled by humans; such devices had an enduring fascination for the students.

Kwiyos lost control of their bodies, in various forms of common mockery, for example, in the practice of *dimuna*. The origin of the term derived, students explained, from the 'blinking' of a car's indicators, controlled at whim by the driver flicking a switch. The flashing indicator light was mimicked through the rapid opening and closing of the palm of the hand with the fingers extended. The *kwiyo* was instructed to perform repetitively a particular action of the body, for example opening and closing his mouth on the mocker's signal. This might take place one on one, but it was more usually performed with a group of senior students looking on, ready to punish any failure to respond 'automatically'. Obedience came in a modern guise, for the 'truly educated'. One is tempted to say that it was the triumph of machine over modern man that was on display.

In the first weeks, the *kwiyo* had to exhibit in his posture and gait an attitude of 'humility'. It was a parody of the local expressions of 'respect' (*umucinshi* in Bemba) demanded of the young by the elders in Zambian village society (cf. Strickland 1995). It was often used in Zambia as a synonym for 'fear'. One should 'fear', that is 'respect', one's parents, especially one's father, and any member of the older generation. New values based upon 'education' and 'intelligence' were schooled into the subject at St Antony's, while others, based upon age and generation and culturally hoary, were renewed from within the boarding-school tradition. This hybridised renewal was a significant aspect of mission school life.

The *kwiyo's* body had to acknowledge his lowly place in the school hierarchy by responding appropriately. Constrained and 'invisible', his body and its movements should not take up too much space. He should not swagger or walk 'like *mishanga* sellers', the young men, 'drop-outs', who sold cigarettes and other items on streets in town. There must not be the slightest indication of 'pomposity' or 'rudeness' which would be read as a direct challenge and dealt with accordingly.

The *kwiyo* would be ordered to crawl on all fours 'like a dog'. Told he was a radio – an instrument of modernity, like the robot and the car – he would be imprisoned inside a locker in the dormitory and required to produce a variety of programmes, the most popular of which was a music programme to the sound of which other *kwiyos* were ordered to dance.

Another form of humiliation, when personal space and the body were intruded upon, and which caused a great deal of distress, was effacement, when a mocker scratched the face of a *kwiyo*. Effacement was done with the hand first extended on the top of the head, and then drawn slowly and deliberately down the length of the face. The distress reported seemed out of proportion to the physical discomfort caused and, I would argue, was linked to the message of the action. Such effacement was, quite literally, a loss of face, scratching away, if only temporarily, the surface of the skin.

About the skin, and, above all, face skin, the students were particularly sensitive. In day-to-day presentation, students paid special attention to the application of oil or, more commonly, Vaseline to the face, hands and arms, in order to make the skin appear smooth and glowing. Smooth, shiny skin embodied and gave proof of 'modernity', health and success. Cosmetics spoke of the organised, ordered self. Their absence spoke of poverty and disorder.

Being a 'nobody', denied ownership rights, the Grade Eight student had his food brought from home snatched forcibly from him by some of the senior students, if he did not hand it over to be 'shared' with house prefects. A *kwiyo*'s 'share' in the dining-hall would be taken from him, and he would instead be 'fed' bits of foam mattress, or given flowers or uncooked maize to eat.

In rites that symbolised biological death and acted as metaphors of dissolution (Turner 1967: 96), the *kwiyo* would be 'shot' with a wire gun or simply with the index and middle finger of the mocker's hand, and then required to act out the process of dying and play dead. This acting-out of physical death, I infer, embodied the symbolic death of childhood and the primary-school existence associated with it. A boundary was drawn against the past, as in the Ndembu *mukanda* rites surrounding the *mukanda* log, 'the place of death' (Turner 1962: 173). In a deliberately ridiculous parody of passage in the Christian rite of baptism, the *kwiyo* would be taken by students of other grades to the showers, dressed or undressed, and 'baptised' with water 'in the name of the Headmaster, the Deputy Headmaster and the body of prefects'. Again, the appropriation of informal authority by parodying the formal, as in the parody of difference in respect for elders, was unmistakable, creating a new hybrid from the 'modern' and the 'traditional'.

Stage two: the rite of speech

Acceptance and incorporation into the house was dependent upon the successful delivery of a biographical speech in English to the other members of the dormitory wing. The narrative outlined the details of the newcomer's past. 'Story-telling' as personal narrative was a major activity in life in 'the boarding'. At the beginning of term, students took a special delight in telling and listening to holiday exploits, and an accomplished story-teller acquired much kudos. In the rite of speech, skill was required in the use of style for presentation, no less than in the selection of content. A proper insight was required into what constituted an appropriate narrative.

Speeches were demanded in the first weeks of a student's arrival. The exercise resonated with age-grade initiation; it was only performed when most of the Grade Eight students had arrived. Newcomers who arrived 'early' were told they would have to wait for their 'friends'. A rota was established by the wing monitor who conducted the proceedings. House and school prefects played no official part, although they would put in an appearance, if they heard that an individual was expected to be particularly entertaining. It was a rite that could not be avoided. Anyone who refused to give a speech was physically punished by the monitor; a reluctant Grade Eight would be slapped, punched and kicked into submission. There were two much-discussed examples of 'rich boys' receiving this treatment during my fieldwork.

The speech was a public event within the house and, even more narrowly, in the *kwiyo's* dormitory wing. Normally the wing alone witnessed the event, but news of reputations, made or lost, spread throughout the house and often beyond. The information gained remained within the student body. The event and reports of it were most carefully kept among the students, and normally away from all the teachers. Awareness of a teacher in the vicinity immediately led to a postponement of the speech. Even in my marginal position, I was unable to officially witness a speech. Once students were aware of my presence in the dormitory, speech-giving was halted. However, I did surreptitiously listen to some speeches standing or crouching in the dark beneath open dormitory windows and I supplemented this by gathering *post facto* accounts from Grade Eights and other students and former students who vividly recalled their presentations. In an inversion of normal school time and activity, the speech was given at night, in darkness and at a time when speech was officially forbidden, so that its location and timing screened it off from any intrusive authoritarian or officially authoritative gaze.

One or two students were called upon each night, after the bell for silence and lights out. Formerly nameless, in that until this point he had been identified by senior house-members merely as a *kwiyo*, the anonymous neophyte's name was now called in the dormitory and he became the centre of attention. His individual account, in all its supposed particularity, was heard by the members of his house, as he attempted to make a name for himself. The individuating nature of the event was highlighted by the lone voice of the novice, who appeared most vulnerable in this test of courage.

He was made to stand alone in the middle of the dormitory, normally wearing only his underpants. Without clothes, the speaker faced an added test of confidence. It also made a statement about being a man among men. Only some wealthy students, and among these, only the youngest and smallest, ever wore pyjamas at school. It was not considered 'manly' to do so. Students were often bare-chested in and around the dormitories in the period before lights-out and, on several occasions, I saw muscular prefects and other house officers remove their shirts before going from wing to wing to make announcements. Shouts of 'volume' and 'focus' (normally used when watching a film), from members of his audience, secure and cosy in their beds, instructed the *kwiyo* to speak sufficiently loudly in order to be heard in all corners of the dormitory.

The Grade Eight was instructed to give an account of his life so far, to render an account of himself, his childhood at home, and his primary school career. It was a defining moment in the schooled presentation of the self. The new boy had to endeavour to construct an acceptable biography, almost confessional in style, witnessing to the life through which he had passed, as he crossed the threshold into the next stage, the new regime of a secondary boarding career. And yet there were strict limits to his inventiveness. He had exemplars to draw upon and adhere to. Of course, in this rite of passage, the possible scripts, the appropriate accounts, were not set down in approved texts, but rather were to be drawn upon from the memory of their transient narrative performance.

An awareness was quickly acquired by an astute *kwiyo*, before he switched from being a silent, passive member of the audience to taking centre stage as the main interlocutor; the categories and roles of 'participant' and members of the 'audience' were subject to change (Kapferer 1979: 7). It was in the successful negotiation of the shift from audience member to participant that the transformation of individual identity was won, and an important stage in the resolution of his ambiguous status was also achieved. The *kwiyo* followed the examples of peers as his immediate predecessors, and heard the welcome for their accounts, from which he learnt.

Approved narratives generated other narratives of the same type, according to perceived criteria of rightness and a recognition of the constraints within which the narrative unfolded (Gilsenan 1994). This was evident in Grade Eights' discussions with me. Newcomers had carefully rehearsed their speeches many times and often offered practically verbatim accounts of them. Below is part of an account given to me by Richard, a stocky eighteen-year old Grade Eight

> So, the speech in the wing. In my speech, they said you had to describe how you started your Grade Seven, the family you come from. I started my speech like this: 'I come from a poor family. Yes, because my father is not well-educated. So we are four in our mother's family,

in my father's family, three girls and one boy.' Then they said, 'You have to tell us how you started school.' 'I started my schooling in 1985, and then completed my Grade Seven in 1991, when I wrote my examination. And the result comes. I've qualified! With 790 marks.' After that they said, 'OK, how many girlfriends do you have?' I said, 'I don't have any girlfriends.' So they started forcing me to tell them about my girlfriends. Then I said, 'OK, I have one girlfriend.' 'Did you chop her?' [i.e. have sex with her] 'Yes, I chopped her.' That's how my speech was.

Thus, such a speech was no mere monologue; the *kwiyo* had to answer for himself, present his own defence – it was an adversary action as a public trial. The ritual involved a transformation of the context (Kapferer 1979); the normally warm, informal, nurturing 'domestic' space of the dormitory wing became a courtroom. Specific types of performative media, the speech and the subsequent cross-examination, were employed, producing a particular frame of action and meaning (Goffman 1961a: 20). The frame employed contained, at the level of discourse, a particular symbolic type, implicitly or explicitly present in the performance of the ritual (Kapferer 1979: 13): the secondary school student as the raw – or rather, now cooked – new boy. The Grade Eight became acutely aware of being measured against that symbolic type. Switching back and forth from being members of the audience to major participants, boys of other grades made assessments and passed judgement. During the course of the *kwiyo's* speech, they gave commentaries, in English and Zambian languages, regarding both form and content and, in student parlance, 'fired' questions at the newcomer from the darkness. In this way other students, apart from newcomers, were also transformed as they gained or enhanced their reputation for oratory or toughness. Grade Nine students, in their anxiety to dissociate themselves from novice status, were always the most active in this, as in other moments of the initiation of the newcomers (for similar observations in English boarding schools, see Wakeford 1969: 114). If judged good-looking, the *kwiyo* would also be required to answer enquiries regarding the number, age and availability of his sisters.

The *kwiyo* had to prove his competence in English, when fielding trick questions which ironically brought up again the theme of death and rebirth. Sometimes the questions played upon the problems encountered when a literal translation from a local language into English was attempted. For example, a common question was, 'How many are you in your mother's womb?', in Bemba, *Mwaba banga muli banoko?* When the *kwiyo* responded with the number of children in his family, he was mockingly asked, 'Are you still in your mother's womb?' Similarly, students were asked, *Banga abapashile (abapitile) kusukulu kumwenu?* The meaning in English was, 'How many passed away from your school?' but the form was used ironically to apparently inquire into the number of Grade Sevens who had won a place at a secondary school, that is, 'How many passed *at* your school?' If the *kwiyo* gave the number and included himself, then he was asked, 'Are you a ghost, then?' When the same question was asked in English, it played upon the use of phrasal verbs, good knowledge of which was possessed by only the most advanced students. In whatever language, all but the most alert and accomplished newcomers were disorientated, and confused into appearing foolish.

A *kwiyo*, poor in English and lacking performative skills, exposed himself to ridicule. Doubts were expressed as to whether he had gained access to secondary school honestly or whether he had cheated in the Grade Seven examination. A student who was suspected to have gained his place through bribery was treated particularly harshly. A competent performance would do much to enhance prestige in the house. It was a moment when the *kwiyo* had to demonstrate, within his wing, using his ability to speak for himself, his moral worth to the school's elite community.

There is no narrative without a moral to it (White 1981: 23). In student personal narrative, mobility was the moral, *par excellence*. The story of a boy emerging from a poor family background, against the odds, together with an expressed desire to improve his life through study, was well received. The dream of upward mobility was held dear. Boys from wealthy backgrounds were often given a less sympathetic hearing. They were judged to have little to struggle against, and were normally the ones most reluctant to expose themselves to this rite.

In a sense the narrative performance became more important than the events narrated. Alves (1993) has noted, in his study of initiation rites among urban Portuguese boys, that this is because

> experiences, unlike the narratives [are] usually beyond the scrutiny of the peer group. In other words, within the context of the storytelling events, the narrative performances were more real than the experiences: it was the *narrative performances* that accorded storytellers more manly status in the peer group.
> (Alves 1993: 894–5)

The 'truth' was an obsession not only of the official discourse of the school. Among the students, 'maturity', upon which acceptance was granted or withheld, was an intimate blend of the intellectual and the sexual. While exceptions were made for very young Grade Eights (the 'mosquitoes'), the *kwiyo* had to claim to be sexually active, acknowledge his sexuality, and indeed disclose accomplishments in his sexual career. The 'proof' of the *kwiyo's* maturity was acted out, in narrative, upon the female body. Venturing beyond the margins of his discourse as a child, the novice had to stake his claim for acceptance by producing an account that attested to the attainment of, in Alves' phrase for Portuguese urban boys' initiation, 'the prestigious qualities of the male Discourse: courage, autonomy, bravery, fearlessness, assertiveness, toughness, resolve' (Alves 1993: 900).

Noticeably absent from Alves' account is the matter of sex. This may be explained, in part, by the fact that his informants were much younger (nine and ten years of age) than the majority of newcomers to St Antony's, whose average age was between sixteen and seventeen. For the Portuguese children, proof of manhood resided in narratives of their 'rampaging' through their Lisbon neighbourhood. Girls and women were not spoken of; rather, accounts centred upon daring violations of others' private property and space. The mockery rite at St Antony's exhibited continuities with African initiation. In such initiation, sex and maturity are inextricably intertwined; the ordeal is a stage towards, or the immediate preparation for, marriage (see Richards 1982: 54; Heald 1989: 60).

The *kwiyo* was required to demonstrate, in Herzfeld's phrase (1985: 16), that he was 'good at' being a man and, in this context, this demanded an account of sexual knowledge and experience. Even before giving the speech, a *kwiyo* was often summoned by senior students, including prefects, and ordered to demonstrate how he 'chopped' girls. In his speech in the wing, he was aware that he must satisfy the inquisitiveness of his interrogators. Winston, an eighteen-year-old Lala, described part of the speech which he had given the night before:

> Then they asked, – because this is the point they want to know – 'How do you play with your girlfriend?' So I told them, 'I also have one girlfriend.' So they asked me, 'Did you chop her?' So I agree, because when you don't agree, they can attack you. So I said, 'I have one girlfriend who I chopped two times.' Laughing, laughing, they laughed! They laughed, happy, happy! Then they asked me that, 'Did you have another girlfriend?' And I said, 'No, only one girlfriend I have.' Then they said, 'OK, you sleep now.' So I slept.

'Play' was a common euphemism for sexual activity, apparently a direct translation from the vernacular, in Bemba, for example, *ukukwangala*. This gave a tone to sexual activity very different from that encountered in much Christian discourse.

The unofficial student discourse of sexual awareness and accomplishment stood in stark opposition to the official school discourse. The official discourse operated with a model of the puerile student; it demanded celibacy from all its inmates. In this respect, while at school, the students were expected to behave like the Catholic Brothers whose celibate lives were dedicated to the Virgin Mary. In student parlance, not surprisingly, the term 'monk' was pejorative. To be a 'monk' suggested to many students that one was strangely not interested in members of the opposite sex or, more commonly, that one was not 'courageous' enough to get one. Although local girls living around the school were resorted to for sex, they tended rather to be despised in students' talk. Not considered to be of the right 'class', being 'uneducated villagers', students said that their peers tended to keep relatively quiet about such liaisons. The most sought-after girls were the students of the Catholic convent in the nearby town. This was because they were considered by St Antony's students to be of more or less the same 'class', that is, mission-educated. Furthermore, because the nuns were known to be 'very strict', there was a better possibility of 'hooking' a virgin. Many students aspired to be seen on closing day, 'moving together' in town with their girls, their 'honeys'. They were assumed to have sexual relations with their 'darlings': nobody wanted to be known as a 'walking-stick', someone who escorted a girl and did not have sex with her. Sexual experience, accomplishment and competence formed a central part of a Grade Eight's credentials of maturity, and therefore of his fitness to attend secondary school and be one of the elite gentlemen.

Stage three: the cutting of tails

During the course of the school year, the student body decided upon the date of the final rite, which proved the social acceptance, and hence incorporation, of Grade Eight students. In the past, this rite had been conducted towards the end of the year, but in the 1990s it was brought forward.[5]

All Grade Eights were said to have invisible tails, needing to be cut or 'docked' by older students. Once the date was decided upon, it was announced, both by word of mouth and through cartoons and threats on blackboards around the school. Grade Eights were repeatedly reminded of the imminent event, as the time approached. Unlike the rites of the first two stages, tail-cutting had a much less serious tone to it. This rite had ludic, and perhaps therapeutic, elements in the manner in which it was performed. Grade Eights no longer had to 'do' anything, beyond briefly submitting themselves to Grade Nine students, among whom they had already made a number of friends. While they objected to tail-cutting, because it entailed a loss of dignity through a process of humiliation, the very fact that they could articulate their irritation was itself a measure of their integration.

The action of cutting was performed in mime, with or without an implement, such as a mattock or a 'slasher'. Grade Eights might run away in a vain attempt to escape, but they did not show the signs of fear exhibited during their first days in the school, and there was rarely any physical violence beyond restraining reluctant individuals. Furthermore, although the rite mostly took place in 'the boarding', it was performed in daylight, in open spaces around the school. It was an activity that could be watched by anyone present, although few teachers regularly spent any time in this area of the school, and so rarely witnessed it.

Most tail-cutting took place at the doors of the dining halls. It was thus thematically linked to other mockery rituals, which inverted the model of the school as nurturing community, the 'family', into one of deprivation. A general announcement was made: 'No one with a tail can enter the dining hall.' The Grade Eight was stopped at the door of the dining hall and was made to turn, with his back to the cutter, who, if he had a mattock, then mimed the action of cutting the tail. If he did not have an implement, he normally slapped the Grade Eight at the base of the spine. It is perhaps not too fanciful to read into this rite echoes of a ritual of circumcision, although no student ever drew such an analogy and, indeed, very few of them were from ethnic groups which had the practice of circumcision.[6] It may well mark the crossing of the divide from being the young of the species to the adult, or from the animal to the human.

Now that the last vestige of his liminal state and status had been removed, the Grade Eight was given permission to step forward across the threshold. In this 'territorial passage' (van Gennep 1960), his social maturity and his right to belong had been confirmed; he was now free to gain his certification because he had shown his worth. His intellectual abilities had been proved: he had not gained entry by deception. His sexual maturity he had acknowledged: he was no longer a virgin. He could speak for himself and tell of himself. He could begin to conduct himself 'like a gentleman'. He could take care of himself, and was apparently no longer emotionally dependent on those he had left behind at home.

His potential for transformation could be read from his deference to those higher than himself in the student order and, therefore, more worthy of 'respect'. In the bourgeois model of the meritocracy, the individual was allowed to 'better himself' through education. He had 'earned' the right to climb the ladder and to establish his place on it. In his civil manner, he demonstrated that he knew his place in the order of things.

CONCLUSION

One of the insightful lads of Hammertown (the pseudonym Paul Willis gives to a town in Northern England) comments, 'It's the f***ing kids who mould you, not the f***ing teachers' (Willis 1977: 25). Admittedly, it is, but only to a certain extent. The Zambian students clearly acted upon the bodies of *kwiyos* for the sake of instruction in the ways of mission secondary life. They fashioned a new sense of self that in some respects, at least, accorded with the orthodox school discourse. In effect, also, they demonstrated how they themselves were, at least partially, caught within one version of mission-school discourse. However, these lessons, whether from 'Commoners' or from prefects, were at times significantly at odds with the values of official school discourse, and provided examples of the spaces students created for themselves, both in collusion with hierarchy and authority and also in resistance to it. For instance, many students denied the value of a celibate existence and, along with Seventh-Day Adventist prefects, made efforts to undermine Catholic teaching, Catholic practice and the Catholics themselves. Their opposition fell short of open disruption of prayers or Catholic ritual. Rather, they were gradually encroaching upon the space of the Catholic chapel and reconverting it into their own. In collusion with hierarchy, the students imposed seniority and obedience to seniors. Here, seniority was two things, hybridised from two disparate traditions. One was the continuity, even in caricature, with everyday respect for seniors and elders, prevalent throughout village Zambia. The other, from the classic boarding-school tradition, was fagging. Taken together as one, the embodiment imprinted authority as arising in the very succession of students themselves, not in a source outside them, or as coming from 'the school authorities', the Brothers or other members of staff.

I have described above the many ways in which, following Foucault (1977), one could portray life in St Antony's as a space in which technologies of self were employed with precision upon the student body in a regime whose leaders' intention was to render it docile. The students of St Antony's demonstrated how they could discriminate and appropriate aspects of competing discourses that were useful or attractive to them. They offered no resistance to that stream of the school discourse which constructed them as 'educated and civilised' through the reception of school knowledge. In their perception, schooling was a vital avenue of social mobility. Hence, much student co-operation was assured; they actively assisted schooling their subjectivity within the process in which they, too, wanted to find themselves – the civilising process.

Student co-operation became uncertain or unwilling, when the institution attempted to discipline the self in other areas of life, particularly for the control of the stimulated body, in sexuality, in alcohol, in marijuana and tobacco. Many students rejected being made in the puerile image, and thus denied the power of the institution's attempts to objectify and subjectify.

In the realm of religion, students actively contested many of the ethical and religious messages that the school authorities attempted to inculcate into them. The Brothers' Founder stressed that the Brothers' goal was the salvation of the student's soul. The question is: Was it the soul or the self that the Catholic mission school saved? Or revealed? Or in some sense produced?

My approach recognises the subjective reality according to which the soul, no less than the self, existed at St Antony's. Merquior (1991) takes Foucault to task for his dismissal of the soul as an illusion, commenting, 'it [the soul] very much exists – it is permanently produced on those punished, supervised, corrected and controlled' (1991: 99). But Foucault does not wish to deny the existence of the soul; his interest lies in the manner of its production. The students of St Antony's certainly affirmed the existence of the soul, although they debated, in different arenas in the school, the ways in which to achieve salvation, and who had the means to do so.

CONTESTS AROUND CHRISTIANITY

'Very few people think of themselves as non-Christians and "conversion" is no longer an issue' (Jansen and MacGaffey 1974: 16). This observation of Jansen and MacGaffey on twentieth-century Kongo religion applied equally to St Antony's, where the teachers and students, almost without exception, declared themselves to be Christians. Yet behind this declaration lay a great debate about conversion from one form of Christianity to another. It was a continuing argument of images, words and texts about who were the 'real' Christians, who was in possession of the 'truth'. Maxwell (1994: 338) describes similar intense debates in schools in north-east Zimbabwe, provoked by new-wave Pentecostalism.

In this chapter I keep in the background the school's officially-established religion, the Christianity of the Spanish Catholic missionaries, in order to foreground its counter-Christianities embodied by the Seventh-Day Adventists, the Scripture Unionists or Born Agains, and other student preachers who acknowledged different Protestant or Pentecostal allegiances and none. These movements – in Gray's (1991) terms, 'African appropriations' of Christianity – continued to develop through a great deal of contestation with each other, no less than with Catholicism as it was officially established at St Antony's. I write of *counter*-Christianity to stress opposition to the officially-established religion. Each movement, as a distinct variety of religious expression within the school, offered an alternative to the structure of leadership, mode of organisation and fellowship fostered by the school authorities. Other spaces were opened up for the creation and recreation of identity, and biblical narratives were taken up as biography and autobiography were reconstructed, entailing alternative styles of oratory and differentiating aesthetics of self.

Each expression of counter-Christianity was encapsulated within a particular apocalyptic discourse, the central features of which were authority, time and evil (O'Leary 1994: 20). Students proclaimed the message of salvation in various arenas within the school, and the particular dynamics of each space normally dictated the way the message was announced and the accent that it was given.

Student preachers' attempts to persuade fellow students of the truth of their message, the play of their tropes, and the preaching styles they employed offered a window of transparency upon the 'civilising mission' in a post-colonial secondary school. They conducted their preaching in the formal setting of the school chapel on the three mornings a week when all students had to attend. Fundamentalist preachers, both student and staff, dominated the scene. Rarely did a Catholic student, a Catholic teacher or a Brother offer themselves to preach. Fundamentalists criticised Catholic students for their reluctance to preach, and thus for their lack of Christian commitment. One popular Seventh-Day Adventist preacher, Henderson, offered this explanation to me concerning Catholic students' reluctance to preach:

> I'll tell you why Catholics don't preach. I can give you a quote from Ellen G. White about devotion. You'll find it in *Testimonies, Volume Two*, page 439: 'Many of them were in great darkness but many seemed sensitive of their situation. They seemed benumbed but much awake to worldly interests. They were cherishing idols in their hearts and practising iniquity in their hearts.' And then, in *Testimony Six*, there is the quotation from Revelation 3: 16 – a warning to those who are indifferent, 'He will spew them out of His mouth'. That's those who are lukewarm, and Catholics – they are lukewarm. So in this way they are led from God who is holy. Now you cannot mix the two things. He cannot mix with the unholy and we cannot mix with them either. The Catholics are lukewarm because they are not interested in saving other people's souls. A Christian has to show love to others, 'Go ye and preach to all nations,' Matthew 28: 18.

All students who chose not to attend the Catholic Mass were required to attend an alternative Sunday service. Again, it was conducted almost entirely by fundamentalist students. A number of Catholic students attended, explaining to me, 'It's a better Mass than the one in the school chapel.' The fact that it was usually much shorter than the Catholic Mass undoubtedly was part of its appeal for some. The service was timetabled to coincide with the Catholic Mass and thus the likelihood of the preaching being monitored by Catholic authorities was reduced. Beyond these formal settings, every night in each dormitory, between the bell for the students to retire to bed and the second bell for silence, a member of the house or the dormitory preached a sermon. Adventist students dominated the dormitory arena. In addition to these opportunities to spread the Word, individual approaches were made to those students judged to be likely candidates for conversion. Members of the different denominations conducted their own services at various points in the week.

I concentrate upon the Seventh-Day Adventists and the Born Agains because they played central roles within St Antony's in the contestation around Christianity. Nominally the largest denomination in the school after the Catholics, the Seventh-Day Adventists multiplied in the 1990s; they were most successful in attracting and retaining converts within the school. In the early history of the school there had been very few Adventist students. In 1974, out of a school population of 460, there were only twenty-six Seventh-Day Adventists in contrast to 243 Catholics and seventy-eight students who recognised allegiance to the United Church of Zambia. In 1980, the figures for Catholics and Seventh-Day Adventists were 230 and fifty-one respectively (School administration files 1974; 1980). In a repeat census that I took in April 1992, of the 330 students whose religious affiliation I had recorded the previous year and who were still studying at St Antony's, thirty-eight stated that they had changed their religious affiliation. The largest net gains were made by the Seventh-Day Adventists who lost two but gained ten. The biggest losses were sustained by the Catholics who gained three but lost twelve. The United Church denomination lost ten but gained nine. Several students who had been born again no longer stated affiliation to any denomination. The number of Born-Again students fluctuated considerably. Their *modus operandi*, lacking the organisational strength of the Seventh-Day Adventist denomination, depended more upon the charisma and commitment of individual preachers.

Citing Sykes (1984), Gray contends that Christianity 'is and has always been "an essentially contested concept" ... the contestants are held together by the conviction that the contest has a single origin in a single, albeit internally complex performance' (1991: 76). At St Antony's the contest took place in a number of arenas as participants attempted to gain supremacy over physical, moral and intellectual space. Student sermons provided the forms for distinct productions of narrative and of self. The self was situated in a particular orientation towards contemporary Zambian society and African cosmologies. The present analysis assumes, of course, that African cosmologies are historical creations, not pristine realities. In this vein, Gray rehearses the orthodoxy of the profound impact of Christian eschatology upon some African cosmologies. Early mission teaching is often said to have produced a 'cosmological revolution' (see, for example, Horton 1971: 102). Gray cites Wilson's reports of the Nyakyusa reaction in the 1930s to the notion of eternal life in heaven. The gospel message proved attractive primarily because of the promise of 'abundant life to come'. Gray goes on to make what appear to be ethnocentric and ahistoric assumptions which in the light of my evidence are dubious:

> Suddenly the hereafter was no longer a faint reflection of this world, no longer was it primarily concerned with the community's survival, no longer would it slip imperceptibly into the forgotten past. The Bible brought to its African readers the idea of history as progress, the concept of linear rather than cyclical time, and with this was linked a liberating yet frightening emphasis on the individual.
> (Gray 1991: 69)

Admittedly, the element of 'individualism', of individuation, the emphasis on the ego, so often identified with 'modernisation' in Africa and elsewhere, featured prominently in the discourse of counter-Christianity, no less than in established Christianity. The theoretical challenge lies, however, in the question of the kind of 'individualism' being displayed and encouraged. A similar point holds for the idea of history and Christianity. At St Antony's, the religious message espoused by many students neither embraced the notion of 'history as progress' nor that of time being linear rather than cyclical. For Seventh-Day Adventists at least, time was clearly cyclical and not linear.

In counter-Christianity the message of human history was decidedly pessimistic. A similar observation is made by Martin (1990: 54) on the shift to Pentecostalism in Latin America. This pessimism was evident, if para-doxically so, in the face of individual student efforts to become 'civilised' and to enjoy a 'better' life. For Seventh-Day Adventists and Born Agains at St Antony's, historical time was about to end. Time was of the essence; in these last days salvation was to be won or lost.

Yet such pessimism was curiously apolitical, or at least non-partisan. Indeed, in the religious discourse of Protestants and, apparently, of Catholics also at St Antony's, debate about Zambian politics was strikingly absent. No one spoke openly about the specifics of politics in sermons, even during the heady days of transition from one-party rule to a multiparty state and the ousting of President Kaunda through the ballot box. In all the preaching I heard and recorded during fieldwork, in varying contexts and with many different audiences, on no occasion did any preacher make a direct appeal on behalf of UNIP, or for any of the many parties that came into existence prior to multiparty elections in October 1991. Preachers did, however, make apocalyptic allusions to the worsening economic situation and the general political climate of mismanagement and corruption at all levels in Zambian society. What such allusion did was draw a contrast between the things of this world and those of the world to come. For example, Roger, a Grade Eleven preacher affiliated to no denomination, commented during a sermon on 'the sheep and the goats':

> You must read the speedometer of the world. The end is coming. You must be ready for the Day of Judgement. No one will escape final judgement ... Some of you have not touched a Bible this year! [some laughter and some murmurs of agreement from the students] There will be no escape – even if you are a good runner, you will not be able to run away from this judgement ... and there will be no bribery. You cannot bribe God! You have to decide now, before it is too late.

Moralising argument and debate about the public future dominated everyday discussions around the school, in student dormitories, at football matches. The majority of students and teachers, like many missionaries, yearned for change. They hoped that MMD would win the election. 'We are only waiting for October,' became the stock phrase that summed up the sense of heightened anticipation in and around the school. The MMD slogan 'The hour has come', normally abbreviated to 'The hour', and the MMD symbol became commonplace at St Antony's as October drew near. But a minority, among both students and teachers, said they did not want change; they feared it. Many expected violence, whatever the outcome from the ballot box. UNIP politicians made 'peace' a major plank in their political platform. With Kaunda the country had enjoyed peace; without him there would be war. 'Tribe' would fight against 'tribe'. The common rejoinder, 'You can't *eat* peace,' pointed to the ever-worsening economic situation.

Religious affiliation offered no reliable guide to political affiliation. One Seventh-Day Adventist preacher told me in conversation that MMD would 'do something' about inflation; another Seventh-Day Adventist preacher told me that MMD would 'only bring confusion'. I am not sure whether this muted political expression meant a determination to keep 'religion' and 'politics' separate. No student preacher ever suggested to me that this would be the correct thing to do. What is undeniable is that old habits died hard. Direct public criticism of the government, especially the President, had been non-existent or very muted, for many years. One did not know whom to trust and who might report back to local party officials. Many feared the consequences of speaking publicly against the ruling party UNIP in case it should 'play tricks', and thus by one means or another retain power following the elections. What is certainly true is that Pentecostal student preachers drew upon events within Zambia and beyond, and they portrayed them to be signs of the impending apocalypse. On the international scene, the Gulf War furnished ample evidence. At national level, AIDS continued to claim many young lives, the *kwacha* tumbled, there was a cholera epidemic. The end could not be far away.

Here there was an autonomy, perhaps a contradiction in self-definition. On the one hand, in these movements, members saw themselves as set apart, bounded entities. They stressed, in different ways, the need to 'leave the world' and to cling to the community of the saved. This opposition between the religious community and the world echoed earlier conceptions of Catholic religious life. It was read by many Zambians in the manner in which the missionaries at St Antony's lived so apart from them.

On the other hand, modernity was a positive good. All students espoused a 'civilising' ideology and valued the 'modern' and the successful. The early mission project at St Antony's was designed to produce educated, useful citizens for the nation; in this, Seventh-Day Adventists and Born Agains also concurred. Indeed, Seventh-Day Adventist student leaders were the best exemplars of 'modernising' men. This orientation was the one to which they consciously aspired.

In my experience, Zambians overwhelmingly associated the 'civilising' ideology with urban life which in turn, according to the young men and women who were students at St Antony's, imitated life in the 'West'. The school, or 'Half-London' in the students' argot, was the stepping stone to this better life. For most their education was a means by which they could put a distance between themselves and their 'past', 'uncivilised', rural, village existence. Instead, it was in the modern urban world that successful students anticipated their future lay. This was reflected in student aspirations for post-school careers. In the junior section the five most popular occupations remained fairly consistent from year to year: (1) doctor, (2) pilot, (3) engineer, (4) secondary school teacher, (5) driver. Female students, without exception, expressed an interest in one of the following three careers: nurse, secretary or air hostess. In the 1970s the most popular aspiration had been pilot, both at St Antony's and indeed throughout boys' schools in Zambia. In the senior school in the 1990s the most popular choice was accountant. These aspirations reflected the desired future orientation of St Antony's away from the rural areas and into town, or even abroad if possible. Similar observations are made by Serpell (1993: 18) (see also Scudder and Colson 1980: 160; Hoppers 1981: 86). Preferred styles of 'modern', 'jacked-up', 'up-to-date' self-presentation were much in evidence in Seventh-Day Adventist practice in particular. However, before I describe such production and presentation of self in apocalyptic discourse, I must turn to a discussion and analysis of Christian fundamentalism.

FUNDAMENTALISM

Seventh-Day Adventists and Born-Again Protestants, or Pentecostals, are often considered to be different entities in scholarly literature on Christianity. In his 1990 discussion of Pentecostalism in Latin America, Martin notes the rapid increase of Adventists whom he describes as 'closely related to the evangelical family' (1990: 52). Rose (1988: xxii) observes how 'slippery and varied' the term 'evangelical' is, but decides to use it for 'fundamentalists and charismatics who share core evangelical beliefs'. I prefer, following Barr (1977), to use the term 'fundamentalist' to describe Adventist, Born-Again and other students at St Antony's who claimed to read the Bible in a literal fashion and who spoke in generally apocalyptic terms. Adventists clearly differed from the Born-Again Pentecostals in several respects, but at St Antony's the movement of the Spirit was equally important in both Born-Again and Seventh-Day Adventist preaching. The most 'powerful' preachers identified by students were those who offered a dramatic narrative of conversion, of being born again, made in a new image, and who, their peers said, were 'spirit-filled'.

I address first the question of 'fundamentalism' before I describe and discuss some manifestations of it at St Antony's. This is not to imply that such manifestations belong exclusively to those who claim allegiance to Seventh-Day Adventism or Pentecostalism. Rather, elements of fundamentalism could be discerned in the practice of some Catholic students also. For example, it was not uncommon for students who declared an interest in becoming Catholics to express their wish in the rhetoric of wanting to be 'saved', or 'born again', or desiring to make Jesus their 'Lord and Saviour'.

What is a suitable definition of 'fundamentalism'? Is fundamentalism a quintessentially modern phenomenon (Caplan 1987: 1–24), even if it is best understood as a strategic response to, a critique of, or a resistance to modernity (Walker 1987: 197)? Several commentators have remarked upon the 'oppositional character' of fundamentalism (Caplan 1987; Webber 1987): it needs to define itself – and actually does define itself – in terms of a significant other 'with which it constantly engages' (Caplan 1987: 9). Caplan argues that the fundamentalists' particular use of the Bible is not simply a question of establishing the authority of the Bible because of its infallibility. The situation is more complex because sacred texts 'may constitute prime symbols of religious identity' (ibid.: 14).

For a starting point, Barr's study is useful in that it precisely delineates certain major concerns. These concerns are the very ones I found to be central in students' own versions of Christianity and in their arguments against the version put forward implicitly or explicitly by the authorities at St Antony's. The importance of the fundamentalist versions has to be seen in the context of a wider trend: Barr foresees a time when groups like the Seventh-Day Adventists will become far more important than churches belonging to '"orthodox" conservative evangelicalism' (1977: 8).

The differences Barr recognises between forms of Christianity – the fundamentalist and the more orthodox – were the very differences through which both Born Agains and Seventh-Day Adventists defined themselves. They used these differences to establish the boundary between themselves and the Catholics: the inerrancy of the Bible, hostility to modern theology and modern critical biblical study, and the firm conviction that others who did not share their religious viewpoint were not really 'true Christians' at all. There was, of course, a certain irony in the fact that this position was not all that far from pre-Second Vatican Council Catholicism, which held, officially, to 'no salvation outside the church' and favoured biblical scholarship of a conservative nature.

The Bible, which Barr also suggests is used as much as a symbol (or in an incantational manner) as a source for establishing 'the truth', constitutes a boundary which is both anti-liberal and anti-modernist (1977: 37). For fundamentalists, the Bible is treated as a fixed and final source of truth. In Grade Eight Religious Education classes at St Antony's, by contrast, students were taught about the Bible, how it was put together at which periods and by which authors. The school's approach to biblical criticism, following the approved syllabus for all secondary schools in Zambia, was modernist. Both Born Agains and Seventh-Day Adventists in the school denounced this and expressions of Catholic doctrine for being 'false teaching'. Catholic expressions such as the devotion to the Virgin Mary, Confession to a priest, and the practice of having crucifixes in classrooms were, in the understanding of Born Agains and Seventh-Day Adventists, a clear contravention of the Second Commandment:

> You shall not make for yourself a graven image, or any likeness of anything that is in heaven above, or that is in the earth beneath, or that is in the water under the earth; you shall not bow down to them or serve them; for I the Lord your God am a jealous God ...
> (Exodus 20: 4–5)

AUTHORITY

The fundamentalists recited the Second and other Commandments from memory and expounded their meaning. Their authority, they stressed, on this matter as on all others, was the Bible. The question of authority was constantly at play in fundamentalist interactions with school authorities. Seventh-Day Adventist prefects imposed a discipline more in keeping with their own religious tenets than with those held by the Catholic missionaries. The apocalyptic discourse was a discourse of authority, indeed of the final authority of God over all creation. Fundamentalist preachers claimed to preach with divine authority. All religious discourse, but perhaps especially that of eschatology and apocalypse, must present itself as divinely authoritative if it is to win fundamentalist acceptance (O'Leary 1994: 51). The preacher must persuade his audience of his prophetic gift, his 'privileged vision of the realm of the sacred' (ibid.: 53). In this, the preacher draws upon a tradition that goes back to the origins of the Protestant Reformation whose emphasis upon *sola scriptura* paradoxically offered great scope for interpretive subjectivity (O'Leary 1994: 55).

At moments when religious opposition to Catholicism became more public in the school, the issue of biblical authority, and thereby the authority of the 'saved', provided a public challenge to Catholic school authorities. When fundamentalist preachers at a Sunday service for non-Catholics denounced the Pope as the Beast of Revelation, matters came to a head.[1]

A CONTEST OF AUTHORITY: THE PREACHERS' MEETING

At a meeting (March 1992) between school authorities and student preachers, the inversion of school and parental authority was a marked feature of the discussions. Preachers arrived, armed with their Bibles, and when the issue of their direct challenge to the Catholic authority in the school was raised, one preacher after another cited Acts 2: 17, where Peter on the day of Pentecost quotes the prophecy of Joel and recognises its fulfilment in the apostles' receiving the Holy Spirit: 'And in the last days, it shall be, God declares, that I will pour out my Spirit upon all flesh, and your sons and your daughters shall prophesy, and your young men shall see visions.'

The meeting lasted some four hours. The argument swung back and forth between the fundamentalist preachers and Brother Henry, the Zambian head of the Religious Education department, supported by Sister Teresa, the Zambian superior of the convent. Among the student preachers, most denominations were represented, but it was Seventh-Day Adventist and Scripture Union preachers who were the most vocal and, at times, the most vociferous. The latter were told by Brother Henry that they were merely 'a club' and could not be recognised as a denomination. In addition, others, like Joseph, not a member of Scripture Union, announced, 'I'm independent. I don't follow any denomination. I'm just following what the Bible says.'

Brother Henry began by explaining that he had called the meeting because 'some denominations' were 'attacking other churches' doctrines'. In particular, student preachers were 'rebuking' Catholics. St Antony's was 'a gift of the Catholics'. The Brothers, dedicated to *Christian* and not simply *Catholic* education, had no desire to 'oppress' anyone but the criticism had to stop; students, in Brother Henry's phrase, 'had to know their place'. Brother Henry then commented on the sermon that was the immediate cause of the meeting:

> Six, six, six and the Pope! I said to myself when I was listening, 'He is young. I have to accept him.' But do you realise you are pupils and you have agreed to follow Catholic education? Accept you are pupils here, or go and become preachers elsewhere … You are young! Even if you say you are not young in the Spirit! If you are not young, move out of the school! We are all learning here. The *words* of the Bible are holy. *We* are not holy – we are growing… we have all accepted the same Christ. It's just wasting time. Why don't you go and preach to the Moslems?

Lovemore, a Grade Eleven student and a member of the Adventist baptism class, called for moderation, appealing to the value of respect due to parents and elders:

> It's like in a family – parents and children. It's like a child who wants to move naked. Well, what will the parents do? We are children here. Me, when I grow up, I'll do what I want. St Antony's is our home. We are children here. We want to finish our education and have a good life. We are in the hands of some people. Let's try to follow the rules. Eat from these pots now – later, there will be time. At school, like at home, we have parents. We don't want to be chased from the house …

Lovemore's contribution provoked a storm of responses, with several preachers speaking at once:

> *Reuben (Seventh-Day Adventist)*: The earth is not your home. You are just passing through. "The fear of God is the beginning of wisdom!" – Proverbs! Parents are not always right! There are certain things that your children can teach you. Remember, Judgement is coming![2]

> *Sister Teresa to Reuben*: You are not the storehouse of truth! Your human limitation interferes with the interpretation of truth. It is possible to misinterpret the Bible. For example, "If your eye causes you to sin, pluck it out". There is need for preachers to be checked. Parents have the right to rule children.

> *Henderson (Seventh-Day Adventist)*: We have to rebuke, to correct. If it's not from the Bible, then it's from the Devil. Scripture is made to keep the child of God. Ezekiel, chapter thirty-three – the preacher – the presenter of the word – he is the watchman. We Christians are free. We want to represent to others who are behind.

> *Samson (Scripture Union)*: The Bible is not after pleasing anyone. If sinners are happy with you, then there is something wrong ... People are annoyed by what they are told from the Bible. I cannot preach what is contrary to what God wants.

> *Gideon (Seventh-Day Adventist)*: Before Jesus left us, he said, "I will send you a helper." Jesus has given us a helper – the Spirit – so the preacher has to give what he has to the people because the Lord has given him the Spirit.

> *Brother Henry*: Are all preachers holy?

> *Gideon (looking very upset)*: Ah, no! Sorry, Brother. Only *God* is holy.[3]

The heated discussion went on in this fashion, ranging from one topic to another, from the correct day of the Sabbath, to the silence of Catholic students who did not put themselves forward to preach, to the unsuitability of teachers who preached at morning assembly despite, some students claimed, being 'drunkards'. Samson asked rhetorically, 'Do you expect these people to preach when they do wrong?'

The challenge to notions of respect (*umucinshi*) due in a gerontocratic tradition could not have been clearer. For Protestant fundamentalists, *all* things are to be made new in the Spirit. Granted a new identity, they are moved to speak with powerful oratory and transported into a new space, inhabited by religious kin, from which to speak. The sins of the fathers are to be brought to light and the perpetrators admonished. It is a world turned upside-down. Van Dijk (1992a), who analyses the significance of youth for

Born-Again preachers in Malawi, shows that 'extraneous identity' offers 'opportunities for the younger generation to assert itself *vis-à-vis* the positions of authority occupied by the elderly' (van Dijk 1992a: 70; cf. Marshall 1993: 25; Maxwell 1994: 345 ff.). Van Dijk (1993: 167) records the words of one young woman's preaching to her elders which neatly encapsulates this inversion: 'You, you are learners today.'

A channel is made available by which the young can give expression to their own assertiveness, capturing the moral high ground, and situating themselves beyond the reach and influence of the potentially malicious forces of the elderly. The young preachers described by van Dijk tended to have had at most only a few years of primary school. Strikingly at St Antony's, the preachers were students about to complete their secondary schooling, some being on the way to university. Their remit to rebuke the faults of others included not only Zambian elders but all, Zambian or expatriate, 'educated' or not, who persisted in failing to follow the Commandments of God (see Ojo 1988, for a description of such preaching on a Nigerian university campus).

At times the tension moved from speech to action. During my fieldwork, a number of classroom crucifixes disappeared, and many of the school authorities suspected Seventh-Day Adventists were to blame. An appeal for the return of the crucifixes was made by Mr Mwila, the Catholic Headmaster, at the weekly school assembly. He reminded the students that St Antony's was a Catholic school and if they did not like that, they could seek transfers to other schools. Some of the Brothers were also concerned by this transgression, Brother Tomas commenting: 'Now, they are going too far. Now, it is too much.' As in earlier Catholic teaching, however, Seventh-Day Adventists and the Born Agains placed much emphasis in their rhetoric upon the crucifixion of Christ and salvation won through his blood.[4] This emphasis on the blood heightened the emotional tone of the persuasive rhetoric of conversion within student sermons. It was employed for dramatic effect, as much as to emphasise a theological point.

TIME

The Question of the Sabbath

Each fundamentalist church foregrounds essential ritual observance or a distinctive symbol, a boundary marker of its own. Ever in the foreground, for the Born Agains, was the necessity of being 'born again'. For the Seventh-Day Adventists, the correct observance of the Sabbath was the religious practice clearly marking apart 'true believers'. Adventist students preached numerous sermons on this topic, normally to the unconverted, drawing upon the writings of Ellen G. White.[5] As a boundary marker, the Sabbath worked powerfully, often being cited by student converts as the most important ground for their conversion to Seventh-Day Adventism:

they realised they had been 'praying on the wrong day'. Their broad conviction, asserted aggressively at times, was that only Seventh-Day Adventists were following the Bible literally. In Barr's view (1977), and it is admittedly somewhat circular, the Seventh-Day Adventists insist on the literality of the seventh-day commandment because their structure of religious authority makes that point a vital one in particular.[6] To ignore the true Sabbath was rebellious, to refuse to acknowledge the authority of Scripture. Seventh-Day Adventist students often explained one could not pick and choose what to believe and what to reject; Christian faith was a matter of all or nothing.

Seventh-Day Adventist students in the school had permission to hold their services and 'schools' on Saturdays. In this way these students very publicly set apart from others, and their time no longer synchronised with school time. The main Seventh-Day Adventist service took place during the time set aside on the timetable for school housework, the period for cleaning the dormitories and the surroundings in preparation for the Sunday school inspection. It was also the time when students washed their uniforms and other clothes. Seventh-Day students who washed their clothes on Saturday were censured by their leaders, who cited Jeremiah 17:21 as their authority, for failing to keep the Sabbath Day holy by refraining from work.

The argument about who was a 'true Christian' was at least twofold in its thrust. First, a particular argumentative use of the Bible established a boundary between insiders and outsiders. Secondly, the argument asserted a provocative challenge to the missionaries who ran the school and to members of other religious groups.

The religious certainty of the argument was itself problematic in post-colonial Zambia. Some of the Brothers, products of a post-Franco, modern, pluralistic society and survivors of a post-Second Vatican Council crisis in Catholic religious life and vocations, were easily alarmed, hurt and, as a matter of conscience, undermined by the certainty and the conviction of the students of other religious persuasions who faced them. Brother Tomas, for example, anxiously asked me on more than one occasion, 'How can the Born Agains be so sure?'

Because of shifts in the Catholic missionaries' understanding of 'mission', their earlier emphasis upon winning converts had largely been replaced, at least in the eyes of the Catholic missionaries themselves, by the 'social gospel' of improving the lives of 'less fortunate' others. The Spanish Brothers were convinced they could do something where they were to make the lives of the people 'better', by educating them. Yet what this new emphasis relegated, or tended to omit, was the channels that offered the potential for purification.

The fundamentalist students who faced the Brothers longed for purification, and they argued that this could be achieved not through good works but only through faith. Indeed they had no 'social action' programmes whereby they could be seen to be putting their faith into 'action'. Or rather, their activity was aimed totally towards maintaining themselves in a state of purity and towards the conversion of others to this condition.[7] For Adventists, this active work for the conversion of others accelerated Christ's Second Coming, and thus the end of the world. Their activity was tied to an apocalyptic eschatology which was at odds with that of the missionary Brothers.

According to the fundamentalist students of St Antony's, things were to get progressively worse before Christ's Second Coming. The media made students and teachers aware that Zambians had the highest per capita debt in the world. In this way, not only did they have the lived experience of a worsening situation, but they were informed that, in some way, *they* were culpable and liable. Every individual in Zambia was said to owe the IMF and other international lenders US$1,000. Instead of the future being oriented towards progress, a millennial mood prevailed. One merely had to read 'the signs of the times'.

Barr notes the essentially twentieth-century nature of such millennialism in which books of the Bible, such as Daniel, Ezekiel and Revelation, are pored over in order to establish the precise sequence of events to come. Profoundly radical in character, such interpretation is totally at odds with notions of progress (Barr 1977: 200). I have noted above the conservative and apolitical tendencies common among many of the Christian churches in Zambia. For example, the Catholic Church in Zambia showed few signs of the liberation theology encountered so powerfully in Latin America, although the Catholic bishops did begin to speak out publicly towards the end of President Kaunda's regime. The opposition profile of the Catholic press was high at that time of climax. After that, Catholic bishops were much more publicly critical of the economic and political situation in the Third Republic. Archbishop Milingo, who was removed from the archdiocese of Lusaka by the Vatican, provided an exception to the earlier rule (see Gray 1991: 109; Ter Haar 1992).

Secondary school students had to confront a central contradiction. Their lives were oriented forward, often quite consciously, towards getting the qualifications that would enable them to have 'better lives', on the one hand. Indeed, I demonstrate below the ways in which, in preaching and worship, student leaders embodied all that was valued and recognised to be 'modern', 'civilised' and 'up-to-date'. On the other hand, their secular perspective remained profoundly pessimistic, even if, at the end of time, the promise of happiness awaited.

History and evolution were intertwined problems in Zambian arguments. Writing with Britain in mind primarily, Barr observes that evolution, once a major focus of fundamentalist controversy, has 'receded from the scene' (1977: 92). Not so in Zambia, where evolution worries 'fundamentalists' and others alike. Furthermore, in England Darwinism did not provoke such a controversy as it did (and continues to do) in America. Marsden links that to great differences between English evangelicalism and American fundamentalism (1980: 222). While allowing that fundamentalism is not unique to America, Marsden contends, in only a slight over-generalisation, 'Nowhere outside America did this particular Protestant response to modernity play such a conspicuous and pervasive role in the culture' (ibid.: 222).

Zambia, like much of Africa, is again exceptional, further evidence perhaps of the mainly North American origins of such fundamentalism. Evolution created a great deal of controversy and discussion in junior-school history classes. Seventh-Day and Born-Again students rejected evolution more or less out of hand, but they were not the only ones. Seventh-Day Adventist teachers on the staff, in their preaching at school assemblies, publicly deplored the teaching of such 'lies' at St Antony's. Beyond that, reluctance to accept the theory of evolution was widespread and not in any way confined to members of certain 'fundamentalist' groups. Many students questioned this part of the syllabus and largely rejected it in favour of the story of Adam and Eve found in Genesis. Students commonly remarked, 'One of them is right and one of them is wrong. They cannot both be right'. Further, for most students, Christians were supposed to 'follow the Bible', and in the Bible the story was clear. Therefore, to accept the theory of evolution was to reject the Bible. To reject the Bible was to cease to be a Christian. Thus Christians were defined as 'people of the Book'. Fundamentalist student preachers constantly reiterated that they taught solely from the Bible, with 'nothing taken out and nothing added'.

EVIL

For fundamentalist students at St Antony's, the world was essentially evil. But evil is not one thing for all. Evil was located, perceived and dealt with differently by Adventists and Born Agains. The difference in their orthodox discourses on evil opened a window upon their quite distinct concepts of personhood. As a matter of policy, Adventists distanced themselves explicitly from the evil of the 'village'; in formal discussions with me, they outspokenly averred little interest in matters of witchcraft and evil spirits. Ellen G. White's doctrine of 'soul sleep' denies the existence of spirits.[8] However, Adventists' everyday talk often revealed a deep interest and excitement in these matters. What they all publicly forswore was the use of 'traditional medicines', although several student converts to Adventism told me that they had unwittingly offended God by using 'traditional medicines' in their childhood. Again, in the writings of the Adventist visionary, Ellen G. White, health and illness are central concerns, especially with regard to the need for adolescents to discipline their bodies. In 1864 she published a tract on the evils of masturbation and excessive sex and recommended a bland diet to curb the urge (Numbers 1976: 151). Avoidance of the temptations of the flesh requires constant vigilance. Dietary laws are primarily a requirement for entry into heaven and only secondarily a means to enjoy a healthy life on earth. Adventist students preached repeatedly on the importance of refraining from tobacco and alcohol and of maintaining a healthy diet.[9] Some Brothers' smoking and drinking were cited as evidence, I stress, that they were not 'true Christians' Tobacco and alcohol, Adventists warned, 'destroy' the body, 'the temple of the Lord'.

The health of the body had to be maintained by watchfulness over appetite, by abstaining from certain food and drink, and by a wholesome diet. Should this care of the body fail, Adventists had resort to the medicines supplied at the clinic or the hospital in town. Born Agains also preached against tobacco and alcohol, but, in contrast to Adventists, they identified illness as satanic in origin and attempted to restore the body to health through exorcism, preferring when possible to forego 'Western' medicine. Prayer and fasting were required to maintain the state of purity required before the Spirit would take up abode.

NARRATIVES OF THE INDIVIDUATED SELF

It has been forcefully argued that 'we' grasp our lives in a narrative (Heidegger 1962; Ricoeur 1984; Bruner 1987; Carr 1986). It is maintained that narrative gives coherence to the otherwise inchoate. Life becomes conceptualised as composed of narratives by which time, past, present and future, is experienced through acts of emplotment (see Taylor 1989: 47).[10] Conversion narratives have a long history in Christian tradition. In his *Confessions*, Augustine describes his conversion through his personal narrative. Influenced by Plato's doctrine, he locates the memory, where an implicit understanding and self-knowledge exist, within the soul (Taylor 1989: 134).

The inspiration for new stories may be found in a variety of texts, and the Bible has always been for many Christians a tremendous source of 'empowering' stories (Frye 1982), figures upon which one can model one's own narrative (de Mijolla 1994: 2). Lives may be recast in a new narrative as individuals find sources that present fresh avenues to articulate feelings or desires. Narrative, at least in Western discourse, projects a future story (Taylor 1989: 47). Peel portrays narrative as a 'critical instrument of human agency' producing 'sociocultural form through an arch of memories, actions and intentions' (1995: 582). The Bible, the 'lively oracles of God' (ibid.: 601), does not only tell of the past; it offers paradigms for the present and the future (cf. Carrithers 1992). 'Representation' and 'reality' are intertextually related (Stanley and Morgan 1993: 3).

Fundamentalist students at St Antony's drew upon biblical narratives in a less mediated manner than their Catholic counterparts. Adventists and Born Agains moved beyond the merely referential when biblical language became constitutive of new selves (see Stromberg 1993: 3). 'Saved' through the blood of Jesus and the power of the Spirit, Fundamentalists took on a prophetic role in which the repeated ritual narrative performance of their own epiphany (see Denzin 1989: 70f) effected self-transformation (Stromberg 1993: 55f.).

In the fundamentalist perspective, only individuals can be redeemed, not the world. Thus what is of paramount importance is conversion of oneself and of others. The two were inextricably intertwined for members of groups such as the Seventh-Day Adventists. An example of this concern for conversion was constantly expressed in Seventh-Day Adventist students' preaching in the school assembly or in the dormitories. The preacher's life narrative became most explicitly modelled upon exemplary biblical figures. The preacher, achieving self-realisation in metaphor (de Mijolla 1994: 11), refigured himself through mimesis into a member of the first Christian community. Formlessness was rejected in conversion narratives, told and retold for the conversion of others; a sense of autobiographic closure was achieved (ibid.: 4) within an aura of certainty and not merely of hope. The Bible inspires because it provides the sense of an ending (see Kermode 1967). In slave narratives (Curtin 1967; Davis and Gates 1985) a state of disconnection and disempowerment become plotted through memory into a new story with a very different ending (Peel 1995: 594). Fundamentalist students repeatedly returned to their enslavement to sin, to the time when they were 'lost', and recalled lost time, when they had placed themselves far from God and, in their phrase, 'walked in other ways'.

The person born again enters a specific narrative, becoming 'a kind of Third Testament' (Harding 1992: 63). Moving beyond a mere web of allusions, intertextuality becomes flesh, beyond mere words, as preachers' lives are framed and shaped by God's Word. The preacher thus enters into biblical time; he traverses a biblical topography. In interviews, the Seventh-Day Adventist Grade Twelve student Henderson repeatedly refigured himself after the exemplar of the apostle Paul. He, too, had experienced the road to Damascus, he told me. At the close of his preaching in the dormitories one night, he drew upon the description of Paul's farewell to the people of Ephesus (Acts 20: 17–38), and he made it his own:

> From verse 25, it says, 'And now, behold, I know that all you among whom I have gone about preaching the kingdom will see my face no more. Therefore I testify to you this day that I am innocent of the blood of all of you, for I did not shrink from declaring to you the whole counsel of God.' *And now also I put myself here* [my emphasis] and I will say to you that I am innocent about your blood, because if you die in sin, it simply means that you have not put, or you did not put, what I have told you into practice. I am innocent because I have revealed to you the way to salvation – I have revealed that to you. It is up to you to

put it into practice ... If you die in sin and if you go to hell, then all the blood that you will shed, well, you will shed it for yourself. It won't go on anyone's head because you have known the truth.

Henderson and Paul became one in their address, each, like the Baptist minister in Harding's account, 'insinuating God's voice in his own' (Harding 1992: 64). In this way, story and event became one (ibid.: 73). This 'taking on', this refiguring of the self into a biblical figure, was a marked feature of fundamentalist preachers at St Antony's. It began with the conversion experience itself, often explicitly a road-to-Damascus experience. When suffering because of their faith, fundamentalist preachers often explicitly imagined and knew themselves according to biblical exemplars.

Only the sinner can save himself. Once saved, each must preach the news of salvation to others. Yet, as Barr argues, this is a very particular kind of 'individualism', tempered as it is by intense group loyalty and expressed in contexts in which their biblical study does not take the form of individual interpretation, but rather a reiteration of the agreed religious interpretation, 'a ritual repetition' (1977: 318). Such intensification of group loyalty fitted well with young Zambians' notions of personhood, in which they placed a high value upon 'moving together'. Strikingly, religious conversion to Seventh-Day Adventism or the Born Agains was often marked at St Antony's by the severing of close friendships. Former friends felt unable to escort the convert upon his new journey. The convert, having the new sense of self that the conversion experience had produced, now saw that his erstwhile companions 'belonged to the world' and 'lived in the flesh'.

Enoch, a sixteen-year-old Grade Eleven student at the beginning of my fieldwork, experienced this loss of friends. Prior to his conversion to Adventism, he used to visit me in company with his best friends, Luke and John. All three attended the Catholic Mass, until Enoch realised that he was praying on the wrong day. He came to this conclusion, he explained, after careful study of Scripture (Matthew 27: 57; Matthew 28: 1–2; Luke 23: 50; Luke 24: 2; Isaiah 50). When he was baptised into the Adventist fellowship, he said he felt a new person, 'forgiven by the Lord, and free to preach and to do the work of the Lord ... I felt touched, attached to the Lord'. He now realised the error of his former ways: he had not kept the Sabbath, he had gone to Catholic services and bowed before idols. While at primary school, he had stolen maize, disobeyed his father, insulted others and committed fornication. In spite of his sinfulness, Enoch had repented and had been saved by the Lord; he had been allowed to live, while others had died. Now he felt it was his duty to preach to his parents and to friends. He explained to me, 'I'm not judging, I am teaching. Only a few will enter the kingdom. The path is narrow.'

Enoch quarrelled with Luke and John, he said, 'because of misunderstandings about religious matters'. They no longer understood him and they persisted in living in a way which, according to Enoch, displeased God. Enoch felt the loss of his friends painfully, but he accepted this loss as part of the cost of discipleship. When I expressed anxiety regarding his position at St Antony's, Enoch, more than once, likened himself to the prophet Daniel. God would look after him, he assured me, as He had protected Daniel in the lions' den (Daniel 6: 16ff.). He told me:

> If you are a follower, you should be happy to be persecuted. If you preach to evil people, they won't welcome you. They may even beat you. Christians should be respectful. They should respect their friends. They don't laugh at their friends. They avoid annoying things like fighting. True friends give each other respect. Christians don't involve themselves in worldly things, like talking about girls and fornication. You see those boys, they talk. They say when they go home, they have to do it. Christians shouldn't talk about such things.

Luke and John told me they did not understand what had happened to their friend, Enoch; he had, they said, become 'a fanatic'. When Enoch's zeal brought him into conflict with the Catholic Deputy Headmaster, and his future at St Antony's was placed in jeopardy, even some members of the Adventist fellowship considered that he had gone too far. Lovemore, a member of the Adventist baptism class, expressed concern that if Enoch continued to clash openly with school authorities he would be expelled. He would thus lose his opportunity to get to university and to have a better future. Material success appeared as important as spiritual progress in Lovemore's estimation: 'No one will listen to Enoch if he is dressed in rags.' The Spirit may therefore lead the convert into the desert, driving a wedge between friends, bringing into question the cherished value of always 'moving together'.

CONCLUSION

The Adventist students at St Antony's offer a noticeable example of switching between opposing, even contradictory, self-images. They constructed a boundary against others, especially the Catholics, who 'prayed on the wrong day', and yet in their command of the prefect hierarchy, they captured the centre ground and imposed their religious discipline upon others. They acknowledged their total unworthiness to God in prayer, and yet they exhibited the finest examples of so much that was admired, being civilised, educated, 'Americanised' gentlemen ('Anglicised' being somewhat passé). Born Agains employed a similar rhetoric of unworthiness and yet claimed to have captured the moral high ground, stridently pointing out the errors of others. Powerless in the student hierarchy, Born-Again preachers became leaders within their own movement and brooked no opposition. Each religious movement stressed that one won or lost salvation upon an individual basis, and each, in their separate ways, denied the ultimate power of witchcraft and the spirit world. Preachers in both movements presented themselves as intellectuals, well-versed in the rhetoric of apocalyptic argument and therefore in command of The Book.

Fundamentalists in America in the 1920s felt themselves to be in a secular society that was 'openly turning away from God' (Marsden 1980: 3). It would be a mistake, however, not to problematise the considerable differences between the American fundamentalists of the 1920s and the Zambians I describe. In virtually every sphere of life, religious activity in both 'mainstream' churches and independents evoked enormous interest and involvement. In everyday life, it seemed almost impossible to avoid encountering 'God talk' of one variety or another. The small world of one mission school gave ample proof of the interest and commitment so many young secondary school students had in openly turning *towards* God.

Talk of modern secularisation and of evolution may have alarmed fundamentalists and 'discontented intellectuals' in America, giving them a sense of profound 'spiritual and cultural crisis' (Marsden 1980: 3). But could it be said that anything comparable had taken place in Zambia? Modernism in the form of a secular disenchantment with religion would seem to have made little headway, and the theory of evolution was generally dismissed out of hand by educated elites and 'drop-outs' alike. In Zambia, the comparable crisis might be that of the state and the evident moral morass. Whichever political party held the reins of power, many Zambians felt it was impossible to transcend their lived experience of corruption and inefficiency at all levels of life.

In a discussion of the appeal of Jehovah's Witnesses on the Copperbelt in the 1950s, Epstein notes how membership helped 'many individuals to develop a new-found and more congenial sense of self' (1992: 121). Fundamentalist converts at St Antony's spoke of gaining a new, and more congenial, sense of self. Students all described their experience of a profound change in character that accompanied conversion, a complete break from the past in which they were made 'new men'. The 'evils' of 'smoking, drinking and fornicating', almost always cited together, were abandoned for this new life. Some noted that it was in this moment they had found the power, the courage, to go and preach to others. Many told that before conversion they had liked to fight and to insult others. From being short-tempered, they became docile, slow to anger, more understanding of others. All spoke of a new-found sense of freedom, a feeling of a burden lifted from them. Where once they had been selfish, they had become generous. Adventism and Pentecostalism created the spaces within which a new sense of self might be produced and presented to others. The modern project of an aesthetics of the self was furnished with discourses, narratives and performances.

8

SCHOOLS WITHIN THE SCHOOL

The fellowship of students labelled 'Scripture Union' or more commonly, by outsiders, 'Born Agains' was one of the two most prominent religious movements at St Antony's. Members rejected such labels themselves, although being 'born again' was a fundamental necessity; they proclaimed it, aggressively, a central truth in their religious discourse and in the narratives by which they constructed alternative identities at St Antony's. For some students this religious enthusiasm was a passing phase which would not continue for long after they had left St Antony's. For others it was the beginning of a commitment which would continue through university and into married life. Joining a new religious family was another marker which set them apart from the religious denomination of their parents, upon whom they sometimes passed moral judgement. Student leaders of both groups described their Catholic fathers as 'drunkards'.

The fundamentalist discourses of the Born Agains and the Seventh-Day Adventists both reinforced the civilising mission, exaggerating the thrust towards discipline and a puritanical world-view while denying the total authority of the missionaries, their teachers and their parents. They also denied the ordinary everyday transgressive moral economy of most of the other students as it was revealed in the custom of mockery, where sexual achievement was a *sine qua non* of mature status, and in the behaviour of some students who went out-of-bounds, drinking beer, smoking marijuana, or 'hunting' for girls.

Of the two movements, the Born Agains were less like an alternative church in organisation. By contrast, the Seventh-Day Adventists had a structure similar to a denomination in which a considerable degree of bureau-cratisation had taken place. On the surface, the Born-Again fellowship had *apparently* more tolerance, more space for the movement of the Spirit, for a member to be filled by the Spirit without the mediation of others. There seemed to be greater opportunity for creative initiative, and for innovation, in religious expression.

This appearance might, in fact, have been deceptive, since tight control was exercised by Born-Again leaders over preaching and healing. The Born-Again fellowship was very authoritarian, its members closely disciplined (see Martin 1990: 22, 168 for this emphasis on authority and discipline among Pentecostal groups in Latin America). A defining feature for members was that they did not constitute a 'denomination'; they belonged to 'no church'. However, this had tended to work against them in the school; they had been told that, because they were not a recognised denomination, they could not be expected to be treated like others who received certain privileges and considerations from the school administration, such as school transport to attend religious meetings outside the school. They were, at times, seen by school authorities as a threat. The grounds for this perception were substantial. The Seventh-Day Adventists were generally circumspect in their criticism of Catholics and others. By contrast, the Born Agains made little or no effort to temper and tailor their message to time or place, arguing that to do so would be hypocritical. Because Born Agains sustained the loosest of structures, the school authorities found it harder to call leaders to account, should their members' preaching and attempts to convert others be deemed to go beyond reasonable bounds. For their part, Born Agains said 'the Spirit blows where it wishes'. They were merely the human channels of God's Spirit; they had a duty to point out sin *wherever* they found it.

Born-Again numbers fluctuated considerably. They tended to be fewer than the Seventh-Day Adventists, averaging twenty to thirty. In the past these numbers had sometimes been much larger, owing to, I suggest, the personal charisma of individual student leaders. Active participation in the group was the *sine qua non* for any claim to membership. One might have had students who did not attend Catholic or Seventh-Day Adventist services, and yet who would describe themselves as either 'Catholic' or 'Seventh-Day Adventist', but it was not possible to claim to be 'Born Again' and not to participate in 'fellowship'. At best, one would be described as a 'backslider'.

The whole tone of the group appeared to be more personal, more face-to-face. With few senior students, the membership tended towards a pattern of seniors, normally Grade Twelve students, holding all the leadership positions – chairman, vice-chairman, treasurer and publicity secretary – and a much larger number of juniors. The fellowship offices mirrored, strikingly, leadership of the many school clubs and organisations, each with their elected chairmen, vice-chairmen and so on. Their organisation exemplified what they much admired: the civic culture of the wider contemporary Zambian society. After the model of the civilised, educated 'gentleman', the Born Again knew how to conduct himself in committee. The post of publicity secretary acknowledged the virtue and power of advertising in the modern world.

The major recruiting ground for converts tended to be newcomers to the school, especially Grade Eights. The leaders targeted the brighter, younger and more academically gifted boys, many of whom came from wealthier urban backgrounds. However, this form of religious expression appealed well beyond the members of the wealthy (*cinondo* or *apamwamba*) families, perhaps all the more so because the Born-Again preacher had the national image of material, and not only spiritual, success.

Among Born Agains, as among Seventh-Day Adventists, the recent growth of their fellowship had benefited from a student leader having family links to leadership in the religious movement beyond the school. The Seventh-Day Adventist choir and group leader's brother was a Seventh-Day Adventist minister. The brother of a Born-Again leader who had recently graduated was a well-known preacher who led crusades and appeared on Zambian television.

FELLOWSHIP MEETINGS

During my fieldwork, the fellowship went through a difficult period. Several prominent members of the congregation left after completing Grade Twelve. Other younger members transferred to other schools. The fellowship was led by two Grade Twelve students, Alfred and Frank, neither of them prefects. The majority of other members were juniors, recently recruited as a consequence of Frank's preaching at the morning school assembly. This leadership profile sharply contrasted with that of the Seventh-Day Adventists whose congregation was dominated by prefects, including the school captain and his vice-captain. The two Born-Again leaders had been fellowship members since their arrival in the school in Grade Eight, although Frank said he had gone through a period of crisis, 'falling away', engaging in 'drinking, smoking and fornicating', but had later seen the error of his ways and returned to the fold. Another friend, now a prefect in the same grade, had appeared the 'most committed' of all, but he had recently become 'lukewarm' and had 'fallen away' from the group. It would seem, at St Antony's at least, that the unpredictability identified with the actions of the Spirit-filled disqualified them from consideration for inclusion in the formal student authority hierarchy. Born Agains openly declared themselves to be a moral alternative to all other structures of authority in the school, deriving their power from no human source.

Fellowship members, like Seventh-Day Adventists, addressed each other as 'Brother', and they gathered nightly in the same room used by the Adventist group on Saturday mornings. There were no girls present. On weekdays they met after the evening meal and before the evening study, which gave them about thirty minutes for their service. At weekends, they had more free time and meetings generally lasted an hour and a half. They came together, by choice, in the dark; this heightened the emotional tone of the proceedings. It promoted, I suggest, a greater sense of release and abandon in those who participated. The practice also implied that the production and performance of self enacted at these moments was, at least in part, in stark contrast to the modes of presentation of self that were generally most admired and valued at St Antony's. Hidden from any established gaze, they turned *inwards* upon themselves for their true selves in the making. And against the accepted silences and sounds, dominant in the school, they made their *own* voices heard raucously.

No one could see the faces of the others, although one could make out general shapes on moonlit nights. The darkness heightened some senses at the expense of others, making performance, above all, intensely oral. Text ceased to be a matter of print. For example, no one arrived armed with a Bible. Texts were quoted from memory by the preachers and no one followed the words in print, line by line, page by page, in the ritualistic manner the Adventists required. The Bible became more an open text, the source of a rather limited, in practice, choice repertoire of stories told and retold at fellowship gatherings. Together with the testimonies of those who repented, the Bible was the pretext for the *spoken*, rather than the written, word. In this, Born-Again practice at St Antony's echoed that of Pentecostal groups elsewhere. Martin notes this 'restoration of the oral' in the Pentecostalism of the Caribbean and Latin America (1990: 177). At St Antony's, the oral remained a privileged means of communication. But 'the restoration of the oral' was a further departure from the visually rich world of Catholic liturgy.

The meeting was always led by one of the two Grade Twelve students, who were elected to the posts of chairman and vice-chairman, they explained to me, like Matthias (Acts 1: 15–26), after prayer and reflection. Again and again, Born Agains, like Adventists, resorted to the Bible for exemplary narratives. Students identified with these narratives and made them their own, by recreating a sense of the self refigured upon biblical characters. A new identity was further reinscribed in ritual spaces (cf. Werbner 1989) when preachers and hearers actively took upon themselves the roles of the early Christians.

As members arrived at the Born-Again gathering, a circle was formed and hymns were sung to the accompaniment of hand-clapping and highly constrained 'dancing', mostly jumping up and down on one spot. Clapping is a reported feature of Pentecostal worship elsewhere and may play a role – especially when done in arhythmical patterns – in inducing a trance-like state (Goodman 1972: 10, 79). It clearly facilitated a state of dissociation, preparing the way for glossolalia. Unlike at Catholic services, drums were not used, suggesting that Born Agains wished to distance themselves, in some respects, from 'village' life. The congregation remained standing throughout. Their body movement to the hymn accompaniment provided a sharp contrast to the 'traditional' dancing of *rumba* and *kwasakwasa*, to Zairean music, which many students who were not Born Again engaged in at weekends in the school hall and which involved a great deal of pelvic thrusts. The embodied religious expression of the Born Agains also provided a marked counterpoint to the rule forbidding dancing in Adventist services. In each case, the body in divine service spoke of the variety of modulations and of shapes in religious formation and expression at St Antony's.

The singing was rough, certainly not polished, compared to the precision of performance at Seventh-Day Adventist services. Born Agains did not meet for choir practice, unlike Adventists who regularly practised established favourites and extended their repertoire. Born-Again singing was not formally acknowledged as a means of converting, of 'touching' others, and yet it played a part in moving members of the fellowship towards states of ecstasy. They had no choir, no forms of musical accompaniment, no set pieces when the congregation sat and listened. The singing itself tended to be repetitive, usually repeating one line or phrase of Scripture, not unlike that of Mexican Pentecostals (Dirksen 1984: 33; Martin 1990: 168). Examples at St Antony's included, 'I rejoiced when I heard them say, "Let us go to the house of the Lord,"' or an exclamation of faith, 'Jesus is risen, Alleluia, Alleluia.' These lines were sung over and over again, the rhythms altering as more and more students arrived and the hand-clapping became divided into different parts, each section seeming to clap against the other. This tended to produce something of an hypnotic effect over time. All the singing was in a Zambian language, most usually Bemba. No hymns were sung in English, although everything else *was* in English. There seemed to be an unspoken agreement to make as much noise as possible. It was an opportunity, I would speculate, to express a sense of release and freedom from the regimented life of the daily school regime, and also an attempt to draw the attention of others to the fact that the service was taking place. The noise could be heard throughout most of the school. Grade Twelve 'Commoners' and, to a lesser extent, juniors, 'voiceless' in the day-to-day running of the school, found and made their voices heard at fellowship (cf. Martin 1990: 163).

Sometimes the meeting consisted solely of the singing described above and an opening and closing prayer. The opening prayer followed a certain formula, like that of the Adventists, reminding those present of man's unworthiness and God's goodness. The closing prayer usually included a request for God's help with studies and with financial problems. More notably, Born Agains sought God's protection through the night against evil spirits and the activities of witches. While Adventists, Catholics and others spoke of the activities of Satan, the Born-Again fellowship was alone in its direct comment upon the activities of 'traditional' malevolent forces and in its attempt to safeguard its members through prayer.[1] For all the potential for being transported by the Spirit to another place, the fellowship provided a very down-to-earth service. For a similar observation of Colombian Pentecostals, see Flora (1980: 85); Martin comments, Pentecostals 'want the removal of those things which (literally) bedevil them ...' (Martin 1990: 84).

Usually, towards the end of the meeting, some time was given over to 'individual prayer'. All those present then vocalised their petitions and prayed simultaneously. It was a moment which paradoxically both focused upon the individual and at the same time subsumed this individuality in a sea of other voices. Some students, normally the leaders and one or two others, spoke in tongues, although, Frank and Alfred assured me, this was not a feature to which a great deal of attention was paid

On some nights, the chairman or, less commonly, the vice-chairman preached upon a theme that was said to be central to becoming a 'true Christian'. Repetition was a striking feature of the preaching style adopted. Often words, phrases and sentences were repeated over and over again. The preachers spoke in the Americanised English much admired at St Antony's. They had had the opportunity to study such preaching through the programmes of American tele-evangelists, and the crusades of Zambian preachers such as Nevers Mumba, screened on Zambian television. Some had also attended crusades in Lusaka and on the Copperbelt.

The choice was starkly put: either you belonged to the world, the flesh and the Devil, in which case you would perish in the coming end of time, or you accepted Jesus as your personal Lord and Saviour and thereby gained salvation and eternal life, by entering the 'kingdom of God'. A Christian was someone possessed by the Spirit of God. Reference, for biblical confirmation, was constantly made to the Letter of Paul to the Romans, especially chapters 7 and 8. The alternative was to have within oneself the spirit of the Devil, who would force a person to do evil deeds. When a person received the Spirit of God, he became 'born again'. The person had first to be living a righteous life in order for the Spirit to enter him. The Spirit could not dwell in an 'evil, unrighteous' person. One could not simply pray for the Spirit and He would come. The Spirit of God, the comforter promised by Christ before his ascension into heaven, would only take possession of a person who had proved himself to be 'righteous before God'.

An archaic, biblical style coloured the language employed by both Born Agains and Seventh-Day Adventists within the context of their preaching, religious services and everyday interaction. This language empowered them to speak God's word at a time when, in the wake of the Second Vatican Council, everyday language had been imposed upon Catholics in place of the mysterious, elevated Latin of the traditional Mass. The different congregations thus formed, in some respects, separate linguistic communities which cut across the linguistic and ethnic divides among students at St Antony's.

Here we see a further example of the distinctively heteroglossic nature of school life at St Antony's. Language was one marker of the boundary between those who were 'lost' and those who were 'saved'. Speech was employed to persuade others of the error of their ways. The language and the concomitant imagery, associating the speaker with the Bible as universal, thus transported him beyond the present confines of Zambian life to the past of the time of Jesus, the sacred early days of the church of Christ's followers, while at the same time anticipating the imminent end of all time. For those born again and granted the gift to speak in tongues, their language moved even further beyond the merely archaic; its very incomprehensibility became, paradoxically, the most potent and significant means of communication. Glossolalia was thus both expressive – it made a statement, situating the speaker within the sacred space of the Saved – and transformative – it drew a tight boundary against the polluting world outside, creating a space of intimacy as a hedge against alienation (Csordas 1997: 250). Indeed, Csordas suggests that speaking in tongues could be thought of as the most characteristically postmodern phenomena, a language 'which means nothing, but which everyone can understand' (Csordas 1997: 58).

A theme that ran through many of the sermons and prayers was the need to return to the sacred time of the early days of the church. This concern reflected an orientation to the past and its re-creation. There was also much talk of the return of Christ, and of how a proper reading of the 'signs of the times' would convince those prepared to see that the end of the world was not far. The leaders spoke quite specifically of the problems and difficulties of 'living in the twentieth century', a time when people 'lived in the flesh' and not 'in the Spirit', disobeying God and meriting the destruction that was about to befall the world. And yet the Apostle Paul repeatedly admonished the faithful to 'walk in the Spirit' (for example, Galatians 5: 16–25). Only in this way could men recognise each other in religious kinship and thus become 'true children of God'. To be born again was to begin life afresh, cleansed of one's sinful past and recognising a spiritual kinship with those who were 'saved'.

Born-Again preachers made constant reference to, and thus situated themselves in, the events recorded in the Acts of the Apostles, when the apostles received the gift of the Holy Spirit and changed from frightened, disappointed followers to courageous, articulate preachers who could perform such wonders as healing others and casting out spirits. The later choice of Stephen as a deacon, 'a man full of faith and the Holy Spirit' (Acts 6: 5), was also cited. To be such a follower, it was said, one had to renounce the world; one could not live 'in the flesh' and 'in the Spirit' at the same time. There was no room for 'compromise'. The boundary was clear. Those who 'backslid' were said to have 'returned to the world'.

In contrast, the 'righteous' were able to walk, talk and live in the Spirit in this life and were then transformed after death into 'spiritual beings'. The Spirit of God was said to enter the good man. Only by being guided by the Holy Spirit in this life could one make 'progress' in Christian life. Sins that offended the Holy Spirit were said to be the most serious of all. To 'grieve the Holy Spirit' was very dangerous. The chairman preached and taught almost exclusively upon the topic of the Holy Spirit. He explained there was no salvation without the Spirit. When a Grade Eight student referred in a question to the Spirit as 'it', he was sharply and firmly rebuked by Alfred: 'Not "it", Brother, but "He".'

Frank and Alfred explained that one could recognise the presence of the Holy Spirit because the Spirit 'bore fruits' in someone's life, thus making the person a 'true', committed Christian. It was in the behaviour of the individual that the presence of the Spirit could be read, although little attention was paid to performing Christian deeds or being involved in Christian social action. In contrast to Seventh-Day Adventists, little emphasis was placed upon the duty all individuals had to work for the conversion of others. This task was reserved, to a great extent, for the leaders of the group who passed through the dormitories at night, making contact on an individual basis with those students thought to be likely candidates for conversion. Although they would speak at the morning school assembly, protected by the manner in which this assembly was framed, Frank and Alfred did not preach to the whole wing of a dormitory at the same time. Often judged by the majority of students to be too extreme and eccentric, it would have been difficult, if not impossible, in some wings at least, for them to receive a sympathetic hearing. This was especially true where dormitory prefects and monitors were Adventists.

HEALING

At the end of most services, students with particular problems were asked to make their needs known to the chairman and vice-chairman. The leader reminded all present of Jesus' promise: whatever was asked for in His name would be granted. Students sought His help in their studies and with financial burdens, especially towards the end of term, at exams and when they waited anxiously for the arrival of money to travel home. They also made requests for healing from headaches, malaria, stomach-aches, coughing and sneezing, chest pains and other ailments.[2] The leader called the sick into the centre to make an inner circle; the congregation formed a larger enclosing ring. Into this ring stepped the chairman and vice-chairman who, in turn, laid hands on each of the sick and prayed over them, casting out 'spirits of sickness'. While the congregation sang a hymn, the chairman and vice-chairman put their hands upon the head and shoulders of the sick. In authoritative tones, they prayed and exorcised, using the following formula: 'In the name of Jesus, in the Spirit of God, I command you, spirit of sickness, spirit of malaria, to leave. God, we, your children, we ask you to command these spirits to leave. Amen?' To which all present replied, 'Amen!'

Such healing practice resonated with indigenous practices of healing, through casting out spirits, that many students were familiar with, and of which some, at least, had had direct experience. The security cordon of the saved displaced the protective circle of mealie-meal flour, commonly found at divination. In the fellowship, however, the meaning of possession and exorcism was transformed; the diviner's mediation and medicine were rejected in favour of direct recourse to God through the power of prayer (cf. Maxwell 1994: 351f.). In an analysis of young Puritan preachers in Blantyre, Malawi, van Dijk cautions against placing Born-Again healing on a rural-to-urban continuum. Neither in form, nor in content, can young Born-Again religious authority be considered a transformation of any equivalent among traditional Malawian diviners. Here is no middle ground for 'tradition' to re-enter:

> In their healing practices the young preachers cannot be compared to diviners, since they do not diagnose the exact cause of affliction, nor do they make use of medicines, concoctions or purified water in administering healing: they do not seek inspiration via the shades or other ancestral spirits, and so forth. They simply lay on hands, and no more. (van Dijk 1992a: 177)

A caution is in order, however. What Born-Again healers at St Antony's demonstrated was that, in their shared experience of displacement, they engaged with rural derived practice not by synthesis or mix but, rather, by negation.

INDUCTION OF NEW BROTHERS

Newcomers were periodically invited to come into the inner circle where they could accept Jesus as their personal Lord and Saviour. The invitation was issued in the following manner: 'Are there any of you who are not born again? Then come here and we will pray for you.'

The leader explained that only the Born Again stood in the right relationship to God. Everything in his relationship with God had to be correct, 'made straight'. Obstacles had to be removed while there was still time. If not, on the Last Day, the Day of Judgement, whoever had not been born again would be 'left out'. Individuation, the notion of the individual standing alone before God, was repeatedly stressed. An example was Alfred's invitation, which I tape-recorded at an evening meeting in the presence of about forty Born Agains:

> You must be born again. And also, again, there may be something in Christianity that is holding you up. You want to stand. You want to strive, but it's something that is holding you up. We can pray together with you and leave God to deliver you … leave God to deliver you. Maybe you want to pray but something is holding you up. That's laziness! That's laziness! Feel very free. Because God actually knows you. You are going to stand before God on your own, and not as we

are meeting here. We are all going to stand before God alone, and each of us will give an account of what we have done, right and wrong. The thing we should know is that we are actually strangers on this earth. We are actually on our way to a certain place that God says He is preparing for us ... If we pass through without settling things, making things right before God, we are heading for destruction. It would be bad for you to come and sing and dance here and then go to hell when you die. Amen?

Preachers made much of common Christian themes of pilgrimage and exile in Born-Again and Adventist rhetoric and narrative, just as they did in the Marian and Catholic. The theme of *strangerhood* ran throughout their selection and repertoire of biblical narratives: Abraham figured himself as a 'stranger and sojourner' among the Hittites (Genesis 23: 4; cf. Hebrews 11: 13); Jesus repeatedly told his followers that the cost of discipleship entailed being a stranger upon the earth, with nowhere to lay one's head (Matthew 8: 20). On earth, however, the surrogate religious family acted as a type of 'personal security cult' (Werbner 1989: 6) in which identity was reinscribed (ibid.: 328). While Catholics resorted to Mary for assistance 'in the hour of our death', the Born Again and Seventh-Day judgement was a much lonelier encounter. All had to remember, as indeed the Brothers' Founder also repeatedly warned, that God saw and knew everything and an account of one's life would be demanded.

Preachers paid a great deal of attention to the idea that there might be 'something holding you up', preventing you from making progress in the growth of the knowledge of God, the life of the Spirit. The need to confess one's sins before God was said to be the *sine qua non* for being born again. Various biblical references were quoted or referred to on this theme (for example, Romans 10: 8–9, 1 John 1: 18–25).

The importance of Confession for Catholics and Anglicans was used to establish a boundary with them. The Born-Again chairman explained to candidates being initiated that in his fellowship brothers confessed their sins to God and not to man, that is, not to a priest. (Ironically, few Catholics actually had recourse to the sacrament of Confession.) In a style common to several Pentecostal crusades in urban areas and shown on Zambian television, the chairman stressed again the individual and direct nature of man's relationship to God. Alfred's words at one reception of ten new members illustrated this emphasis:

We are not like these others. They confess to man and not to God. We must only confess to God, tell God who we are and God will visit us. I'm going to lead the prayer, but don't look to me, look to God. He's the one who saves. He's the one who saves. I want you to concentrate on the cross of Calvary. Look on the Lamb of God! Look on the Lamb of God! Don't look at me. I am a servant of God. I am not able to save you. The one who can save you is God. Look to God for your salvation. If any of you feel shy, well, God says, 'If you feel shy, I'm going to feel shy to you.' Don't be shy! The door is open! The door is open! Amen?

Several general prayers followed which stressed God's goodness and man's unworthiness. Loud voices spoke of the rejoicing in heaven when one sinner repented, and the chairman asked God to send the Holy Spirit upon the candidates in the inner circle:

Lord, may you rejoice with the angels this evening over the souls that are coming back to you. In the name of Jesus! Bring down your strong arm against the Devil! In the name of Jesus! Break every kind of bondage from the Devil. In Jesus' name! You know their failures, their weaknesses. You are the one who knows their inner mind, oh God! Oh God, I want to pray [now shouting loudly] that you set them free from the bondage of sin, from the bondage of sin. In the name of Jesus, set them free from the chains of Satan, set them free from the chains of Satan. In the name of Jesus! Erase all kinds of demons in the name of Jesus! Amen?

Preachers used physical force and loud vocalisation in their attempt to release newcomers from Satan's power. The chairman, empowered by the Holy Spirit, had the authority to request this from God.

After this prayer, the candidates were then required to repeat the following prayer, said aloud first, phrase by phrase, by Alfred:

Dear Jesus, we come to you this evening, knowing that we are sinners and that we can't save ourselves. As we come before you this evening, forgive us, oh Lord. Forgive us, oh Lord, wash us, wash us with your blood. Wash us with your blood. We call upon the name of Jesus to come into our lives. We welcome the Holy Spirit. We welcome the Holy Spirit into our lives. In the name of Jesus, I accept Jesus as my personal Lord and Saviour. I accept Jesus as my personal Lord and Saviour. Take control of my life. Take control of my life right now. I renounce the Devil, in the name of Jesus. I call upon the blood of Jesus! I call upon the blood of Jesus! I thank God I am now free. I thank God that I am born again! Amen! Amen!

Personal culpability was a strong feature in the Born-Again fellowship, as it was in Adventism. The dramatic imagery of salvation through Christ's blood was similarly regularly mobilised in their preaching. Only the blood of Christ could wash away sin. Through verbal metaphor and metonym, believers were brought orally into a direct relation with the suffering body of Jesus. The suffering was rarely visualised and never physically incorporated.[3]

Following the prayer of induction came a period of 'individual prayer', with everyone in the room shouting out prayers and petitions at the same time. Some wept aloud. The noise grew louder and louder, and out of it one could only catch snatches of prayer: 'Oh God set us free ... In the blood of Jesus ... Break the bonds of Satan ... Break the bonds of darkness ...'

Some spoke in tongues, especially Frank and Alfred, whose voices, gradually increasing in volume, dominated throughout. At no point were they 'out-shouted' by the other members of the congregation. Frank and Alfred spoke, in an urgent manner, in brief, staccato, repetitive phrases, taking short, shallow breaths. Having achieved a sustained crescendo, their voices started to fall away and gradually became quieter. Their shift in volume signalled to the others to become also more restrained; then all was silence. No particular attention was paid to the glossolalia; no one attempted to interpret what was being said. I would speculate, however, that the leaders' ability to speak in tongues proved their credentials to the fellowship as effectively as their persuasive rhetoric.

Alfred then spoke for some time, giving general advice to the newly born again, who had 'recently come out of the world', warning them in particular that now that they were 'true Christians', they would be special targets for Satan's attacks. The Devil did not need to bother with the others, many of whom said they were Christians but who were, in fact, already working at his beck and call. Serious temptations would come but they could be defeated by constant prayer. The newly Born Again must become a 'prayer warrior' and spend all his available time reading the Bible in order to gain the strength he needed to overcome the work of the Devil.[4] The sides were only two: God's and the Devil's. The newly Born Again had to choose, either to be controlled by 'nature' [that is, sinful human nature], or by the Spirit.[5] No compromise with the world was possible.

Then followed another period of prayers over the new members and general petitions offered for those present. The meeting broke up with a final refrain, 'Walk with Jesus', sung in Bemba.

The reception of new members illustrated the difference in induction between Born-Again fellowship on the one hand, and the Catholic and Adventist, on the other. Born Agains, unlike the others, had no long process of doctrinal teaching. They offered a different kind of education. The Born-Again novice was trained, first and foremost, through participation in fellowship. Here embodied practice was fundamentally important; the newcomer learnt, without formal taught instruction but rather through direct imitation of bodily expression, how to clap, how to 'dance', how to breathe, how to pray with hands upraised and, if he was blessed in this way, how to speak in tongues. What was important was 'baptism in the Spirit'. Every few months, new members were offered 'baptism by water' through visits arranged to a nearby Born-Again fellowship which was led by a pastor.

However, leaders stressed that this was *only* baptism in water; its importance was secondary. In this way, student leaders retained the ultimate authority. By contrast, the Catholic Sacrament of baptism by water was the entry to full membership and reception of the Sacraments. Seventh-Day Adventists placed great importance on baptism by complete immersion and students, especially preachers, reported to me the immediate gift of the Spirit that baptism gave them.

DISCIPLINING THE BODY

Important as their differences were, the Seventh-Day Adventists and the Born Agains were remarkably similar, especially in the creation of the boundary between them and others and in the injunction to make the body fit to be 'the temple of the Holy Spirit'. From this flowed injunctions against smoking and drinking, activities Catholics were known to allow: one should not put alcohol or smoke into the body where the Spirit of God dwelt. Two Spanish Brothers at fault were often singled out for criticism. Frank and Alfred, while valuing the teaching and administrative capabilities of missionary Brothers, piously regretted that, as a community, they 'showed no signs of the Spirit of God'.

The Born-Again leaders and some of their followers took the need to control and to subdue the body a stage further by engaging in fasting to 'live more fully in the Spirit'. They explained that fasting made you ready to enter into 'deep prayer', the time for much speaking in tongues. The leaders used it as a strategy to make prayer for the conversion of others more efficacious. Depriving the body of food was also a means of asking God to 'bind all the evil dreams' and thoughts of women. They identified sexual desire to be the most likely cause of young people 'falling into sin'. Frank was one of many student preachers to speak both in sermons and in conversations about such temptations. In an interview with me, he spoke at length upon the Apostle Paul's advice to offer oneself as a living sacrifice to God:

> You see, you find that, if you are not strong in your Christianity, you'll tend to think about girls, and you start regretting: 'Why did I become a Christian?' You have to fast. You have to pray hard. Before you sleep, you pray 'Father, bind all the evil dreams.' You see, like at home, you wake up in the morning, you pray – because it's only through prayer that you achieve that, only through prayer. Mind you, the Devil can't be seen – maybe you'll just try to throw a girl and then you commit fornication. That's why many people have found it difficult to be born again.

'Worldly' music and dancing, 'the work of the devil' were also condemned for arousing such desire. Behaviour and speech unmistakeably marked apart the one having the Spirit of God within him. The 'Spirit-filled' person had the power to 'touch' others with his words about God. Examples were given from Zambian television, both the national crusades of Zambian preachers and the programmes of such American tele-evangelists as Jimmy Swaggart. When they preached, Born Agains said, 'You really felt it.'

The notion of the boundary, of being separated off from others who were not 'true Christians', was much stronger, or at least more explicit and outspoken, in the rhetoric of the Born Agains. First, to repeat for clarity, Born Agains, unlike the Seventh-Day Adventists, were not recognised by the school authorities as a 'denomination'. Further, they were conscious of, and indeed drew part of their identity from, their sense of being ostracised and 'mocked' by others. This was, for them, a sign that they were doing God's will: they faced trials and temptations, and they were denounced 'fanatics' by other students, simply because they were unwilling to 'compromise with the world'.

Born Agains were highly conscious of the need to keep their fellowship pure and uncompromised. When one of their number went astray, they brought heavy moral pressure to bear. First, they approached the 'backslider' in ones and twos. If this pressure failed, all came together to try and 'convince' the one who had gone astray. They recognised, however, that some individuals so hardened their hearts that there was nothing further to do but to 'cast them off', 'set them aside', 'send them away'.

The accusation Born Agains levelled against all the other churches was that they took some parts of the Bible seriously, and not others. The Born Agains claimed to be the only ones who faithfully followed everything in the Bible. As for the Seventh-Day Adventists, the Born Agains said that they ignored the requirement, specifically stated by Jesus, of being 'born again' in order to enter the kingdom of God. They also criticised the Seventh-Day Adventists for keeping the Sabbath on Saturday, a requirement only for the 'Israelites', not for the Gentiles. They explained, 'We are not part of Israel.' The Born Agains were particularly outspoken in their anti-Catholic stand (cf. Martin 1990: 236; Maxwell 1994: 334). Catholics, they protested, worshipped Mary, and ignored the role of Jesus and the necessity to be born again 'of the Spirit' and 'in Jesus' blood', a spiritual baptism rather than simply a baptism with water.

STAFF INVOLVEMENT

Like the other religious groups in the school, apart from the Catholics, the Born Agains organised themselves with only minimal contact with sympathetic members of staff or with religious groups beyond the school. During the period of my fieldwork one staff member, Mr Otoro, a Ugandan exile, gave the Born-Again group encouragement and support. In an interview, Mr Otoro refigured himself according to the exemplary narratives of the biblical prophets and, indeed, of Jesus Himself. He did not attend any fellowship meetings, because he feared a 'spy network' of teachers and boys, 'hypocrites' who greeted him but who were monitoring groups other than the Catholics. He told me one should not be surprised: there had always been 'Judases'. Mr Otoro held gatherings in his home for interested students, who formed a breakaway Pentecostal group of their own, and here he discussed the Bible with them. Brother Henry had threatened him, in an oblique manner, with removal from the school following the baptism of some students, one of them a Catholic, in the local river. Mr Otoro had contacted some Pentecostal associates in the nearby town, members of the Assemblies of God, and, together with them, he had organised the baptism.

Mr Otoro had also clashed with a number of other teachers, and he denounced their 'sexual immorality'. He had also quarrelled with the parents of some of the girl day scholars, people who, he said, 'appeared very serious in church' [that is, the Catholic church] but who actually encouraged their daughters to engage in 'sexual immorality' for material gain. Pointing to the fact that about half the girls failed to finish their junior secondary school because of pregnancy, he suggested that those who managed to complete only did so because they had abortions.

Mr Otoro placed great stress upon the idea that he belonged to no church; all that was needed was to read and understand the Bible. As a history teacher, he said he knew that the Spanish had always been cruel people, and he saw these Catholic missionaries, in particular, as people who did not 'know' the Bible properly, people who had replaced the Bible with 'theology'. They were 'very far from Scripture', having only 'theories' to work with. Declaring himself to be 'one who will not live by theology but by practical Bible studies', he foresaw the time when the Catholics, who, he said, were now 'holding back', would one day 'rule' the World Council of Churches. Denominationalism was 'against God's word' and denominationalism had started with the Catholics in Rome. He had other serious reservations about the Catholics, such as the rule of celibacy of the clergy and religious which, in his opinion, simply encouraged immorality, and the teaching that Mary remained a Virgin until her death, something he believed was clearly contradicted by even the most cursory reading of the Bible. Against the Bible also were the images in the church and the sanctuary lamp that claimed that Christ was present in the tabernacle. But the end was coming very soon, he said, and then all would be revealed. One could read the signs of the times because here again were 'days of sexual promiscuity as in the days of Noah and Lot'.

Mr Otoro's dealings with the school authorities and with Brother Henry reflected his determination not to compromise with the world and to point out sin wherever it was to be found. In this he resembled the majority of Pentecostal students. By contrast, the three male Seventh-Day Adventist teachers were equally opposed to the 'threat of Catholic domination', but they normally conducted themselves in an extremely circumspect manner.

EXTERNAL RELATIONS

The Born-Again group had contacts with two local Pentecostal congregations in nearby villages where healing and casting out spirits featured prominently. It was to one of these that new members went to receive 'the baptism of water' from the pastor there. It was also from these that they received some of their literature, published by 'Gospel Sunrise, Inc.', in Virginia. Their literature-based Christianity, like that of the Seventh-Day Adventists, had its origins in North America. If all St Antony's students lived in a world curiously 'made in England' (Veliz 1983), for some more than for others it was a world *remade* in North America, and existentially, I would add, further refashioned by themselves in Zambia. The Born-Again material consisted of short pamphlets, with titles like *Jesus Said ... 'Save your life – or lose it'*. They dealt with different aspects of teaching, but always focused on the need to choose between this world and the kingdom of God, and on the need to be born again to enter the kingdom.

During the eighteen months of my fieldwork, the Zambian pastor of the local Pentecostal fellowship paid one visit to the school. Some twenty students attended, among them a significant number of Zimbabweans. The pastor pointed to the poor attendance as evidence of the Devil's work of keeping people away from the truth. Still, the fact that they were few did not actually matter, he explained. In fact, the notion of 'being few', of being 'the remnant' was a major theme in both Born-Again and Adventist identity and self-portrayal. A long biblical tradition was drawn upon to support this, from God's destruction of Sodom and Gomorrah (Genesis 18: 19), through to John the Baptist's 'voice crying in the wilderness' (Matthew 3: 3; cf. Isaiah 40: 3) and Jesus' warning: 'Many are called, but few are chosen' (Matthew 22: 14).

The visit of the pastor took place on a Saturday morning and the accomplished, and at times exuberant, singing of the Seventh-Day Adventist service could be clearly heard throughout the Born-Again fellowship meeting. The whole atmosphere in the school hall where the meeting took place was, by contrast, subdued. The pastor tried to instil a little enthusiasm by leading the singing, performing little dances, strutting across the stage in the hall and repeating again and again, 'Ah! You people! What's the matter? Aren't you happy?' In his late twenties, he was dressed smartly, with black trousers, new, highly polished shoes, an expensive-looking open-necked shirt and a white zip-up jersey. He was accompanied by three others, one of whom he introduced as his interpreter. He, too, was smartly dressed in white trousers, a jacket in pastel shades, good shoes, and the dark glasses much admired by the students, which they associated with American 'cool'. The pastor and his interpreter thus exhibited in their attire, stance, gait and posture the very embodiment of all the trappings of desirable modernity, American-style.

All present could follow perfectly well in English, but the preacher had everything translated by his interpreter into Bemba. The interpreter followed the pastor as he moved around during his preaching and from time to time they faced, almost confronted, each other. There was a sense in which they appeared to work off one another, and the mode of translation employed added a dramatic dimension to the proceedings.[6] Having text in American-accented English and interpretation in Bemba was dynamic, productive of tension, representing a movement not merely across languages, but across worlds of the imagination.

The pastor, speaking English but with the 'American' accent much admired in Zambia, chose as his theme the need for faith, illustrating it with many references to both the Old and the New Testament. Talk was easy, he explained. Prostitutes, homosexuals and bishops called themselves Christians, but they were not 'true Christians' because they had not been born again; they had not accepted Jesus as their personal Lord and Saviour. About thirty minutes into his sermon, he recounted a visit he had recently made to another secondary school. There he had encountered a girl possessed by demons and having an affair with a married man. He had prayed over her and cast out the demons, and she had repented, ended the affair, and gone to the man's wife to ask for forgiveness. The power of the Spirit had been demonstrated, he concluded.

He then issued an invitation for anyone who wished to be born again to come forward. Nobody moved. Another hymn was sung in a rather desultory fashion and the invitation reissued. Again there was no response. After consultation with the chairman, the pastor invited anyone who 'had problems' to come forward to be prayed over. For some time there was no movement. Then a Grade Twelve student, not a regular member of the fellowship, went forward. He appeared to indicate that he had something wrong with his head, pointing to his sinuses. The pastor and his assistants laid hands on the student and explained that a spirit was causing the problem. He commanded the spirit to come out, and instructed the student to shake his head vigorously from side to side. This procedure was repeated twice. After each attempt the student indicated that he did not feel any improvement. After the third unsuccessful attempt the pastor, rather unceremoniously, instructed the student to return to his seat. No explanation was offered for this failed performance. After several more hymns, and with no one else coming forward, Alfred announced that the service was over. Having thanked all those who attended, he reminded the members about the evening meeting where, he said, 'We shall deal with the Devil.' The pastor then had a meeting with the chairman and the vice-chairman. Before his departure, he distributed some more pamphlets, singling out for me a pamphlet on the fate of 'backsliders'.

The Born-Again leadership at St Antony's maintained a vociferous, critical commentary on the sins of others, and they marked out for them-selves a separate space from which to speak. Seizing the moral high ground, they poured scorn on 'the things of this world' and yet, paradoxically, in their presentation of self, especially through preaching and healing, they revealed the ways in which they continue to aspire to the status then exemplified in the person of the Born-Again President.

SEVENTH-DAY ADVENTISM

The Adventists, by contrast, were a denomination which negotiated more successfully – according to popular response to them – the problem of living in this world while preparing for the world that was to come. Again Seventh-Day Adventist aspirations to 'civilised' status, associated with the *musungu*, were once more to the fore. This connection would appear to be of some years standing. Colson, speaking of the Plateau Tonga, notes that Mwansa Chieftaincy, where many of the people were Seventh-Day Adventists, was 'considered by the Tonga as progressive, as a place where people are trying to live like Europeans' (1958: xii–xiii).

The Seventh-Day Adventists were the most active and the most visible exponents of the Protestant counter-discourse at St Antony's. They domin-ated the preaching at morning assemblies and the alternative Sunday service. Adventists also did most of the dormitory preaching at night. Adventist preachers, such as Henderson, gained considerable reputations in this way. The Adventist choir was greatly admired by many students and staff. Choir members were regularly called upon to sing hymns to mark the opening and closing of school celebrations, such as Youth Day and Africa Freedom Day, taking second place on the programme only to the rendition of the national anthem. They also sang at morning assemblies whenever there was an Adventist student preacher.

Among staff members, two of the three male Adventist teachers demon-strated a keen interest in preaching at the school assembly. They were joined in this by the Adventist school secretary, Mr Chisenga, who preached regularly and to considerable effect. Because of his access to so much local knowledge from both the teachers' and the students' communities, Mr Chisenga's sermons were peppered with apt illustrations; he addressed the concerns that, he knew well, occupied the minds of his student audience. Always greeting the students as 'sons of God', Mr Chisenga, like Mr Mwila, often omitted acknowledgement of the presence of the few female day scholars. He sometimes preached upon the importance of keeping *all* the Commandments, which meant, of course, observing the Sabbath on the correct day. While he cited the Bible as his source of authority, he, like most Adventist student preachers, made no public criticism, at assemblies, of Catholics for 'praying on the wrong day'. Such direct censure was more generally made by Adventist preachers in the dormitories at night.

The subject to which Mr Chisenga returned again and again was the imminent end of the world. Around that he wove repeatedly the main themes of formation at St Antony's: education for citizenship, the links between Christianity and gentlemanly conduct, and the account and the accounting of the self, full of consequences both in this world and the world to come. He reminded his hearers, 'Jesus will come like a thief in the night.' Even the angels did not know the hour of Jesus' return, but, Mr Chisenga warned and I recorded:

> You may be found doing the wrong thing! ... You must check where you are standing. Maybe you are in the middle – lukewarm. Well, if you are lukewarm, God says, 'I will spit you out'. So you must be very serious, how you accept the Spirit of God in your body. Remember, your body – it's the temple of God! So you can't insult or mock or beat your friend – like your Grade Eight friends, no! We are all one in Christ. If your friend is sick, you must help him. You can't just say, 'No, my friend, maybe you've just eaten too much *chikwangwa* [the crust of *nshima* from the bottom of the cooking pots], because you are a shunter [a food committee member]'. No! [Laughter from the students.] No, remember the last day is coming. The angels of God and the angels of evil are now sealing their people! Be careful! Once you've got the seal, it will be too late! Now is the time to be reformed, to become very serious students of St Antony's ... And once you are converted, the prefects and the administration will have no problems with you. You won't blast [use vernacular], you won't steal your friend's share. You won't lose control. Each of you must control yourself. Now is the time. You must show yourselves responsible citizens, good boys and girls. Remember the testimonials will follow you when you go to look for a job – they'll follow you, even to Livingstone! Even to Mongu! ...

Adventist student preachers generally also concentrated on the themes of the Sabbath and the end of the world. Many pointed to the year 2000 as the most likely time for the cosmic cataclysm. At night, in the dormitories, some preachers were more explicit in their denunciation of Catholic errors. Here Catholics were warned of the consequences of failing to keep the Sabbath Commandment. A particular target for attack in dormitory preaching was the Pope who was regularly identified to be 'the Beast, Six, Six, Six' of the apocalyptic vision (Revelation 13: 18). On the wall of his cubicle, Henderson had posted a large sheet of paper on which was written the Pope's title in Latin, *vicarius filii dei*, 'the vicar of the Son of God'. Arrows indicated how parts of the words, VIC, IIII DI, could supposedly be read as Roman numerals indicating the number 666. Below the Latin words, Henderson had written: '666 = the Beast!'

The official line in the school, expressed to me by Adventist prefects, was that everyone was free to follow their own conscience, although, they invariably added, a *correct* reading of the Bible was also necessary. They assured me that they were happy at St Antony's; there were 'no problems'. Because the school administration was 'very understanding', there was freedom of worship. In fact, Adventists capitalised on the space this freedom offered them to preach their message to fellow students, and thereby hasten Christ's return. The secular authority that they had attained through the prefect system was mirrored by the moral authority they claimed through their reading of 'the signs of the times' and through 'praying on the right day'.

THE SEVENTH-DAY SABBATH SERVICE

The conduct of the Seventh-Day Adventist Sabbath service exhibited many features of the civilising process as it was an ideological desire of the students themselves. Most striking was the particular accent given by Seventh-Day Adventists to the civilising process in the production, presentation and performance of self at St Antony's. In the order of service, the civilised body could be viewed here in perhaps its most accomplished form – socialised into pacification, rationalised and individualised (Elias 1979: 201, 253–7; 1983: 243).[7] At St Antony's many of these features of modernity were observable in the various arenas of school life I have already described. The Seventh-Day Adventist service offered a salient example of civilising in a remarkably achieved moment.

Sabbath activities demonstrated the manner in which another type of schooling, another avenue of formation, was revealed at St Antony's in spaces controlled and maintained once more by the students themselves. The weekly service took place on Saturday mornings from 9 a.m. to noon.[8] Varying slightly during my fieldwork, attendance was between thirty-five and forty-five students, and everything was done by the students themselves. Seventh-Day Adventist teachers and Mr Chisenga did not attend. They preferred to worship with a local Seventh-Day Adventist congregation, four kilometres from the school, which the students, particularly the choir, also joined on special occasions such as field camps. During my fieldwork, no Adventist minister visited St Antony's.

The students' service took place in the same room, known as the 'Art Room', used by the Born Agains. Now used mainly for option classes and for personal study, since art had not been taught at St Antony's for many years, the room was allocated for Adventist use at this time by the school administration. There were no girls present. As with all religious and other gatherings in Zambia, students drifted in, in twos and threes, during the first twenty minutes or so, while hymn-singing was led by one of the choir-masters of the group. Everyone joined in, and sometimes hymns were sung in two or even three languages simultaneously. This hymn-singing, involving all present, was quite different from the hymns performed by the Adventist choir as set-pieces at later stages in the service. The choir's singing was much admired within and beyond the group, and such singing was held to be the main way, along with preaching, in which converts were 'touched' and 'moved' to seek Seventh-Day Adventist membership.

The standard of the official choir's singing was extremely high. They sang *a capella* and rejected the drum accompaniment common among Catholic, United Church and other choirs because, in their view, it was highly inappropriate for religious worship. In this they also explicitly distanced themselves from the drumming at beer parties and other celebrations and from the drum rhythms of affliction and healing (see Turner 1968). This was considered by them to be part of the 'traditional' 'things of the village' such as spirits, witchcraft, and a concomitant understanding of illness and misfortune, from which the Seventh-Day Adventist students wished to dissociate themselves. They cited the Bible as their source for this practice, explaining that biblical descriptions of the use of drums demonstrated that drums were 'used to celebrate, but in church you are supposed to *pray*'. Peter, School-Captain and Seventh-Day Adventist preacher, explained to me the need to discipline the body and control its emotions and their expression: 'You see, if you use a drum, some people will become full of emotion. They may get carried away and even think of dancing.'

An extraordinary amount of time and effort was put into choir practice at weekends and on free evenings. One or two copies of the Seventh-Day Adventist hymnal, without musical notation, circulated among members. Words were normally transcribed into exercise books by choir members. Apart from the hymnal, choir members learnt new hymns directly from tapes purchased through Adventist House or, more commonly, received from Adventist pen-friends in America or South Africa. Favourite hymns, sung in English, Bemba, Tonga and Nyanja, were rehearsed again and again in an almost obsessive quest to achieve a sense of perfection and completion.

The choir sang mostly in three-part or four-part close harmony, with bass, baritone and two tenors. Their repertoire exhibited different styles. Many hymns were in the marching mode of Methodist and Anglican hymnody or in the genre of Negro Spirituals. Others were in the call and response mode, the style of much 'traditional' African singing. Here soloists, normally the bass, were answered by the others in three-part harmony. Syncopation was a marked feature of much of their singing.

Adventists expressed a desire to create a distance between themselves and local African practice. Ironically, however, their inadvertent introduction of latent syncopation into Methodist hymnody provided clear evidence of African retentions.[9] In spite of themselves, they could not discard 'Africa' so easily. Or perhaps, one might say that 'Africa' returned in what they perceived to be an acceptable, controlled, refined mode of expression. The singing had a great deal of repetition; *ostinato* (where the melodic figure is repeated through all or part of the piece) is, again, a marked feature of African singing. The key and melody rarely changed, but the harmonies increased and became more complicated in certain hymns.

A hymn was often sung through first in its basic pattern. The main themes were elaborated upon through notational variation, sequence and repetition, the tempo changing and the harmonies becoming increasingly more complex. Most singing was in four-four, three-four or six-eight time. Singing in three-four time, the choir often inadvertently stretched the tempo. Choir members sang emotionally and passionately, but theirs was always a restrained passion.

The choir, dressed smartly in dark trousers, white shirts and black ties, exuded a sense of professional order, of drilled competence. Disciplined in their deep and regular breathing, completely motionless, they stood in a semi-circle, their feet slightly apart. They faced the congregation, but did not engage in eye-contact with them. Intent upon the achievement of harmony, their facial expression revealed transcendence: it was as if they had been transported to another place. The lyrics and imagery of the hymns told of the dramatic events about to unfold. Choir members explained that the hymns had to have a message in order to 'convince people'. The official hymn repertoire delineated an apocalyptic topography and rehearsed, again and again, the most prominent themes of Seventh-Day Adventism: the Second Coming, the Last Judgement, the need to choose between good and evil, heaven and hell, and Christ's Death on the Cross for the salvation of mankind.

Foucault's description of the modern self caught within a penal account-ancy had many resonances in Adventist hymns. It was an accounting and an account that stretched into eternity. Not only did God see everything, He recorded everything, too. It was this knowledge of the record of one's life, a narrative beyond the control and the manipulation of the subject, that held a special dread for the sinner, called to account at the end of time. The choir's rendition of 'How shall You Stand on that Great Day?', resonant with the drama of the final *individual* accounting, was a particular favourite both with Seventh-Day and with other students. The hymn was first sung through twice in four-part close harmony. A baritone solo then repeated the verses, accompanied by other choir members humming in three-part harmony:

> The Judgement has set, the books have been opened.
> How shall you stand in that great day,
> When every thought and word and action
> God, the righteous judge shall weigh?

Chorus
How shall you stand in that great day?
How shall you stand in that great day?
Shall you be found before Him wanting,
Or with your sins all washed away?

The work is begun to those who are sleeping.
Soon will the living here be tried.
Out of the books of God's remembrance,
His decision to abide.

Chorus repeated:
How shall you stand on that great day...

O, how shall you stand that moment of searching,
When all our sins those books reveal?
When from that court, each case decided,
Shall be granted no appeal?

The hymn, attributed to F. E. Belden and dated 1886, is a standard piece taken from *The Seventh-Day Adventist Hymnal*, published in the United States. The hymnal indicates the Scripture references contained in the text of the hymn. The references – in this hymn, Daniel 5: 27, 7: 10; Matthew 12: 36; 2 Timothy 4: 8; 1 Peter 4: 17 – situated Adventists within the apocalyptic discourse and topography which enfolded all preaching and singing. Of outstanding interest, in this particular example, was the treatment of the original theme, 'How shall *we* stand ...' The dramatic tone had been heightened by the change of pronoun to '*you*'; the address was thus transformed into a direct individual appeal to hearers of the hymn: *repent*. In their narratives of conversion, several students, Adventist and Born Again, spoke of the power contained in such an address. They reported their sense that preaching or singing directed very personally at them *alone* was the defining moment in their decision to repent: they became conscious, as never before, of their own culpability. Fundamentalist students remarked upon this repeatedly. Alfred, the Born-Again chairman, recalled for me the moment he realised his sinfulness:

> It came about when one time I attended the Crusade by certain Brothers from Livingstone, hosted by the Pentecostal Ministries in Northmead [Lusaka]. I just went there to listen to some music. They had some instruments there. When I reached there I sang, danced, then it was the time for preaching. He preached and then after he preached, it was like everything that the preacher said was against me. He said everything that I used to do – on that I said, 'No, maybe it's God speaking to me.' So I had to reconcile.

Written in chalk on the board in the Art Room was the theme of the day's service, a verse from the Bible. This theme followed that found in the Seventh-Day Adventist literature obtained from a Seventh-Day Adventist 'field office'; the nearest office, staffed by Zambians, was located thirty kilometres away in the nearby town. Material was also sent by post from Lusaka. During the first half of my fieldwork, Edward, the leader of the Seventh-Day Adventist student group and also chief choirmaster, had a brother, a Seventh-Day Adventist minister on the Copperbelt, who kept him supplied with the relevant material. Several student preachers had their own small library of Seventh-Day Adventist texts. They also copied out by hand extensive parts of Adventist literature into exercise books, and it was normally these books that they used as *aide-memoires*, if need be, during their sermons. They sometimes read direct from this material while preaching.

Preachers' personal libraries and students' study books demonstrated the external sources of most of the Seventh-Day Adventist material: North America and South Africa. Apart from the Seventh-Day Adventist Church manual, the most common books were the writings of Ellen G. White, whose visions were often described in student preaching. The writings included *The Greatest Love*, *The Desire of Ages*, *Health and Happiness* (used as a source for sermon material on the topic of 'temperance'), and *The Great Controversy*, the latter part of which, 'The Final Warning' focuses upon 'the things to come'. All these are published by Inspiration Books of Phoenix, Arizona. Popular also were the works of other writers, especially those dealing with the final struggle between good and evil, for example *The Revelation of Things to Come*, by R. J. Wieland (Sentinel Press, Capetown), and *The Lucifer Files* by K. McFarland (Pacific Press, Ontario). As imported books, they were expensive for students to purchase and their possession spoke of a member's willingness to invest in things not of this world. With the exception of students from wealthy families, most students had very few personal books. What was available was passed from friend to friend and, in fellowship, from brother to brother.

In the Seventh-Day Adventist student archive were guides to assist in the task of 'awakening the world from sleeping'. Preachers were advised how to prepare to meet and 'canvass Mr Prospect', the potential convert. The preparation was divided into 'spiritual, mental and physical'. The importance of 'the art of salesmanship', that is 'the skilful application of organised knowledge', and 'literature ministry' were stressed. The pedagogy of preaching was couched in idioms of advertising and commerce. The section on 'literature ministry', which began with criticism of Catholicism, foregrounded the historical importance of the printing press in the Reformation's drive to rectify 'the evils of Catholicism'. What emerged was the enormous value placed upon reading literature and consequently the ability to read and develop the skills of argument and debate.[10]

THE FORMAL BEGINNING OF THE SERVICE

When a reasonable number of students were present, the ones in charge of conducting the service assembled outside the room and then made a solemn formal entrance, taking up positions at a long table facing the congregation. Their formal comportment gave a business-like air to the start of the proceedings. The congregation rose to greet their arrival. An introductory prayer was said and the congregation sat to hear the first sermon. It was usually quite brief and given by someone who was still rather junior in the leadership hierarchy.

Most of those who preached, at this point, were Grade Ten students. Many of them later became both accomplished preachers and prefects in the school. Thus a forum was provided for trainee preachers to practise an art, valued in different arenas of school life, in front of the sympathetic congregation of fellow Adventists, before facing the wider audience in the school assembly. I observed, over my time at St Antony's, how much individual preachers gained in confidence and expertise, qualities that could be read as much in their poise and gesture, as in their command of persuasive rhetoric. They normally progressed from diffident early attempts to bravura performances. Hesitancy, lack of eye contact, unvarying and unmodulated speaking tone, over-reliance on written notes and nervous posture were, within a short space of time, abandoned. Preachers developed into adept evangelists who employed body and voice in their efforts to move their congregation. In their skilled presentation and confident stance, they employed a range of rhetorical devices: they modulated their voices, at times whispering, at times speaking loudly, and they varied their speech rhythms, heightening suspense for dramatic effect.[11]

All student preaching in the school was in English. Whatever the context, the Seventh-Day Adventist preachers always began with a formula prayer that stressed the unworthiness of all men to address God or to preach about Him: 'We come before you, Father, seated at the mercy seat, with nothing but our sins.'

As in the Born-Again fellowship, members were introduced, addressed and referred to as 'Brothers' or 'Brethren' during the service, and at other times in day-to-day school life outside the classroom, in recognition of their shared spiritual kinship, recreated and strengthened in such moments. Thus, in fundamentalists' eyes, there was not only one group of 'Brothers' at St Antony's. Fundamentalists, both Born Agains and Adventists, claimed the moral high ground for themselves, referring to the Spanish Brothers as 'the so-called Brothers' in interviews with me and pointing to their estimation of the Catholic missionaries in the moral equation.

The end of the first sermon was often presented in a low-key manner by the probationary preacher. He had yet to develop the skills which would demonstrate his competence at modulating and manipulating emotional tones. He had to do this in a restrained fashion, and yet with sufficient conviction and passion to reveal the presence of the Spirit within him. The conclusion was greeted by all present with a shout of 'Amen!'

Seventh-Day Adventist students all agreed that the good preacher was inspired by the Spirit of God. They acknowledged that not all who preached were in possession of, or possessed by, such inspiration. The most 'sinful' before their conversion were generally judged to have the greatest power to move others. Henderson was a good example of a preacher to whom students attributed power because of his sinful past. He readily rehearsed his past in sermons and in conversations. In an interview with me, he remarked:

> Before I was saved, I used to be a smoker – ordinary cigarettes and *dagga* [marijuana], a drunkard and a thief. I developed all these habits here at school. I used to move with a group of last year's Grade Twelves. Then, on 1 October 1991, at Choma, my life changed.

All converts to Seventh-Day Adventism said baptism, the time when they received the Holy Spirit in a special way, changed them as people, generally making them more gentle and understanding. They became pacified, and went on to develop the control of body and spirit required of the righteous. This pacification had particular resonances in the Zambian context. Bemba students, for example, were ambivalent about their alleged warlike personality. They took a certain pride in their historical narrative of legendary physical strength and courage and yet, in modern-day Zambia, they wished to distance themselves from that, preferring the image of civilised, literate gentlemen. The value placed upon gentleness – and gentlemanliness – in action was placed equally upon gentleness in words among both Zambian students and teachers. Verbal insults were always judged by students to be particularly serious and, in everyday school life, quickly led to personal violence. Garvey (1974: 190) notes that Bemba Catholics at the beginning of this century valued Confession as a means of cult purification after infringement of a religious law. He observes:

> In the Bemba view ... *icipyu* or deep-rooted anger and spite was the root of most evil and is the reason for the seriousness with which an insult is regarded by the Bemba as well as the frequent confession of insults before Catholic priests whose traditions do not lead them to view them in the same serious vein.

After the first sermon came the first of two collections, during which the hymn 'Bringing in the Sheaves' was sung by the whole congregation, which stood during its rendition. Hymns were sung in English, Bemba, Nyanja or Tonga, and often in more than one language by different sections or individuals in the congregation. The collection rarely amounted to more than a few *kwacha* (a few pence), but it was brought up to the front with great ceremony to the accompaniment of a further hymn and a prayer of offering. Then came, usually, the first of several opportunities for the choir to move forward to sing, again in one of the languages cited above. Members of the congregation sat and listened appreciatively. The choir normally consisted of five to ten members. The conclusion to each hymn, most of which were established favourites that were repeated weekly, was again greeted by shouts of 'Amen'. Other choirs, normally not so accomplished, were given the opportunity to sing and, on occasion, a member of the congregation would perform a solo.

SABBATH STUDY

The set-pieces sung by the choir were followed by a period of study time, which usually lasted from thirty to forty-five minutes. The transition from worship to study was marked by a prayer for those who were to teach that God might enlighten their hearts and minds. The congregation was divided into two parts: the baptised, and those who were being prepared for baptism. Each group was led by a student who had been given the responsibility by the Seventh-Day Adventist committee, while the one who led the whole group tended to be the one who taught the baptised group. Here was a formal occasion on which students explicitly took on the role of teacher.

The baptised group followed a Bible-study programme which, during my fieldwork, focused upon the prophetic and apocalyptic books of the Bible, particularly the Book of Daniel and the Book of Revelation. Each member of the group was expected to have his copy of the Bible with him, and to follow attentively the readings and the teacher's commentary.[12]

During the first part of my fieldwork, when I attended services, the text chosen for study was the Book of Daniel. At the commencement of this study, the leader, Edward, invited those present to open their Bibles and started by giving a general outline of the structure of the Book of Daniel and its main themes. He then embarked upon a line-by-line reading and commentary on the beginning of the first chapter, the apprenticeship of Daniel, Hananiah, Mishael and Azariah at the court of King Nebuchadnezzar. Edward departed from the text regularly to fire questions at his listeners, speaking sharply when they failed to answer his queries or showed signs of inattention: 'You, ah! You're Bible students, you!' (meaning, 'You are supposed to know the answers to these questions.') Or, 'You've all got Bibles, you!' (meaning, 'You can always find the answer there.')

Typically, the leader used the interactive method of teaching – virtually call and response – followed widely by many Zambian teachers and public speakers, among them politicians. The leader began a sentence, and the audience was expected to complete it. For example, Edward would say 'When the Israelites prospered they forgot about … forgot about …' and several students would answer in chorus, 'God'.

Edward followed this response with an expression of agreement, 'Eh-heh', in a tone of approval. Like other student preachers, Edward employed the typical stance of a man of learning. The teacher, and thus the preacher, spoke holding a copy of the Bible in one hand and a pencil or pen in the other. Edward commanded a strong sense of controlled, dominant presence, especially in his stance, his use of eye contact and hand gestures. Fundamentalist teaching and preaching opened a space for students to produce and assert themselves in authoritative roles. Their authority was at least twofold. First, they were 'intellectuals', displaying, quoting and cross-referencing their 'deep knowledge' of biblical texts. Secondly, and more importantly, being led by the Spirit, they were in possession of, and possessed by, a power far greater than any merely human authority. By contrast, these avenues of self-expression were not open to Catholic students who silently and passively attended to the Word preached by the school chaplain at Sunday Mass.

The students listened carefully. Many of them made notes of the key points illustrated by the teacher. They responded well to questions, raising their hands to offer answers and generally reacting in a lively way to what they heard. They often expressed some scepticism on topics which were not considered crucial and which seemed to contradict a value of their own. One example of this occurred early in the study of the Book of Daniel, where it is recounted that King Nebuchadnezzar ordered his chief eunuch to provide Daniel and the other youths of the people of Israel with a daily portion of rich food and wine which contravened the dietary provisions of the Law. Daniel prevailed upon the chief eunuch to allow him and his companions a diet of vegetables to eat and water to drink: 'At the end of ten days it was seen that they were better in appearance and fatter in flesh than all the youths who ate the king's rich food' (Daniel 1: 15).

At issue here was a cornerstone of Ellen G. White's teaching on the need to temper the body through disciplined diet. The temperate diet ensured the purity of the body and strengthened it against the temptations that were ever present in 'the battle within'. In Zambia, the additional gain of improved physical appearance had particular appeal. However, most students placed a high value upon eating meat, particularly beef, which they believed made a person strong and which was also a sign of success, living well and having money – of being, in a word, elite. Within the school community, one example always cited as proof that things had 'gone down' was the scarcity, indeed the near absence, of meat in the school diet. Thus the leader was met with a great deal of murmuring and laughter when he recounted this tale and individuals in the congregation shouted out, 'Don't cheat us!' and 'Oh no!'

Challenged, the leader digressed to discuss attitudes in the school. He stressed the diet was now one of 'vegetables throughout', and that when students complained about the school diet, the cry was always, 'No beef, no beef!' Faced with further sceptical murmuring, he repeated his point, skilfully drawing upon local examples and employing student argot: 'It's true! No cutters, [pieces of meat], no Big Bites' [a reference to the name of a cafe in the nearby town where hamburgers were served].

Clearly, the students were not simply passive conduits for Seventh-Day Adventist teaching. Here, too, there was a tension between an orthodox and a practical discourse. Where the values expressed contradicted the students' own values, students found such teaching difficult to accept and were ready to express dissent. However, being an adept teacher, Edward managed to retain the initiative through his apt local reference, drawing out the under-lying message: the body had to be subdued, or it might lead one to sin; sacrifice was necessary, and God rewarded those who were obedient to Him.

Preparation for Baptism

The baptised held their Bible study outdoors, which left the room free for the preparation of the others for baptism. Here the procedure was even more pedagogical in style. Unlike the baptised who sat in a circle during Bible study, candidates for baptism sat in rows, as they did during ordinary class time. The teacher read out a list of questions and invited the class to answer. Each correct answer won signs of the teacher's approval. The format was much tighter, more controlled than that of the baptised class, with less room for diversion from the main themes; indeed, it was very similar to the earlier forms of catechism class used by Roman Catholics. To concise questions of doctrine, brief 'correct' answers were sought and given. In this class the members were addressed as 'Mr' rather than 'Brother', marking their unbaptised, and therefore not fully incorporated, status in the group.

The teacher read from a prepared list, copied down from Seventh-Day Adventist manuals. Each numbered question was part of a drill, often repeated. Here is the transcript of part of one such class which I attended, led by Robert, a Grade Ten student at the time but later the school Vice-Captain. This part of instruction began with the Holy Spirit and then recapped the narrative of the fall of Satan, once the brightest of all the angels in heaven. Answers were given in chorus, although the same three students tended to give all the right answers:

> *Teacher*: Question 19. What is the unforgivable sin?
> *Class*: The sin against the Holy Spirit.
> *Teacher*: That's right. Question 20. What is sin?
> *Class*: It's the transgression of the law.
> *Teacher*: Aha. Correct. Question 21. Who are demons?
> *Class*: The Devil's angels.
> *Teacher*: Yes. What was the post of Satan?

Class: Archangel.
Teacher: Correct.

At this point there was no attempt to explore any of the theological intri-
cacies. Robert cited the numbers, I suggest, to emphasise that the questions
were not his own. The questions and answers were from the higher
authority of the Adventist manual. Quite simply, class members gave the
correct answers as they would in their everyday classroom interaction. The
teacher moved swiftly on, until the class became puzzled and began to falter
concerning the problem of evil. Robert continued:

> Yes Satan was an archangel, but then, what happened? [Silence] He
> was guilty of ...? He was guilty of ...? [No response] Backsliding! But
> why did God not stop him? [Silence] Because God gave him the
> chance. Like us. He gives us a chance to decide ... He gave us all the
> chance to see the works of the Devil.

Here Robert had to supply all the answers. He introduced the class to new
terminology such as 'backsliding' and began to draw out the dramatic theme
of individual choice between good and evil. Robert then turned to more
apparently straightforward issues and the class responded quickly and
confidently:

> *Teacher*: Who created all things?
> *Class*: God.
> *Teacher*: Aha. Through who do all things exist?
> *Class*: The Holy Spirit and Jesus Christ.
> *Teacher*: Yes. Good. What was the crowning act of creation – that's
> question number 25 – the last thing to be created?
> *Class*: Man.
> *Teacher*: Yes. Now, when Adam and Eve sinned, what part of the Law
> did they break? [Silence] What part of the Law did they break?

This proved a difficult question for the class. There was a prolonged silence
until one student volunteered; 'Honour thy father and mother.' Robert was
evidently unprepared for this answer. But he retained his warm manner,
gently probing for clarification, before discovering a way to embrace this
answer within the wider scheme of Adventist acceptance of the totality of
the biblical teaching, and to draw additional support by reference to an earlier
answer. There was thus a cumulative acquisition of the correct knowledge.

> *Teacher*: How? [Silence] Do you agree with him, Mr ... Is he correct?
> [Silence] Well, yes, the Bible says if you break one law, you break all of
> them. So Adam and Eve, they broke all ... In the Garden of Eden all
> the ten commandments were broken. There was only one rule, 'Don't
> do it.' But they touched that part where they were not supposed to

touch. They transgressed the Law. And we heard that the transgression of the Law is sin. So that's how they sinned. The Bible says if you break one, you're guilty of all. Question 27. How did the curse of sin affect the whole of Creation?
Class: Death.
Teacher: Yes, death. Any other answers?
Class: Trouble.
Teacher: Yes, death and trouble. Adam and Eve were the parents of sin. Now, how did God help us?
Class: Sending Jesus Christ who had no sin.
Teacher: Yes, he died to atone for our sins. He died and because of this we will resurrect. He died and rose from the dead. Now, why did God send Jesus Christ?
Class: He wanted to show his love.
Teacher: Yes. Anything else. Any other answers?
Class: No angel sacrificed to come.
Teacher: Yes. All those are answers. Yes, the heavenly host was quiet. No one would do it. The angels said, 'We can't go to die.' Now, what promise encouraged man after they had sinned?
Class: God promised to send a redeemer.
Teacher: Hmm. Yes. It's in Genesis 3: 15. To send a redeemer to crush the snake. Next question, number 31. Why do all men die? Why do all men die when only two sinned?
Class: We have all sinned.
Teacher: Correct. We have all sinned. We read in the Bible, yes, we are the offspring of those who sinned.

Throughout all the classes I observed, nearly all the questions were answered by the same two or three students. These students later became noted preachers and, in two cases, prefects, in the school.

It would be wrong to suggest that all classes proceeded without contradiction on the students' part. For example, students were eager to point out inconsistencies between the lessons of different weeks. On one occasion, a lively discussion arose on the reason for the expulsion of Satan and 'the other devils' from heaven to earth. The teacher first explained:

> There was simply no room … because there were millions and millions of angels loyal to God. And, at that time, the only other place that existed apart from heaven was earth, where Adam and Eve lived – so that's why they were sent there.

A young Grade Nine student responded:

> But that's not what we were taught last week. Last week you said that Satan and his followers were driven out into the atmosphere, but his

followers complained because he had promised to take them to a new place and that's why Satan then decided to come to earth.

Robert looked unruffled. Smiling in a knowing manner, he confidently countered:

> Look, you are misunderstanding what really happened. You should read *One Hundred Worlds* [by Ellen G White], then you will understand. You see, 'worlds' are not worlds as we understand them – no!

Robert's explanation and resort to authoritative text appeared to satisfy the class, and he moved on to the next question. It was, perhaps, an example of 'edification by puzzlement' (Fernandez 1982: 512). The answer itself was a riddle which had the power to entangle the hearer. The student mistakenly thought 'worlds' were the 'worlds' that he was already familiar with. The teacher's skill was just as vital an element here as in any other form of teaching. Robert remained securely in charge of proceedings. He smiled a great deal and rewarded correct answers with facial and vocal expressions of approval.

The lesson proceeded until the leader was informed that the senior group had completed their Bible study and were ready to return. Among themes constantly rehearsed were the need to have faith and to pray by reading and studying the Bible as many times a day as possible.

Worship Resumed

Upon the return of the senior group, came another interlude of hymn singing, usually by the entire congregation, but the moment also gave junior choirs the opportunity to come to the front and demonstrate their talents. Another selection of hymns from the official choir usually followed.

After the hymns came the announcements. The officials then left again, in single file, and returned while another hymn was sung by the entire congregation. This time, the officials were accompanied by the committee's chosen preacher for the main sermon. First, a prayer was offered, followed by more hymn singing and a second collection. Yet more hymns followed and then a further prayer before the preacher delivered his sermon. This sermon reflected the theme of the service that was written upon the board. The most commonly recurring themes were the suffering and death of Jesus Christ, salvation through his blood, and the need for repentance in order to be ready for the events surrounding his Second Coming.

Towards the end of the sermon, a hymn was struck up. The music enveloped the sermon. The preacher continued delivering his message while the congregation or choir sang appropriate verses. Call and response gave way to counterpoint. The final message took on a heightened emotional tone, the words of the preacher spoken above the forceful yet subdued singing of his congregation. One Sabbath, for example, the congregation sang 'Wash all my sins away ... I'll turn to sin no more', while the preacher repeated the story of 'the good thief on the Cross who was cleansed by the blood of the Lamb', sporadically interjecting a direct address to his audience: 'Are *you* going to be able to stand before Him [God] on the Last Day?'

This preaching was followed by a closing prayer and a recessional hymn, during which all members of the congregation left the room in single file. They formed a circle outside, greeting each other with a handshake as they took up their places. Locating each student no longer as a stranger but as a member of the religious family, their circle offered a sense of unity and completion. It established their apartness, the boundary between them and the rest of the school community. This rite marked the end of the morning service, after which, in the afternoon, came further gatherings for 'Sabbath school', more Bible study, and hymn singing.

CONCLUSION

In Seventh-Day Adventist and Born-Again student movements, Christian narratives were seized upon deliberately for re-creation of self and subject-ivity. The Bible was their primary source for alternative texts of identity. Members of the movements were aware – indeed, highly conscious – of achieving a new sense of self. Their old selves they cast off, judged morally wanting. Their new selves they produced and empowered in preaching, teaching and in many other encounters in everyday life. Their making of an alternative moral topography advanced the resituation of the self. It was an alternative moral topography that was redrafted by competing apocalyptic arguments of authority, time and evil and within a new religious family of brothers. Here mimesis was important and so was the recognition of differ-ence. Using mimesis, preachers and hearers refigured themselves according to the exemplars of Old and New Testament figures. By the same token, the self was recognised negatively by who one was not. Each movement distinctively offered a specific structure of religious formation and religious expression counter to the Catholic and Marian. Each movement converted, schooled and emotively indoctrinated individual students in values and practices deeply at variance with the orthodox and practical discourse of the school.

Such practical and imaginative re-creation took place at times within, and at times beyond, the sight of school authorities. The Seventh-Day Adventists were more subtly successful in treading the fine line between the appearance of conformity and the expression of open resistance. Born Agains, if apparently less successful, were in fact extremely successful, in their own apocalyptic mission, in carving out a special niche for their very own identity. Into signs of contradiction, of relative isolation, of being marginalised, the Born Agains read the doom which promised their ultimate triumph: of the Word over the flesh.

9

CONCLUSION: 'AND AFTER THIS, OUR EXILE'

On 28 October 1997, the day after a rise in the price of maize flour was announced, an army officer calling himself 'Captain Solo', in concert with some fellow junior officers, briefly took control of the Zambian state radio. 'Captain Solo' announced that, inspired by an angel, he had taken power as leader of a National Redemption Council, in a military coup he named 'Operation Born Again', in order to put an end to the corruption rampant in Zambian public life. Such details of this abortive coup provided a deadly serious and yet strikingly ironic parody of the situation that faced St Antony's students and all Zambians in the 1990s.

The attempted coup, if it can be so described, lasted little more than two hours. The army, loyal to President Chiluba, quickly regained control of the radio station. A number of army officers and others suspected to have been involved were arrested and a state of emergency proclaimed. By Christmas ex-President Kaunda was also under arrest.[1]

For many in Zambia, including the students and former students of St Antony's, 'national redemption' looked more and more like 'mission impossible', so closely did the prevailing political order of MMD resemble the old order of UNIP. To the discourse of failure, another trope had been added. If only 'Half-London' could be transformed into 'Whole' London or, even better, New York! The students of St Antony's longed to be different, to live differently, to escape from what they perceived as the self-inflicted failure and the moral morass of Zambia to what they imagined to be the truly 'civilised' West. In their refashioning of selves, however, students revealed that they were willingly caught within at least part of the contested discourse. In their ambivalence towards their Africanness, they exposed the distance they desired to place between themselves and their rural origins. Their blackness was indeed often read by them as a curse. They put their trust in the 'civilising mission' to provide an avenue of escape. They longed to be transformed into 'jacked-up' 'intellectuals', modern Christian gentlemen who could succeed in urban life.

Mudimbe records how his students' dismay at events in Africa required him, very reluctantly, to revisit the 'old affair' of the curse of Ham: 'A young African in Brazzaville, Helouya, asked me if all our present miseries (drought, political dictators of the worst kind, AIDS and other calamities) were not simply signs of an ancient curse' (1994a: 180). His response, informed by a Foucauldian perspective, is an unequivocal 'no', and he embarks upon an examination of this myth and its origins, troubled by the regularity with which this question of a curse re-emerges. Yet he ponders how an African can escape the prison of such alienation. Wondering if he ever believed in the existence of God, Mudimbe, former seminarian and former Benedictine monk, now reads a Christian identity as one sign of the alienation that Africans must struggle to free themselves from, so bound-up is Christianity in Africa with the construction of the African as the sign of absolute difference (1994a: 75).

Yet, perhaps Mudimbe's verdict is too pessimistic, especially in the light of his account of his own revolts against the gaze in the regimes of the minor seminary or the Benedictine monastery. My ethnography of St Antony's demonstrates the limits of the gaze of authority. Yes, in some ways St Antony's may be depicted as a 'total institution' in which the 'civilising process' of mission education is received in the full glare of the missionaries' panoptic gaze. Yet students, from the earliest days, demonstrated that they were quite able to retain a sense of agency in the face of official Catholic authority. In demonstrating the fragility of school discipline, they retained a space for themselves, in which to fashion their own desire, namely the identity of mission-educated, Christian gentlemen, of future leaders, of an elite in the making, even in uncertain times. Technologies of discipline met with counter-technologies of resistance, at times openly, at times covertly. While willing to accept Catholic mission discipline to some degree, in order to achieve their desire for a 'good education', in the 1990s young Zambian men no longer felt they had to hide their religious affiliations, as some pioneer students did when they pretended to be Catholics to gain entry to St Antony's. Indeed, the contrary became true as fundamentalist students challenged Catholic dogma and practice, choosing alternative religious discourses, alternative technologies of self.

At St Antony's, there was not one all-encompassing gaze. Rather there was a multiplicity of gazes and of competing discourses, demonstrating resistance and achieving, if not total, at least partial, subversion. The picture is a complex one. Foucault's early totalising discourse cannot help theoretically to delineate the movements and counter-movements, the arguments of words, signs and images that was the quotidian practice in this post-colonial mission school. Foucault, a very 'specific intellectual' (Spivak 1988: 4), whose texts are 'without Africans' (Richlin 1998: 139) may not be the best of guides for an exploration of the postcolonial condition in Africa, nor perhaps for the colonial one either (see Vaughan 1991: 8). Yet while 'failing to acknowledge the gendered nature of the religious practices', in his recognition of religion as both a political power and a 'technology of self', Foucault does provide 'new ways to allow "difference" and the "other" a voice' (Carrette 1999: 9).

Missionary uncertainty and doubt were in evidence in the challenge to give St Antony's a Catholic and Marian atmosphere, conspicuously so in the face of fundamentalist contestation from some students and teachers. Catholic religious authority was subverted and denied. 'Making Mary known and loved' appeared an impossible task to many Brothers. Even Mary, after all, was 'only a woman'. The Brothers' Catholic Marian discourse was muted, their mission project constrained and hedged about with doubt, both from without and within. From without, the Brothers had contended with the quotidian experience of living in colonial and postcolonial Zambia. They had shifted their project to meet the secular demands of the state, in the requirements of the Ministry of Education, and to meet the expectations of parents and students. From within, in the wake of the Second Vatican Council, the Brothers lived in an uncertain world, in which their Founder's beautiful notion of 'presence' to others became deeply problematic. The missionary presence, strikingly full of doubt, encountered a situation of deep uncertainty, so unlike the religious conviction of the fundamentalist students under, in theory, their charge. The Brothers, officially the managers, the agency, of the school, did not hold the centre ground in the competition for souls; indeed, theirs was a profound sense of displacement.

St Antony's provided a site for the disjunctive proximity, if not the meeting, of disparate 'traditions' and for different orders of strangers. Bauman (1993) suggests that postmodern life is implicated with meetings that are not quite meetings; indeed, he prefers the term 'mismeeting' (ibid.: 154) to convey the absence of fit between social and physical spaces, the incongruity of social intercourse with strangers. This mismeeting, this dwelling among strangers makes for 'a precarious, unnerving and testing life' (ibid.: 160). It is a context 'pregnant with the danger of false steps' (ibid.: 149) as individuals strive to deal with and, perhaps, contain the strangeness of strangers. Well before the turn to the postmodern as the order of our epoch, Simmel (1978) remarked that modern life cannot do without strangers, and this appears to be doubly true of postcolonial Zambia. The expatriate Brothers were a case in point, one among the many Christian missionary organisations engaged in education, health and 'development' work. Yet these Brothers were at least doubly alien, working in a school founded in accord with colonial requirements and upon the model of the British public school, and in the foreign mission field of Zambia. Furthermore, they were not only strangers but estrangers (Skinner 1979: 282; Werbner 1989: 302) with the potential to alienate Zambians from themselves.

In his archaeology of the idea of Africa, his message to his children, Mudimbe comments : 'I have been talking about alienations' (1994b: 209). Estrangement from others but also, more crucially, from one's self, if once a colonial predicament, is now the postcolonial predicament *par excellence*. The desire for education is a desire to become Other in all kinds of ways.

The St Antony's students' dream of education became their own 'voyage out' from their childhood pasts and towards a desired place of 'reciprocal recognitions' (cf. Fanon 1986: 218), in the order of the postcolonial state which paradoxically exhibited all the hallmarks of disorder.

At St Antony's contesting Christian discourses opened up a space in which students could refigure and refashion alternative selves, choosing technologies of self other than the Catholic and the Marian. The Word was made flesh in many ways, each in opposition to the others, each vying to gain control and hold the moral high ground. The 'Salve Regina' speaks of the cries of pain from those who experience exile – the quintessentially Christian condition - in their pilgrimage through this world which is a valley of tears. This hymn to the Virgin Mary resonated with a kind of truthfulness in the world of the postcolonial mission school that is 'Half-London'/St Antony's.

NOTES

CHAPTER 1 INTRODUCTION: 'HALF-LONDON'

1. The United National Independence Party had been committed to one-party rule since taking control (Gertzel et al. 1984: 2).
2. 'The hour has come' was the election campaign slogan of the MMD party.
3. President Chiluba's declaration of Zambia as a Christian nation (29 December 1991) was greeted enthusiastically by Born-Agains but immediately led to considerable controversy among other Christians and non-Christians (see Gifford 1998: 197–205).
4. Throughout the 1990s and into the new millennium the *kwacha* went into free fall. By late 2002, the rate was well over 7,000 *kwacha* to the pound.
5. See Mitchell (1988) on colonial education in Egypt, and Comaroff and Comaroff (1989, 1991) on colonial attempts to recreate the Tswana.
6. The numbers and locations of the Brothers worldwide, according to their 1990 census, were as follows: Africa 443, Europe 2,068, Oceania 615, Asia 187, Latin America 1,653, North America 526. These figures indicate a sharp decline in the total number of Brothers from a peak of 9,227 in 1960. 1991 statistics for the eighteen African countries in which the Brothers maintained a presence put the total at 445, 280 of whom were African and 171 missionaries.
7. The term 'compound' refers to the no-income/low-income/medium-income parts of towns where the vast majority of Zambians live, as opposed to the 'residential' areas of people who have money.

CHAPTER 2 CATHOLIC FORMATION: CHANGE AND CONTEST

1. For example, the report of a Catholic Headmasters' meeting in 1972, noted:
   Concern was expressed by some Heads at the growing percentage of non-Catholic children who are admitted to Catholic-managed schools in the context of their desire to maintain a Catholic atmosphere in their schools. It was generally agreed that in the situation obtaining in Zambia it was impossible to call our Secondary Schools Catholic Schools; the more correct description would be that they are schools which are managed by Catholic agencies. An enquiry conducted in 1968 revealed that we do in fact manage the equivalent of four non-Catholic schools. It was agreed that the problem of maintaining a Catholic atmosphere must be tackled in the admission of our existence in a pluralistic society of which the Catholics constitute but one-fifth of the population.
   (School administration files 1972)
2. *Gravissimum educationis*, the Second Vatican Council's most important document concerning education, defined the Catholic school in the following manner:
   The Catholic school pursues cultural goals and the natural development of youth to the same degree as any other school. What makes the Catholic

school distinctive is its attempt to generate a community climate in the school which is permeated by the Gospel spirit of freedom and love. It tries to guide the adolescents in such a way that personality development goes hand in hand with the development of the 'new creature' that each one has become through baptism. It tries to relate all of human culture to the good news of salvation so that the light of faith will illumine everything that the students will gradually come to learn about the world, about life and about the human person.
(*Gravissimum educationis*: 8)

According to a more recent official church document, *The Religious Dimension of Education in a Catholic School* (Congregation for Catholic Education 1988), the 'school climate' should be pervaded by 'the religious dimension' in the 'constitutive elements such as persons, space, time, relationships, teaching, study and various activities' (ibid.: 12). In this climate, 'everyone should be aware of the living presence of Jesus the "Master" ... the one genuine "Teacher", the perfect Man in whom all human values find their fullest expression' (ibid.: 12). Having crucifixes in the school is one way in which the presence of Jesus is to be acknowledged (ibid.: 13).

3. The 'Salve Regina' first appears in a Cistercian antiphonarium compiled in 1140. It has been attributed to Adhemar, bishop of Le Puy, who led the first crusade and died at Antioch in 1098. Among the relics in the cathedral at Le Puy was housed the Virgin's girdle. The Founder was born and spent most of his life in the Massif Central region not far from Le Puy.

4. Rosary beads were sometimes worn around the neck by local Catholics; some of them asserted that this custom protected them from mystical harm.

5. The school chaplain was a priest appointed to the school by the Archbishop of Lusaka to cater for the school, the Community of nuns who ran the clinic, the local parish and its numerous outstations. The chaplain lived apart from the Brothers in his own house beside the church.

6. The Legion of Mary, a Catholic lay organisation, was founded by Frank Duff in Dublin in 1921 to encourage devotion to Mary.

7. Linden and Linden (1974) discuss Chewa Catholic acceptance of the cult of the Virgin Mary in Nyasaland in the early part of the twentieth century. They note the many plaster statues in churches in Nyasaland, the blue-eyed Virgin with a cream complexion and report:

grown men would fall to their knees before it and consider it a representation of a woman second only to Jesus. While certainly an archetype of Western Catholicism, it represented an elevation of womanhood which profoundly impressed African Catholics. They soon saw that African women could aspire to, and live successfully, a conscious imitation of the life of the Virgin Mary.

In their discussion of nuns, the Lindens note that the idea of a Bride of God was not unknown to Chewa religion in connection with women's service at the rain shrine of Msinja. By contrast, Hinfelaar (1994) describes the difficulties encountered by Catholic missionaries among the Bemba when they attempted to promote the value of virginity. The Bemba considered virginity a curse, breaking the chain of fecundity and thereby destroying the past and the future (Hinfelaar 1994; personal communication 1995).

8. At one staff meeting, during my fieldwork, Adventist and some other (male) teachers complained that pregnant Grade Nine students were being allowed to take the Junior School Leaving Exam.

9. For an account of the circumstances surrounding Archbishop Milingo's removal by Vatican authorities, see ter Haar (1992).

CHAPTER 3 ORDER AND DISCIPLINE

1. Foucault has been taken to task by several commentators who question his rendition of the history of Revolutionary and post-Revolutionary France. While Taylor (1986: 82) admits that part of Foucault's attraction is that of '*terrible simplificateur*', Merquior (1991) describes *Discipline and Punish* as a work of '(philosophical) history at once less reckless and more shoddy than *The Order of Things*' (ibid.: 96). He argues that because Foucault's history is always 'une histoire à thèse' (ibid.: 144), it is always unreliable, especially in this case in its 'Marcusean account of the eighteenth century', 'a brazen historical caricature' (ibid.: 98) which in its Manichaean simplicity reduces to a uniform gloss a mixed, and more complex, historical record.
2. See Jones, R. (1990) and Gemie (1992). For striking parallels with contemporary events in Britain, see also Jones, D. (1990).
3. The De La Salle Brothers were founded in 1680 in France by Jean-Baptiste de la Salle whose theological training had been undertaken in Paris at the seminary of St Sulpice and the Sorbonne (Hamilton 1989: 58). As McMahon (1992: 142) notes, de la Salle paid great attention to the slightest detail: 'A life ruled by constant attention to minutiae was held to be a better demonstration of faith than a life punctuated by occasional acts of heroism' (Hamilton 1989: 68; cf. McMahon 1992: 142; Hamilton 1989: 9; York 1986: 1).
4. For the origins and development of the prefect system in British public schools, see Weinberg (1967) and Bamford (1967). For a fictional account of prefects and privilege in a Zambian boys' boarding school, see Sinyangwe (1993).
5. Letter from Director of Education to Provincial Commission, 20 November 1957. Copy in School administration files 1957. See Coombe (1967–8), and Mwanakatwe (1968) for accounts of the development of secondary education in Zambia.
6. Correspondence between Archbishop and the Brothers' Superiors in Southern Rhodesia, School administration files 1957.
7. District Commissioner to Education Secretary, 24 March 1958, School administration files 1958.
8. Correspondence, Provincial Education Officer to the Headmaster, School administration files 1960.
9. The identification and punishment of ringleaders in student disturbances were often difficult issues to resolve between the school administration and the Ministry of Education.
10. Brother Jean-Pierre, for example, commented regarding the first cohorts of students:

    The first group we had, well, you really couldn't choose. In 1960 we just took the rejects. Then when we came to Form Three, Grade Ten today, we had the same problem. Nobody would trust a new school. So, the first group of Form Fives were very poor, although there were some good individuals. After, of course, when the results come, people say, 'So that school, it's not so bad after all'. That's when people flocked to us.
11. All quotations taken from the Inspectors' Report, May 1964.
12. The daily routine reported for the Inspection Statistics Return for 1968 was as follows:

    Monday to Friday: 6.00 Rising; 6.25 Morning Prayer followed by Mass (free). Those who do not wish to attend Mass go to class for prep.; 7.00 Breakfast; 8.00–10.00 Class; 10.00 Break (tea and buns); 10.30–12.30 Class; 12.30 Lunch; 1.30–2.50 Class; 3.00 Manual Work/Sport/Prep.; 3.40 Recreation;

3.45 Interhouse Football/Volleyball; 4.30 End of games: showers and pre-paration for prep.; 5.00 Prep. (different subject for each day); 5.45 Evening Prayer; 6.00 Supper; 7.15 Evening prep. (different subject for each day); 8.15 End of prep. – Recreation; 9.00 Everybody goes to his dormitory and silence starts; 9.15 Lights out (Form Fives may study in their classroom until 10.00).

Saturday: 6.30 Rising; 7.00 Prayer, Mass/Study; 7.30 Breakfast; 8.30 Conference by the Principal, followed by work around the houses; 10.00 Cocoa and buns and Recreation; 12.00 Lunch; Free afternoon – interhouse games; 5.30 Prayer; 7.00 Film or dancing in the hall; 9.00 Dormitory, silence; 9.15 Lights out.

Sunday: 6.30 Rising; 7.00 Compulsory religious service; 7.30 Breakfast; 9.00 Prep./Scouting; 10.00 Cocoa and buns; 10.30 House Inspection by Principal, followed by games; 12.00 Lunch; 3.00 Games; 5.30 Evening Prayer; 6.00 Supper; 7.00 Film or dancing in the hall; 9.00 Dormitory, silence; 9.15 Lights out.

13. Compare Carmody 1990, for plans for the development of an indigenous Catholic clergy whose training was to be in no way inferior to that offered to aspirants in Europe and North America.

14. The Catholic Education Secretary to the Provincial Education Officer, 23 June 1964, School administration files.

15. The importance of sport in the rise of the English public school is well documented (for example, Gathorne-Hardy 1979: 158ff.; Wakeford 1969: 104; Bourdieu 1978: 824–32). Gathorne-Hardy describes how housemasters frequently broke down and wept when their houses lost (1979: 158). Bourdieu, commenting on the shift from 'games' to 'sport', notes the role sport played in the 'exaltation of manhood' and the 'cult of "team spirit"', as well as the use of team sports as a technique of supervision. Extracts from the Headmaster's 1970 rules regarding sporting events explicitly link sport and character formation, e.g.:

   1. A friendly spirit must be maintained at all times.

   2. Playing the game is more important than the result.

   7. Players must never argue or be rude in any way to the referee.

  11. Under no circumstances whatsoever would a team ever refuse to continue a game because they thought they had been given a bad decision.

  12. The losers should be the first to congratulate the winners and the captains should always thank the referee.

  13. Education neither begins nor ends in the classroom and it is essential that both players and spectators behave in a seemly manner at all times.

The analogy of sports competition and life as a race featured in some of the Brothers' religious posters around the school. It is an analogy commonly found elsewhere, for example, in the Letter to the Hebrews: 'With so many witnesses in a great cloud on every side of us, we too, then, should throw off everything that hinders us, especially sin that clings so easily, and keep running steadily in the race we have started' (Hebrews 12: 1). It is an analogy, parodied to great effect by Alan Bennett in *Beyond the Fringe*, in the Grantland Rice poem 'Alumnus Football':

For when the One Great Scorer comes
To write against your name,
He marks – not that you won or lost –
But how you played the game.

16. The Catholic Education Secretary, in his written reply to the Brothers' refusal to consider expansion, commented: 'There were no schools that didn't have some

reservations about the efficiency of a boarding school that would go beyond 600. However, you were the only ones who completely rejected the proposal' (copy of letter dated 28 March 1968, School administration files).

17. Headmaster to Catholic Education Secretary, 3 March 1968, School adminis-tration files.

18. A 1975 School Inspection Report concluded: 'St Antony's is a very good school. As a result a large number of people among the well-to-do in the province justifiably classify St Antony's as Priority Number One for their sons. This has generated a great deal of pressure on the school.'

19. The numbers remained small: 1986: twenty-one boys; 1987: thirty-seven boys; 1988: eighteen boys and eighteen girls; 1989: twenty-two boys and seventeen girls; 1990: twenty-two boys and sixteen girls; 1991: twenty-one boys and four girls.

20. Ministry of Education rhetoric, as exemplified in various circulars and Ministers' statements to parliament during the period, furnish many examples of the linkage between character formation, self-discipline, 'education for citizenship' and the 'sacred task' of 'nation building'. Independence Day was to be comme-morated in schools with 'a solemn act of rededication under the flag' by all students. In answer to Ministry queries, the Headmaster reported in 1969 that the school had no Watchtower students, for whom refusing to salute the flag had become a matter of conscience.

21. For similar observations, see Carmody (1990) on the Jesuits in Zambia, and Angus (1986) on the Christian Brothers in Australia.

22. Bourdieu's work in the sociology of education is perhaps the most widely read of all his writing. However, it has been pointed out that this work, relying as it does on the notions of 'habitus' and 'dispositions', is also prone to be obscure and contradictory. Jenkins (1992: 123) highlights a serious lacuna in Bourdieu's ideas in this area: the absence of a sociological model of institutions and how they work. Bourdieu mobilises the term 'disposition' in his theory of practice, although dispositions become complex, if not contradictory, in his exegesis, where the word is alternately employed to mean: 'the result of an organising action', a 'way of being', a 'habitual state'; a 'tendency', 'propensity', an 'inclina-tion' (Bourdieu 1977: 214). Jenkins is among those commentators on Bourdieu's work who have highlighted the inherent tautology in this and other definitions offered by Bourdieu. Bourdieu's quest is to find a way out of the agency-structure, the subjective-objective labyrinth, in his words, 'the absurd opposition between individual and society' (Bourdieu 1990: 31). His Ariadnean thread is the body which, in his scheme, becomes a mnemonic device, upon which and by which 'culture' is imprinted through experience. There appears little or no space for the calculation of actors, no room to manoeuvre, no scope for deviance. In all this I hear echoes of Foucault's early discussions of the subject in discourse. For 'discourse' read 'habitus'. The subject is not trapped in a discourse, but rather 'disposed' through the 'habitus' to generate some practices, but not others. How this is achieved remains unclear.

Bourdieu's 'habitus' has been depicted to be nothing more than a 'black box' (Connell 1983: 151), the mechanics of which remain unexplained (Elster 1983: 106). Bourdieu does speak of 'strategies' and repeatedly employs the metaphor of a game, both of which, one might think, imply some sense of purposeful choice. However, in Bourdieu's model, a 'strategy' does not allow for the possibility of conscious decision-making. Rather the term is mobilised in a rather idiosyncratic manner which leads Jenkins to question whether it is justifiable for Bourdieu to use the word, as he does, to describe 'the ongoing result of the interaction between the dispositions of the habitus and the constraints and possibilities which are the reality of any given social field – whether it be cultural consumption, landholding, education or whatever' (Jenkins 1992: 83).

For the purposes of my argument, while attention to the habits of the body and to 'the infinitely small' (Bourdieu 1983: 112) is central to my delineation of subjectivity and self-invention, Bourdieu's notion of habitus appears too mono-lithic and deterministic, *pace* his rejection of such labelling (Bourdieu 1990: 116). I do not wish to deny that much practice is performed without conscious deliberation; my problem is that, at least at St Antony's, this was evidently not the whole story.

CHAPTER 4 SPACE AND COMMUNITY

1. Associations of dwelling in the home underpin Bourdieu's key concept of 'habitus', of 'systems of durable, transposable dispositions' (1977: 72). 'Habitus' is a generative and structuring principle of both collective strategies and social practices. Natives rely upon their 'habitus' to reproduce existing structures without fully being aware of how structures are in turn affected. For Bourdieu (ibid.: 2), as for others (Giddens 1979; Heidegger 1962), culture is seen to exist foremost in what people do, not in what they think or say they do. Hence, in Bourdieu's usage, 'habitus' highlights the role of action, or praxis, in the production and reproduction of meaning and structures in sociopolitical orders. In generating practices, the 'habitus' reproduces the conditions that gave rise to it initially; in this way, 'habitus' is both product and producer of history. Bourdieu locates a principle mechanism for inculcating 'habitus' in the objectification of symbolic oppositions found inside the house where everyone learns not by assimilating mental structures but by imitating the actions of others (cf. Lawrence and Low 1990: 469). The domestic world always carries with it extradomestic implications (cf. Pader 1993: 114; Robben 1989).

2. The division of male students into 'broilers' and 'layers' is an example of the way in which students were divided into different masculinities. See Connell (1987: 177), for similar divisions in an Australian school.

3. The argument I am pursuing here follows Taylor's suggestion that orientation in moral space is similar to orientation in physical space. This suggestion neces-sarily involves the question of one's identity, tied to the identification of a defining community and glossed by Taylor as 'where you answer from' (1989: 29).

4. Moore (1986: 75), following Fernandez, maintains:
   Metaphor is held to locate itself in the gap between what is said and what is meant. It proceeds from the literal to the figurative, and in so doing it creates meaning. Metaphors are, therefore, repositories of affectivity and feeling. They permit apprehension. They make the unsayable into the comprehen-sible, however fleetingly.

5. In Sepik, distance may have been a 'critical component of the missionaries' mystique and the power accorded to the religion they preached' (Huber 1988: 204). However, Huber points out that a question that deserves to be raised is the degree to which local people have actively collaborated in maintaining this distance: 'Distance contributes not only to the strangers' aura of power, but also to people's autonomy from strangers as well' (Huber 1988: 204).

CHAPTER 5 EVERYDAY STUDENT REGIMENTATION

1. In a 1967 circular from the Ministry of Education, reference was made to a UNESCO and World Bank report which criticised the 'lavish scale' of school accommodation compared to other African countries, causing the capital cost per pupil place to be 'very high' (School Ministry Files 1967).

2. The age of entry to primary school (Grade One) varied enormously, especially in rural areas. A substantial number of students repeated the last grade of primary school (Grade Seven), sometimes more than once; in the 1991 and 1992 intakes at St Antony's to Grade Eight (the first year of secondary school), more then 25 per cent of the students were 'Repeaters'. The ages in a Grade Eight class normally ranged from around fourteen to around eighteen.

3. In Bourdieu's theory, children of elites who had had much more exposure to both spoken and written English throughout early childhood, should experience little or no gap between the 'practical mastery' of language transmitted at home and the 'symbolic mastery' demanded by the school (Bourdieu and Passeron 1990: 117).

4. In general, the body plays an important part in the acquisition of school knowledge. Such knowledge is never acquired independently of the means of instruction (Turner and Bruner 1986: 308). Instructional rituals within the classroom thus involve a type of communication which is both intramuscular as well as cerebral (McLaren 1986: 202).

5. Table 1: Student intake to Grade Eight: rural/urban split

	Rural	Urban
1982–90	1381 (89.7%)	158 (10.3%)
1991	131 (81.8%)	29 (18.2%)
1992	107 (78.1%)	30 (21.9%)

Note that the increases in the percentage of urban students in the period 1991–1992 reflected a difference in policy between the Brothers and the lay administration that handled admissions in the later period.

Table 2: 1992 intake: home backgrounds of 134 Grade Eight Students

Percentage of students' homes in which the following could be found:

piped water	24%
electricity	24%
radio	85%
TV	19.5%

Table 3: number of primary pupils selected for secondary schools

Year	Number of candidates	Number selected	Progression rate (%)
1977	107,000	21,308	19.9
1978	115,000	21,406	18.6
1984	176,680	38,094	21.6
1989	180,826	49,010	27.1
1990	182,318	56,539	31.01

The source of the 1977 and 1978 figures is Serpell (1993). The other figures are from a copy of a 1991 press release from the Minister of Education (St Antony's Ministry Files 1991). The apparent marked improvement in educational opportunities for Grade Seven leavers was almost entirely due to the opening of 'Basic' schools, which involved primary schools opening junior secondary sections, normally on a 'self-help' basis. While some of these schools proved quite successful, they often lacked even the most basic educational aids and material.

Table 4: Student ethnic identities (1991) by first language choice (see note below)

	Number	%
Bemba	111	21
Tonga	89	17
Lenje	69	13
Lala	26	5
Chewa	26	5
Lozi	23	4.5
Nsenga	17	3.2
Tumbuka	16	3
Ila	14	2.6
Kaonde	14	2.6
Shona	12	2.3
Ngoni	12	2.3

Less than 2% each: Ndebele, Soli, Namwanga, Lamba, Sala, Swaka, Mambwe, Aushi, Luvale, Kunda, Acholi, Bisa, Luchazi, Nkoya, Nyika.
No information: 40 students (7.6%)
Note that to establish students' ethnic identity in any simple way was not possible, as a large proportion of students are the product of inter-ethnic unions. The 1992 intake reported their first language as indicated below in Table 5.

Table 5: Students' first languages (Grade Eight intake 1992)

Bemba	37
Tonga	27
Lenje	23
Lala	8
Shona	7
Nsenga	6
Ndebele	5

Less than 5 students: Swaka, Xhosa, Ngoni, Sala, Tumbuka, Lamba, Namwanga, Kaonde, Mbunda, Ila, Lozi, Soli.

However, of the 136 students for whom information was available, no fewer than fifty-seven were the children of parents with differing first languages, or children whose first language differed from either parent. Various factors, including place of residence, played some part in which language became the first language for the students, although the father's language predominated.

The 1993 intake revealed a similar diversity with fifty-six out of 122 students reporting that their parents had different first languages.

Table 6: Boarding students' normal place of residence (1992 intake)

Area	Number of students
Lusaka urban	25
Lusaka rural	23
Mkushi rural	22
Kabwe rural	17
Mumbwa rural	16
Kabwe urban	7
Copperbelt urban	4

Other areas represented: Serenje Rural, Kafue, Mazabuka, Monze, Samfya, Chinsali, Kapiri Mposhi.

In general, students were drawn from a smaller catchment area than previously had been the case. Destinations of students for the holidays at the end of term, although not necessarily indicating normal places of residence, demonstrated that students in the 1970s travelled to and from the most distant provinces of Zambia. At the end of the second term of 1976, for example, students' destinations were recorded, for transport requirements purposes, as follows:

Lusaka, Kafue, Chipata:	180
Copperbelt, Ndola, Kitwe:	109
Mbala, Mpika:	16
Kabwe:	111
Mumbwa:	18
Mkushi, Serenje:	41

(School administration files 1976)

6. Bullivant (1978: 147), teaching geography at an Orthodox Jewish school in Australia, was corrected by students regarding the age of the earth:

    'The Silurian rocks in this region were laid down some 400 million years ago,' I would state, only to have one or the other of the most Orthodox boys challenge the statement. 'This cannot be. In *Chumash* it says that the world was created 5,729 years ago.' For the young Chassid it became something of an obsession to correct me each time. 'We know the truth,' he would say emphatically, 'because Moses has given it to us. Yours is only a theory, and like all theories can easily be proved wrong. We have the truth.'

7. The parallel is to Bourdieu's suggested homology between the school system and the church (Bourdieu and Passeron 1990: 109).

8. This has been noted elsewhere, for example among Catholic teachers of Portuguese immigrant children in Canada (McLaren 1986: 101), in their interaction and in their revealed attitudes towards the students.

9. One problem was securing and keeping a qualified teacher. Bemba was started in the 1970s in Grade Eight but was abandoned when the teacher left for further studies and a replacement could not be found.

10. The subjects offered were: English, Mathematics, Science, Agricultural Science, History, Geography, Civics, Book-Keeping and Religious Education. In the senior school, Science was divided into Physics, Chemistry (or Physical Science) and Biology. Literature was also offered, normally as an alternative to History. Students could also enter themselves for exams in a Zambian language, normally Bemba, Nyanja or Tonga, although very few of them did so.

11. Such reactions were reported in boarding schools elsewhere in Zambia, for example at Munali during the colonial period (Greig 1985), and at the Jewish Orthodox school described by Bullivant (1978: 123).

12. Marx, in his *Critique of Hegel's Doctrine of the State* (quoted in Bourdieu and Passeron 1990: 141), described the exam as 'nothing but the bureaucratic baptism of knowledge, the official recognition of the transubstantiation of profane knowledge into sacred knowledge.'

13. Within each house, senior students were appointed by the Housemaster, in consultation with the prefects, to act as house monitors. There was normally one monitor for each wing of each dormitory. Together with the wing vice-monitor, the monitor was responsible for order in his wing.

14. See Shipman (1968) for the influence of secretaries in British schools.

15. English and Mathematics were allocated the largest number of periods per week, normally eight each in the junior school and seven each in the senior school. Other subjects were normally allocated three, although science subjects might get four to accommodate laboratory experiments. Subjects such as History, Geography and Religious Education normally had three periods a week.

16. Ironically, the Brothers' preferred work clothes, denim jeans, were the kind of clothes that marked out a young Zambian as fashionable. Students expressed genuine dismay when I told them of the fashion in Britain to cut slits in jeans at the knee and elsewhere.

17. The wearing of any type of glasses was generally considered a sign of intelligence. Some students fashioned a pair of lens-less 'spectacles' out of wire and wore them while studying.

18. Belts and sticks appeared to be something of a school tradition. There were a number of headmasters' memos in the school files forbidding these items on holidays.

19. Grade Eights were required to bring their own mattresses in addition to linen and blankets. The general run-down appearance of the dormitories was often commented upon by visiting former students. However, many other visitors, aware of the far worse conditions in many state schools, marvelled at the fact that most of the windows in the school were still intact.

20. As a sign of respect, students tended automatically to button up open shirts if they encountered teachers around the school compound or out-of-bounds.

21. It was noticeable how the students always readily bowed their heads in prayer whenever invited to do so, appearing to take moments of prayer very seriously.

22. The Parent-Teachers Association started to become a force in the late 1970s and grew in influence as the general economic situation in Zambia deteriorated; fees were reintroduced and rose year by year. In 1991 school fees were 574 *kwacha* (about £25) per term.

23. The enormous strength of feeling expressed towards thieves seemed only equalled by that expressed towards witches. Heald (1986) intriguingly explores the connections in these expressions of deviance using evidence from her own fieldwork among the Gisu.

24. This rule had a practical reason: it was a measure to try to prevent toilets getting blocked.

CHAPTER 6 THE STUDENTS' ORDER OF THINGS

1. There was a lot of evidence of this pride in the school, both in the contemporary talk of the students and in the school records. Here, for example, is an extract from one Chief Education Officer's letter to the Headmaster (dated 18 January 1974), conveying his congratulations on the school team's success in the provincial athletics:

> Your boys looked very impressive. They dwarfed every school ... They were able to achieve this because they were highly-spirited, and they rightly

boasted that they were Spirited People, Sugar People, Supermen. These are very funny words but the message is very clear: your boys are really spirited ... Also your results and the way the school is looked after. When I last visited your school, there was a meeting that day, and the boys proudly told me that they were going to the National Assembly. There were referring to their school hall!

2. Fights, whether staged in dramatic performances and films or in 'real life' always appeared to arouse a great deal of excitement among the students, each blow being greeted with roars. Wherever one was on the school compound, one could immediately identify the occurrence of a fight from the student onlookers' reactions.

3. The theme of the school as a 'family ' ran through the official school discourse throughout the life of the school, as it did in the Founder's teaching. The theme was especially invoked around the time of the annual reception of new students, by successive headmasters at school assemblies. Here is an example from the notes of the French-Canadian, Brother Jean-Pierre, who was Headmaster in 1975:

> To students at assembly:
> 'Your place is with the group. You are sociable and you must get used to live [sic.] in a family. Each house is a family, fathers, brothers, big and small. Members in a family must not be selfish. They must help one another, and take very good care of the babies; the babies must not get hurt. He is not a real brother to laugh at, ridicule, mock, make fun of his younger brother. Form Ones are coming on Tuesday. Receive them well. This school is not only a school with good results, it is also a school known for its hospitality and good manners.'
> Memo to staff:
> 'This school is a family. Do not tolerate mockery. It will come mostly from Form Twos and Form Threes. If you see it, do not lose your temper, but act. Do not over-react! "Zeze" means newcomer. Do not accept it. "Kwiyo" is not acceptable. Imitation of babies crying: not acceptable. If I am not mistaken, the boys should be reasonable this year, but you never know.'

Mr Mwila, the Headmaster, also similarly invoked the notion of family at assemblies, although he added, in the multiparty, post-election period: 'There should be no mockery now. This is the Third Republic.'

4. See John Dewey on the emergence of self and character (Wirth 1966: 246–7).

5. During fieldwork, the cutting of tails coincided with April Fool's Day, a custom of mockery familiar only to those few students from 'apamwamba' families who had travelled abroad or who had had contacts with 'European' people and 'customs' in some way. In general, knowledge about Britain and the British seemed to be diminishing in the school. I was, for example, surprised by the number of students who did not know the capital of England, or the currency used.

6. Bowie (1985), in her study of a Catholic mission among the Bangwa of south-west Cameroon, describes 'institutionalised teasing' of First Years ('Foxes') by Fifth Formers. In a footnote, she comments (1985: 196):

> The term 'Foxes', used in connection with first year students, may date from the German colonial period. The term is used in German student 'brother-hoods' ('bruderschaften') to refer to the newest members. The phrase used by students in Seat Of Wisdom College, 'foxes have tails', may be a pun on the German word 'schwanz', which means both 'tail' and 'penis'.

CHAPTER 7 CONTESTS AROUND CHRISTIANITY

1. The identification of the Pope with the number of the Beast, 666, that is the Antichrist (Revelation 13: 18), has a long history. O'Leary (1994: 82) cites McGinn's (1979) translation of a text of the Dominican friar Arnold who supported the Hohenstaufen emperor Frederick II in his struggle against Pope Innocent IV in the late 1240s.

2. Reuben's quotation was in fact from Psalm 111: 10.

3. Gideon's 'Sorry' was his polite way of contradicting Brother Henry. It was not an apology for his earlier remarks.

4. For a discussion of the crucifixion in ritual allegory, as against rhetoric, see Werbner 1997.

5. The Seventh-Day Sabbath was also one of the points of departure between the Millerites and the Seventh-Day Adventists, confirmed by the visions of Ellen G. White in the aftermath of the 'Great Disappointment' of 1844, and made part of the 'new test', as described by Numbers (1976: 15):

   > In heaven, [Ellen G. White] said, Jesus had allowed her to see the tables of stone on which the Ten Commandments were inscribed. To her amazement, the Fourth Commandment, requiring observance of the seventh day was 'in the very centre of the ten precepts, with a soft halo of light encircling it'. An angel kindly explained to the puzzled young woman that the Millerites must begin keeping the 'true Sabbath' before Christ would come.

6. This point is also explored in detail by Hoekema (1973: 51–2; 89f.). Sabbatarianism becomes a badge, the significance of which is linked to its particular history in the Protestant tradition. Marsden (1980: 13) reminds us of the Puritan roots of this concern with the Sabbath, describing it as 'probably the most distinctive symbol of evangelical civilisation in the English-speaking world [remaining] a major reform issue where religious and social interests coincided.' Similarly, Butler points out that, for nineteenth-century American Adventists, sabbatarianism was 'imbued with pivotal significance' (1987: 202).

7. See Werbner (1989) on Zionists and a purity movement.

8. The doctrine of 'soul sleep', or 'conditional mortality', was first proposed by the Millerite George Storrs (Butler 1987: 203), and then affirmed by Ellen G. White. This teaches that there is no inherent immortality in the human race; a human being may only gain eternal life from the immortal God. According to this teaching, a person, whether good or bad, remains in the grave after death in a state of 'unconsciousness' until resurrection at the end of the world, when two resurrections will occur, separated by a period of time called 'the millennium'. At the beginning of this period, the 'righteous dead' will be restored to life and, with the 'living righteous', live for 1,000 years in heaven. At the end of this period, the wicked will be brought back to life and, together with Satan, the originator of death, will be destroyed along with all evil. An 'investigative judgement' is believed to be now in session in heaven (see below, the Seventh-Day Adventist hymn, 'How shall you stand?'). This judgement decides whether an individual will live forever, or be eternally blotted out (see Hagstotz 1935: 11).

   Butler suggests that the promotion of the doctrine of 'soul sleep' represents the anti-Calvinist rejection of eternal punishment, but that it may also have been an attempt on the part of Ellen G. White to deal with competition from contemporary spiritualists. Butler comments (1987: 203):

   > The encroachment of female spiritualist mediums sociologically identical to Mrs White (her 'counterfeit' in Adventist terms) aroused the visionary's

severest criticism. The doctrine of soul-sleep therefore sought to silence the cacophonic voices of the spirit world by disclaiming their existence.

9. Numbers (1976) tells the life-story of Ellen G. White under the title *Prophetess of Health*. White suffered a great deal of ill-health in the early period of her life, but she was initially opposed to 'earthly physicians'. Believing that illness was sometimes satanic in origin, she preferred to follow the instruction from James 5: 14–15:

> Is any among you sick? Let him call for the elders of the church, and let them pray over him, anointing him with oil in the name of the Lord; and the prayer of faith will save the sick man, and the Lord will raise him up; and if he has forgiven sins, he will be forgiven.
>
> (Numbers 1976: 32)

Ellen G. White ceased advocating this policy, however, after the publicity surrounding the death of a devout Sister who was allowed to die without receiving medical help. She also changed her thoughts on this matter after the cure of her two sons' fever using Dr J. C. Jackson's 'water treatment' during the diptheria epidemic of 1862–3. Dr Jackson's tracts on 'healthful living' rejected the use of drugs, however, in favour of ten natural remedies: air, food, water, sunlight, dress, exercise, sleep, rest, social influence and mental and moral forces (Numbers 1976: 74). She had several visions from 1848 onwards regarding 'healthful living' and wrote numerous tracts on the values of temperance and sexual abstinence and against the evils of tobacco, alcohol and coffee. Following a dispute among her followers about tea and pork, she decided not to make abstinence from these 'a test of faith' (ibid.: 38f.).

10. There is considerable debate about what constitutes 'narrative' and whether certain universal features of narrative apply. See, for example, the vitriolic exchange between Peel (1992: 382f.; 1995: 586f.) and Comaroff and Comaroff (1997: 42f.). The Personal Narratives Group (1989: 13) and Stanley (1993: 46) are among those who argue against the assumption that narrative must give evidence of coherent emplotment, a notion, they suggest, that might be the product of androcentric bias.

CHAPTER 8 SCHOOLS WITHIN THE SCHOOL

1. However, the Office of Compline, the traditional final prayer of the Catholic church, includes the request that God protect those present from the evils of the night.
2. 'Chest pains', which caused considerable anxiety for some students at St Antony's, were a commonly reported symptom.
3. On the absence of *physical* embodiment in contemporary African religious movements, see Werbner 1997.
4. Rose (1988: 61) records the use of the term 'prayer warrior' in her ethnography of two American evangelical fellowships. See also Peshkin (1986) for an ethnography of a fundamentalist school.
5. President Kaunda often employed the term 'the animal in man' when speaking about human evil.
6. I have observed this preaching style among Pentecostal street preachers in Harare, Zimbabwe.
7. Elias's history of the body in Europe identifies sixteenth-century court society as the space where the process of monitoring and controlling the body was developed and which set the tone for the perception of the body in modernity.
8. Since the completion of my fieldwork, the Seventh-Day Adventist student

fellowship, together with Adventist teachers and some local Adventists, have erected a church just beyond the boundary of the school. I attended and recorded services there during a return visit in October 1993. Students continued to play the main roles of preaching and instruction.

9. I am grateful to Geraldine Connor, a musician and an ethnomusicologist, who kindly analysed tapes of Adventist singing for me. My remarks concerning the technical aspects of Adventist singing are drawn from her analysis (Geraldine Connor, personal communication 1995).

10. The Adventist instructions in the student manual read as follows:

> *The Importance of Literature Ministry*
> During Dark Ages: The papacy, roaring like a lion, did not spare any group of people, as individuals who tried to expose sins existing in its organisation.
>   People tried to find ways of exposing these errors without risking their lives. The invention of the printing press, with its consequent wider dissemination of literature, was one of the most potent forces in the advancement of the Protestant reformation.
> See *Encyclopedia Britannica* 19 on reformation ...
>
> Its importance:
> 1. The most effective method of reaching people with the message.
> 2. It is one of our most successful pioneer agencies in the homeland and in the foreign countries.
> 3. It greatly increases the success of public preaching efforts.
> 4. It is the source of income to our publishing houses.
> 5. It offers opportunities of self sponsorship.
> 6. It offers missionary employment.
> 7. It develops a deep spiritual experience in our young people.
> 8. It has materially aided in developing spiritual and courageous missionary leadership.

11. I recorded many examples of this in Adventist preaching, especially with regard to the entry of the Israelites into the Promised Land. The imagery of God's Chosen separated from the Promised Land by the River Jordan was employed repeatedly to describe salvation that was tantalisingly within reach for the fortunate few if only they would obey God's Commandments.

12. By necessity students used various translations of the Bible. At the Sabbath study, most students had either the *Revised Standard Version, The New English Bible* or the Catholic *Good News for Modern Man*, issued to them for their religious education course.

CHAPTER 9 CONCLUSION: 'AND AFTER THIS, OUR EXILE'

1. Within weeks Kenneth Kaunda was released without charge. At the time of writing Captain Stephen Lungu – 'Captain Solo' – remains on death row with a number of fellow conspirators, having been found guilty of treason. During his time in Mukobeko Maximum Security Prison, Captain Lungu has been born again and has pleaded for clemency, not for himself, but for the others involved in the attempted coup.

BIBLIOGRAPHY

Alves, J. 1993. 'Transgressions and transformations: initiation rites among urban Portuguese boys', *American Anthropologist*, 95 (4).

Angus, L. B. (ed.). 1986. *Class, Culture and Curriculum: a study of continuity and change in a Catholic school*. Victoria, Australia: Deakin University Press.

Angus, L. B. 1988. *Continuity and Change in Catholic Schooling*. London: Falmer Press.

Arbuckle, G. 1991. 'Through chaos to prophecy', *Tablet*, 245: 7851, 42–3.

Bachelard, G. [1958] 1994. *The Poetics of Space*, trans. Maria Jolas, new foreword by J. R. Stilgoe. Beacon Press: Boston.

Bakhtin, M. M. 1981. *The Dialogic Imagination*, trans. C. Emerson and M. Holquist. Austin.

Bakhtin, M. M. 1984. *Rabelais and His World*, trans. H. Iswolksy. Bloomington: Indiana University Press.

Ball, S. I. (ed.). 1990. *Foucault and Education: disciplines and knowledge*. London: Routledge.

Bamford, T. W. 1967. *The Rise of the Public Schools*. London: Nelson.

Barr, J. 1977. *Fundamentalism*. London: SCM Press.

Bauman, Z. 1993. *Postmodern Ethics*. Oxford: Blackwell.

Berger, P. and T. Luckmann. 1971. *The Social Construction of Reality*. Harmondsworth: Penguin University Books.

Bernstein, B. 1971. 'On the classification and framing of educational knowledge,' in M. F. D. Young (ed.), *Knowledge and Control*. London: Collier Macmillan.

Bernstein, B. 1975. 'Class and pedagogies' in B. Bernstein (ed.), *Class Codes and Control*, vol. 3. London: Routledge and Kegan Paul.

Blier, S. P. 1987. *The Anatomy of Architecture*. Cambridge: Cambridge University Press.

Bloch, M. 1975. 'Introduction', in M. Bloch (ed.), *Political Language and Oratory in Traditional Society*. London and New York: Academic Press.

Bourdieu, P. 1971. 'Intellectual field and creative process', in M. F. D. Young (ed.), *Knowledge and Control*. London: Collier Macmillan.

Bourdieu, P. 1973. 'The Berber house' in M. Douglas (ed.), *Rules and Meanings*. Harmondsworth: Penguin.

Bourdieu, P. 1977. *Outline of a Theory of Practice*. Cambridge: Cambridge University Press.

Bourdieu, P. 1978. 'Sport and social class', *Social Science Information*, 17, 6. London: Sage.

Bourdieu, P. 1983. 'Erving Goffman, discoverer of the infinitely small', *Theory, Culture and Society*, 2: 112–13.

Bourdieu, P. 1984. *Distinction: a social critique of the judgement of taste*. London: Routledge and Kegan Paul.

Bourdieu, P. 1990. *In Other Words: essays towards a reflexive sociology*. Cambridge: Polity Press.

Bourdieu, P. and L. Boltanski. 1978. 'Changes in social structure and changes in the demand for education', in S. Giper and M. Archer (eds), *Contemporary Europe: social structures and cultural patterns*. London: Routledge and Kegan Paul.

Bourdieu, P. and J. Passeron. [1977] 1990. *Reproduction in Education, Society and Culture*. London: Sage.

Bowie, F. 1985. 'A Social and Historical Study of Christian Missions among the Bangwa of South-West Cameroon', unpublished D. Phil. thesis, University of Oxford.

Boyne, R. 1990. *Foucault and Derrida: the other side of reason*. London: Unwin Hyman.

Bruce, S. 2000. *Fundamentalism*. Cambridge: Polity Press.

Bruner, J. 1987. 'Life as narrative', *Social Research*, 54 (1): 11–32.

Bullivant, B. M. 1978. *The Way of Tradition*. Victoria: ACER.

Burke, J. F. 1990. 'The Sisters of Notre Dame de Namur in Lower Zaire: a social and historical study', unpublished D. Phil. thesis, University of Oxford.

Burridge, K. 1978. 'Missionary occasions', in J. Boutilier et al. (eds), *Mission, Church and Sect in Oceania*. Ann Arbor: University of Michigan Press.

Burridge, K. 1990. *In the Way: a study of Christian missionary endeavours*. Vancouver: University of British Columbia Press; London: University College London Press.

Butler, J. M. 1987. 'The making of a new order: Millerism and the origins of Seventh-Day Adventism', in R. L. Numbers and J. M. Butler (eds), *The Disappointed: Millerism and Millenarianism in the nineteenth century*. Bloomington: Indiana University Press.

Caplan, G. L. 1970. *The Elites of Barotseland, 1878–1969*. London: Hurst.

Caplan, L. 1987. 'Introduction', in L. Caplan (ed.), *Studies in Religious Fundamentalism*. London: Macmillan.

Carmody, B. 1988. 'Conversion and school at Chikuni, 1905–1939', *Africa* 58 (2).

Carmody, B. 1990. 'Denominational secondary schooling in post-Independence Zambia: a case study,' *African Affairs*, 89: 355, 247–63.

Carmody, B. 1992. *Conversion and Jesuit Schooling in Zambia*. Leiden: E. J. Brill.

Carr, D. 1986. *Time, Narrative and History*. Bloomington: Indiana University Press.

Carrette, J. R. (ed.). 1999. *Religion and Culture by Michel Foucault*. Manchester: Manchester University Press.

Carrithers, M. 1992. *Why Humans Have Cultures*. Oxford: Oxford University Press.

Christian, W. A. [1972] 1989. *Person and God in a Spanish Valley*. Princeton: Princeton University Press.

Clifford, J. 1984. 'Encounters with the exotic', *Times Literary Supplement*, 22 June, 1984, 683–4.

Colson, E. 1958. *Marriage and the Family among the Plateau Tonga of Northern Rhodesia*. Manchester: Manchester University Press.

Comaroff, J. and J. Comaroff. 1989. 'The colonization of consciousness in Southern Africa', *Economy and Society* (18): 267–95.

Comaroff, J. and J. Comaroff. 1991. *Of Revelation and Revolution: Christianity, colonialism and consciousness in South Africa*, vol. 1. Chicago: University of Chicago Press.

Comaroff, J. and J. Comaroff. 1992. *Ethnography and the Historical Imagination*. Boulder: Westview Press.

Comaroff, J. and J. Comaroff. 1997. *Of Revelation and Revolution*, vol. 2. Chicago: University of Chicago Press.

Congregation for Catholic Education. 1988. *The Religious Dimension of Education in a Catholic School: guidelines for reflection and renewal*. Rome and Nairobi: St Paul Press.

Connell, R. W. 1983. *Which Way is Up?* Sydney: George Allen and Unwin.

Connell, R. W. 1987. *Gender and Power*. Cambridge: Polity Press.

Coombe, T. 1967–8. 'The origins of secondary education in Zambia', *African Social Research*, 3, 4 and 5.

Corrigan, P., B. Curtis and R. Lanning. 1986. 'The political space of schooling', in T. Wotherspoon (ed.), *The Political Economy of Canadian Schooling*. London: Methuen.

Coser, L. A. 1974. *Greedy Institutions*. New York: Free Press.

Csordas, T. J. 1997. *Language, Charisma and Creativity: ritual life of a religious movement*. Berkeley; London: University of California Press.

Curtin, P. 1967. *Africa Remembered: narratives by West Africans from the era of the Slave Trade*. Madison: University of Wisconsin Press.

Davis, C. T. and H. L. Gates Jr. (eds). 1985. *The Slave's Narrative*. New York: Oxford University Press.

Delamont, S. (ed.). [1976] 1983. *Interaction in the classroom*. London: Methuen.

Delamont, S. 1984. *Readings on the Interaction in the Classroom*. London: Methuen.

Delamont, S. 1992. *Fieldwork in Educational Settings: methods, pitfalls and perspectives*. London: The Falmer Press.

Delamont, S. and M. Galton. 1986. *Inside the Secondary Classroom*. London: Routledge and Kegan Paul.

de Mijolla, E. 1994. *Autobiographical Quests: Augustine, Montaigne, Rousseau, and Wordsworth*. Charlotteville and London: University Press of Virginia.

Denzin, N. 1989. *Interpretative Biography*. London: Sage.

de Saussure, F. 1949. *Cours de Linguistique Générale*, C. Bally and A. Sechehaye (eds). Paris: Payot.

Dews, P. 1979. 'The Nouvelle Philosophie and Foucault', *Economy and Society*, 8: 2.

Dews, P. 1984. 'Power and subjectivity in Foucault', *New Left Review*, 144, March/April.

Dirksen, M. O. 1984. 'Pentecostal Healing: a facet of the personalistic health system in Pakal-Na, a village in southern Mexico', unpublished PhD thesis, University of Tennessee, Knoxville.

Dore, R. 1976. *The Diploma Disease*. London: Allen and Unwin.

Dreyfus, H. L. and P. Rabinow. 1982. *Michel Foucault, Beyond Structuralism and Hermeneutics*, with an afterword by M. Foucault. Brighton, Sussex: The Harvester Press.

Dreyfus, H. L. and P. Rabinow. 1986. 'What is Maturity? Habermas and Foucault on "What is Enlightenment?"' in D. C. Hoy (ed.), *Foucault: a critical reader*. Oxford: Basil Blackwell.

Edwards, A. D. 1976. *Language in Culture and Classroom*. London: Heinemann.

Eickelman, D. 1985. *Knowledge and Power in Morocco*. Princeton: Princeton University Press.

Elias, N. [1939] 1979. *The Civilising Process, vol. 1: the history of manners*. Oxford: Basil Blackwell.

Elias, N. 1983. *The Court Society*. Oxford: Basil Blackwell.

Elster, J. 1983. *Sour Grapes: studies in the subversion of rationality*. Cambridge: Cambridge University Press.

Epstein, A. L. 1992. *Scenes from African Urban Life*. Edinburgh: Edinburgh University Press.

Fabian, J. 1983. *Time and the Other, how anthropology makes its object*. New York: Columbia University Press.

Fanon, F. [1961] 1972. *The Wretched of the Earth*. Harmondsworth: Penguin.
Fanon, F. [1970] 1986. *Black Skin, White Masks*, with an introduction by H. K. Bhabha. London: Pluto.
Farrell, K. 1984. *Achievement from the Depths*. Drummoyne: Marian Brothers.
Ferguson, J. 1997. 'Country and city on the Copperbelt', in A. Gupta and J. Ferguson (eds), *Culture, Power, Place*. Durham and London: Duke University Press.
Ferguson, J. 1999. *Expectations of Modernity: myths and meanings of urban life on the Zambian Copperbelt*. Berkeley: University of California Press.
Fernandez, J. W. [1974] 1986. *Persuasions and Performances: the play of tropes in culture*. Bloomington: Indiana University Press.
Fernandez, J. W. 1982. *Bwiti: an ethnography of the religious imagination in Africa*. Princeton: Princeton University Press.
Fields, K. E. 1985. *Revival and Rebellion in Colonial Central Africa*. Princeton: Princeton University Press.
Flora, C. B. 1980. *Pentecostalism and Development: the Colombian case*, in S. D. Glazier (ed.), *Perspectives on Pentecostalism*. Washington, DC: University Press of America.
Foucault, M. 1970. *The Order of Things: an archaeology of the human sciences*. New York: Random House; trans. Alan Sheridan-Smith of *Les mots et les choses: une archéologie des sciences humaines*. Paris: Gallimard, 1966.
Foucault, M. 1972. *The Archaeology of Knowledge*. New York: Harper and Row; trans. A. M. Sheridan-Smith of *L'Archéologie du savoir*. Paris: Gallimard.
Foucault, M. [1969] 1977. *Discipline and Punish: the birth of the prison*. New York: Pantheon; trans. Alan Sheridan-Smith of *Surveillir et punir: naissance de la prison*. Paris: Gallimard.
Foucault, M. [1975] 1978. *The History of Sexuality*, vol. 1. New York: Pantheon; trans. R. Hurley of *Histoire de la sexualité*, 1. Paris: Gallimard.
Foucault, M. 1980. *Power/Knowledge: selected interviews and other writings, 1972–1977*, ed. with a preface by C. Gordon, L. Marshall, I. Meplam and K. Soper. Brighton, Sussex: The Harvester Press.
Foucault, M. 1984. *The Use of Pleasure: history of sexuality*, vol. 2. New York: Pantheon; trans. R. Hurley of *L'usage des plaisirs: histoire de la sexualité*, 2. Paris: Gallimard.
Foucault, M. 1986. *The Care of the Self: history of sexuality*, vol. 3. New York: Pantheon; trans. R. Hurley of *Le souci de soi: histoire de la sexualité* 3. Paris: Gallimard.
Foucault, M. and R. Sennett. 1982. 'Sexuality and solitude', *Humanities in Review*, vol. 1. Cambridge: Cambridge University Press.
Freire, P. 1972. *The Pedagogy of the Oppressed*, trans. M. B. Ramos. London: Sheed and Ward.
Frost, M. 1963. 'Inshimi and Imilumbe: structural expectations in Bemba oral imaginative performances', unpublished PhD thesis, University of Wisconsin.
Frye, N. 1982. *The Great Code*. London: Academic Press.
Gann, L. H. 1968. *The Birth of a Plural Society: the development of Northern Rhodesia under the British South Africa Company, 1894–1914*. Manchester: Manchester University Press.
Garvey, B. 1974. 'The Development of the White Fathers' Mission among the Bemba-speaking Peoples: 1891–1964', unpublished PhD thesis, University of London.
Gathorne-Hardy, I. [1977] 1979. *The Public School Phenomenon*. Harmondsworth: Penguin Books.
Gemie, S. 1992. 'What is a school? Defining and controlling primary schooling in

early nineteenth-century France', *History of Education*, 21, 2, June.

Gertzel, C., C. Baylies and M. Szeftel. 1984. *The Dynamics of the One-Party State in Zambia*. Manchester: Manchester University Press.

Giddens, A. 1979. *Central Problems in Social Theory: action, structure and contradiction in social analysis*. London: Macmillan.

Giddens, A. 1982. *Profiles and Critiques in Social Theory*. London: Macmillan.

Giddens, A. 1984. *Outline of a Theory of Structuration*. Cambridge: Polity Press.

Gifford, P. (ed.). 1990. *Christianity: to save or enslave?* Harare: EDICESA.

Gifford, P. (ed.). [1992] 1993. *New Dimensions in African Christianity*. Ibadan: SEFE; first published by the All-Africa Conference of Churches, Nairobi.

Gifford, P. 1993. *Christianity and Politics in Doe's Liberia*. Cambridge: Cambridge University Press.

Gifford, P. (ed.). 1995. *The Christian Churches and the Democratisation of Africa*. Leiden: E. J. Brill.

Gifford, P. 1998. *African Christianity: its public role*. London: C. Hurst.

Gilsenan, M. 1994. 'Nightmares on the Brain of the Living', paper presented at ICCCR Workshop, University of Manchester.

Giroux, H. 1983. 'Theories of reproduction and resistance in the new sociology of education: a critical analysis', *Harvard Educational Review* 53, 3, 257–93.

Goffman, E. 1959. *The Presentation of Self in Everyday Life*. Garden City, NY: Doubleday Anchor.

Goffman, E. 1961a. *Encounters: two studies in the sociology of interaction*. Harmondsworth: Penguin.

Goffman, E. 1961b. *Asylums: essays on the social situation of mental patients and other inmates*. Garden City, NY: Doubleday.

Goffman, E. 1969. *Strategic Interaction*. Oxford: Basil Blackwell.

Goffman, E. 1974. *Frame Analysis: an essay on the organisation of experience*. New York: Harper and Row.

Goodman, F. D. 1972. *Speaking in Tongues: a cross-cultural study of glossolalia*. Chicago and London: University of Chicago Press.

Goody, J. 1977. *The Domestication of the Savage Mind*. Cambridge: Cambridge University Press.

Gordon, C. et al. (eds). 1980. *Power/Knowledge: selected interviews and other writings of Michel Foucault, 1972–1977*. Brighton, Sussex: The Harvester Press.

Goubert, P. 1991. *The Course of French History*. London: Routledge.

Gray, R. 1991. *Black Christians and White Missionaries*. New Haven: Yale University Press.

Greig, J. C. E. 1985. *Education in Northern Rhodesia and Nyasaland Pre-Independence Periods*. Oxford: Oxford Development Records Project Report 13, Rhodes House Library.

Hagstotz, G. D. 1935. *The Seventh-Day Adventists in the British Isles, 1878–1933*. Missouri: University of Missouri.

Hall, E. 1959. *The Silent Language*. New York: Double Day.

Hamilton, D. 1989. *Towards a Theory of Schooling*. London: Falmer Press.

Hansen, K. 1989. *Distant Companions*. Ithaca: Cornell University Press.

Harding, S. 1992. 'The afterlife of stories: genesis of a man of God', in G. L. Rosenwald and R. L. Ochberg (eds), *Storied Lives: the cultural politics of self-understanding*. New Haven and London: Yale University Press.

Hastrup, K. 1992. 'Writing ethnography: state of the art', in J. Okely and H. Callaway (eds), *Anthropology and Autobiography*. London: Routledge.

Heald, S. 1982. 'The making of men: the relevance of vernacular psychology to the interpretation of a Gisu ritual', *Africa* 52.

Heald, S. 1986. 'Witches and thieves: deviant motivations in Gisu society', *Man*, NS, 21 (1).

Heald, S. 1989. *Controlling Anger: the sociology of Gisu violence*. Manchester: Manchester University Press for the International African Institute.

Heffernan, M. 1992. 'Literacy and the life cycle in nineteenth-century provincial France: some evidence from the département of Ille-et-Vilaine', *History of Education* 21, 2, June.

Heidegger, M. [1927] 1962. *Being and Time*, trans. J. Macquarrie and E. S. Robinson. New York: Harper and Row; London: SCM Press.

Heidegger, M. 1971. *Poetry, Language, Thought*, trans. A. Hofstadter. New York: Harper and Row.

Herzfeld, M. 1985. *The Poetics of Manhood: contest and identity in a Cretan mountain village*. Princeton: Princeton University Press.

Hinfelaar, H. F. 1994. *Bemba-speaking Women in a Century of Religious Change*. Leiden: Brill.

Hoekema, A. A. 1973. *Seventh-Day Adventism*. Exeter: The Paternoster Press.

Hollenweger, W. J. 1972. *The Pentecostals: the Charismatic Movement in the churches*. Minneapolis: Augsburg Publishing House.

Holt, J. 1969. *How Children Fail*. Harmondsworth: Penguin.

Holmes, T. 1994. *Journey to Livingstone: exploration of an imperial myth*. Edinburgh: Canongate.

Hoppers, W. 1981. *Education in a Rural Society: primary pupils and school leavers in Mwinilunga, Zambia*. The Hague: CESO.

Horton, R. 1971. 'African conversion', *Africa* 41 (2) 85–108.

Horton, R. 1975. 'On the rationality of conversion', parts 1 and 2, *Africa* 45 (3) 219–35 and (4) 373–99.

Huber, M. 1988. *The Bishop's Progress*. Washington: Smithsonian Institution Press.

Ingold, T. 1991. 'Against the motion', in T. Ingold (ed.), *Human Worlds are Culturally Constructed*. Manchester: Group for Debates in Anthropological Theory.

Ingold, T. 1995. 'Building, dwelling, living: how animals and people make themselves at home in the world,' in M. Strathern (ed.), *Shifting Contexts*. London: Routledge.

Jackson, P. 1968. *Life in Classrooms*. New York: Holt, Rinehart and Winston.

Jackson, P. 1971. 'The students' world', in M. Silberman (ed.), *The Experience of Schooling*. Eastbourne: Holt, Rinehart and Winston.

Jamba, S. 1989. 'The African disease', *The Spectator*, 9 September 1989.

Jansen, J. M. and W. MacGaffey. 1974. *An Anthology of Kongo Religion*. Lawrence, KS: University of Kansas Press.

Jay, M. 1986. 'In the empire of The Gaze: Foucault and the denigration of vision in twentieth century French thought', in D. C. Hoy (ed.), *Foucault: a critical reader*. Oxford: Basil Blackwell.

Jenkins, R. 1992. *Pierre Bourdieu*. London: Routledge.

Jones, C. and R. Porter. 1994. 'Introduction' in C. Jones and R. Porter (eds), *Reassessing Foucault: power, medicine and the body*. London: Routledge.

Jones, D. 1990. 'The genealogy of the urban school teacher', in S. J. Ball, 1990 (ed.), *Foucault and Education*. London: Routledge.

Jones, R. 1990. 'Educational practices and scientific knowledge: a genealogical reinterpretation of the emergence of physiology in post-revolutionary France', in S. J. Ball (ed.), *Foucault and Education*. London: Routledge.

Jones, T. J. 1925. *Education in East Africa*. New York: Phelps-Stokes Fund.

Kapferer, B. 1979. 'The ritual process and the transformation of context', *Social Analysis*, 1.

Keddie, N. 1971. 'Classroom knowledge', in M. F. D. Young (ed.), *Knowledge and Control*. London: Collier Macmillan.

Kermode, F. 1967. *The Sense of an Ending*. New York: Oxford University Press.

Kleinfeld, I. S. 1979. *Eskimo School on the Andreafsky*. New York: Praeger.

Kohl, H. 1970. *The Open Classroom*. London: Methuen.

Kritzman, L. D. (ed.) 1988. *Michel Foucault: politics, philosophy, culture, interviews und other writings, 1977–1984*. London: Routledge.

Lawrence, D. L. and S. M. Low. 1990. 'The built environment and spatial form', *Annual Review of Anthropology*, 19: 453–505.

Leach, E. 1989. 'Tribal ethnography: past, present and future', in E. Tonkin, M. McDonald and M. Chapman (eds), *History and Ethnicity*. London: Routledge.

Levinas, E. 1987. *Collected Philosophical Papers*, trans. A. Lingis. Dordrecht: Nijhoff.

Linden, I. and I. Linden. 1974. *Catholics, Peasants and Chewa Resistance in Nyasaland, 1889–1939*. London: Heinemann Educational.

Livingstone, D. 1857. *Missionary Travels*. London: Murray.

Lonergan, B. 1972. *Method in Theology*. London: Darton, Longman and Todd.

Manning, P. 1992. *Erving Goffman and Modern Sociology*. Cambridge: Polity Press.

Marian Brothers. 1947. *Life of Father Founder*. Rome: Marian Brothers.

Marian Brothers. 1986. *Constitutions and Statutes*. Rome: Marian Brothers.

Marian Brothers. 1986. *Formation Guide*. Rome: Marian Brothers.

Marian Brothers. 1989. *Life of Father Founder*. Rome: Marian Brothers.

Marsden, G. 1980. *Fundamentalism and American Culture*. New York: Oxford University Press.

Marsh, P., E. Rosser and R. Harre. 1978. *The Rules of Disorder*. London: Routledge and Kegan Paul.

Marshall, R. 1993. 'Power in the name of Jesus: social transformation and Pentecostalism in Western Nigeria revisited', in T. Ranger and O. Vaughan (eds), *Legitimacy and the State in 20th Century Africa*. Oxford: St Antony's Macmillan Series, pp. 213–46.

Martin, D. 1990. *Tongues of Fire: the explosion of Protestantism in Latin America*. Oxford: Basil Blackwell.

Martin, D. 2002. *Pentecostalism: the world their parish*. Oxford: Blackwell Publishers.

Maxwell, D. 1994. 'A Social and Conceptual History of North-East Zimbabwe, 1890–1990', unpublished PhD thesis, University of Oxford.

Mbembe, A. 1992. 'Provisional notes on the postcolony', *Africa* 62 (1) 3–37.

McCulloch, N., B. Baulch and M. Cherel-Robson. 2000. *Poverty, Inequality and Growth in Zambia during the 1990s*. Brighton: IDS Publications.

McGinn, B. 1979. *Visions of the End: apocalyptic traditions in the Middle Ages*. New York: Columbia University Press.

McLaren, P. 1986. *Schooling as a Ritual Performance*. London: Routledge and Kegan Paul.

McMahon, F. 1988. *Strong Mind, Gentle Heart*. Drummoyne: Marian Brothers.

McMahon, J. R. 1992. 'Educational Vision: a Marist perspective', unpublished PhD thesis, University of London, Institute of Education.

McNay, L. 1992. *Foucault and Feminism*. Cambridge: Cambridge University Press.

McNay, L. 1994. *Foucault: a critical introduction*. Cambridge: Polity Press.

Merquior, J. G. [1985] 1991. *Foucault*. London: Fontana Press.

Mitchell, T. 1988. *Colonising Egypt*. Berkeley: University of California Press.

Moore, H. 1986. *Space, Text and Gender*. Cambridge: Cambridge University Press.

Moore, H. 1990. 'Paul Ricoeur: action, meaning and text', in C. Tilley (ed.), *Reading Material Culture*. Oxford: Blackwell.

Mudimbe, V. Y. 1988. *The Invention of Africa*, Bloomington: Indiana University Press.

Mudimbe, V. Y. 1994a. *Les Corps Glorieux des Mots et des Etres: esquisse d'un jardin africain à la Bénédictine*. Montreal: Humanitas; Paris: Presence Africaine.
Mudimbe, V. Y. 1994b. *The Idea of Africa*. Bloomington: Indiana University Press.
Mulrain, G. M. 1984. *Theology in Folk Culture: the theological significance of Haitian folk religion*. New York: Peter Lang.
Mwanakatwe, J. M. 1968. *The Growth of Education in Zambia since Independence*. Oxford: Oxford University Press.
Norris, C. 1993. *The Truth about Postmodernism*. Oxford: Blackwell.
Numbers, R. L. 1976. *Prophetess of Health: Ellen G. White*. New York: Harper and Row.
Numbers, R. L. and J. M. Butler (eds). 1987. *The Disappointed: Millerism and Millenarianism in the 19th century*. Bloomington: Indiana University Press.
Ojo, M. A. 1986. 'The Growth of Campus Christianity and Charismatic Movements in Western Nigeria', unpublished PhD thesis, University of London.
Ojo. M. A. 1988. 'Deeper life Christian ministry: a case study of the charismatic movements in Western Nigeria', *Journal of Religion in Africa*, 18, 141–62.
Okely, J. 1978. 'Privileged, schooled and finished: boarding education for girls', in S. Ardener (ed.), *Defining Females*. Oxford: Croom Helm.
Okely, J. 1992. 'Anthropology and autobiography: participatory experience and embodied knowledge', in J. Okely and H. Callaway (eds), *Anthropology and Autobiography*. London and New York: Routledge.
Okely, J. and H. Callaway (eds). 1992. *Anthropology and Autobiography*. London and New York: Routledge.
O'Leary, S. D. 1994. *Arguing The Apocalypse: a theory of millennial rhetoric*. New York and Oxford: Oxford University Press.
Pader, E. J. 1993. 'Spatiality and social change: domestic space use in Mexico and the United States', *American Ethnologist*, 20 (1).
Peel, J. D. Y. 1992. 'The colonization of consciousness, Review of *Of Revelation and Revolution*, vol. 1', *Journal of African History*, 33: 328–9.
Peel, J. D. Y. 1995. '"For who hath despised the day of small things?", Missionary narratives and historical anthropology,' *Comparative Studies in Society and History*, 37 (3): 581–607.
Personal Narratives Group (eds). 1989. *Interpreting Women's Lives*. Bloomington: Indiana University Press.
Peshkin, A. 1986. *God's Choice: the total world of a fundamentalist Christian school*. Chicago: The University Press.
Piveteau, D. 1967. 'Catholic education in France', in J. Lee (ed.), *Catholic Education in the Western World*. Notre Dame: University of Notre Dame.
Proust, M. 1954. *Du côté de chez Swann*. Paris: Editions Gallimard.
Rabinow, P. (ed.). 1984. *The Foucault Reader*. Harmondsworth: Penguin.
Racevskis, K. 1983. *Michel Foucault and the Subversion of Intellect*. Ithaca: Cornell University Press.
Ranger, T. 1965. 'The Ethiopian Episode in Barotseland 1900–1905', *Rhodes-Livingstone Journal*, 31: 26–41.
Ranger, T. 1996. 'Postscript: colonial and postcolonial identities', in R. Werbner and T. Ranger (eds), *Postcolonial Identities in Africa*. London: Zed Books.
Richards, A. 1939. *Land, Labour and Diet in Northern Rhodesia: an economic study of the Bemba tribe*. London: Oxford University Press for the International African Institute.
Richards, A. [1956] 1982. *Chisungu*. London: Tavistock Publications.
Richlin, A. 1998. 'Foucault's *History of Sexuality*: a useful theory for women?' in D. H. Larmour et al. (eds), *Rethinking Sexuality: Foucault and classical antiquity*. Princeton: Princeton University Press.

Ricoeur, P. 1984. *Time and Narrative*. Chicago: University of Chicago Press.

Robben, A. 1989. 'Habits of the home: spatial hegemony and the structuration of house and society in Brazil', *American Anthropologist*, vol. 91, pt 2.

Roberts, A. D. 1973. *The History of the Bemba: political growth and change in North-Eastern Zambia before 1900*. London: Longman.

Rose, S. D. 1988. *Keeping Them Out of the Hands of Satan*. London and New York: Routledge, Chapman and Hall Inc.

Rosenwald, G. C. and R. L. Ochberg (eds) 1992. *Storied Lives: the cultural politics of self-understanding*. New Haven: Yale University Press.

Rotberg, R. I. 1965. *Christian Missionaries and the Creation of Northern Rhodesia, 1880–1924*. Princeton: Princeton University Press.

Scudder, T. and E. Colson. 1980. *Secondary Education and the Formation of an Elite: the impact of education on Gwembe District, Zambia*. New York: Academic Press.

Serpell, R. 1993. *The Significance of Schooling*. Cambridge: Cambridge University Press.

Seventh-Day Adventists. 1985. *Seventh-Day Adventist Hymnal*. Washington, DC: Review & Herald Publishing Assoc.

Shipman, M. D. 1968. *The Sociology of the School*. London: Longmans.

Shorter, A. 1988. *Toward a Theology of Inculturation*. London: Geoffrey Chapman.

Simmel, G. 1950. *The Sociology of Georg Simmel*, trans. K. H. Wolff. New York: Free Press.

Simmel, G. 1978. *The Philosophy of Money*, trans. T. Bottomore and D. Frisby. London: Routledge.

Simpson, A. J. 1990. 'The Impact of Catholic Mission Education on the Religious Ideas of Young Zambians: a case study', unpublished MA thesis, University of Manchester.

Simpson, A. J. 1996. 'Religious formations in a postcolony', unpublished PhD thesis, University of Manchester.

Sinyangwe, B. 1993. *Quills of Desire*. Harare: Baobab Books.

Skinner, E. P. 1979. 'Conclusions', in W. A. Shack and E. P. Skinner (eds), *Strangers in African Societies*. Berkeley: University of Chicago Press.

Spivak, G. C. 1988. *The Post-Colonial Critic: interviews, dialogues*, S. Harasym (ed.). New York and London: Routledge.

Stanley, L. 1993. 'On auto/biography in sociology', *Sociology* 27 (1), 41–52.

Stanley, L. and D. Morgan. 1993. 'Editorial introduction', *Sociology* 27 (1), 1–4.

Stilgoe, R. 1994. 'Foreword', in G. Bachelard, *The Poetics of Space*, trans. M. Jolas. Boston: Beacon Press.

Stoller, P. 1995. *Embodying Colonial Memories: spirit possession, power and the Hauka in West Africa*. New York and London: Routledge.

Strathern, M. 1991. *Partial connections*. Savage, MD: Rowman and Littlefield.

Strickland, B. 1995. 'Makhalidwe wa Akunda as Kunda Ways of Staying: productions and management of knowledge, agency and power among the Kunda of Eastern Zambia', unpublished PhD thesis, University of North Carolina at Chapel Hill.

Stromberg, P. G. 1993. *Language and Self-transformation*. Cambridge: Cambridge University Press.

Sykes, S. 1984. *The Identity of Christianity: theologians and the essence of Christianity from Schleiermacher to Barth*. London: SPCK.

Taylor, C. 1986. 'Foucault on freedom and truth', in D. C. Hoy (ed.), *Foucault: a critical reader*. Oxford: Basil Blackwell.

Taylor, C. 1989. *Sources of the Self. The making of the modern identity*. Cambridge: Cambridge University Press.

Ter Haar, G. 1992. *Spirit of Africa: the healing ministry of Archbishop Milingo of Zambia*. London: Hurst and Company.

Tonkin, E. 1992. *Narrating our Pasts*. Cambridge: Cambridge University Press.

Turner, V. W. 1962. 'Three symbols of passage in Ndembu circumcision ritual: an interpretation', in M. Gluckman (ed.), *Essays on the Ritual of Social Relations*. Manchester: Manchester University Press.

Turner, V. W. 1967. *The Forest of Symbols: Aspects of Ndembu Ritual*. Ithaca: Cornell University Press.

Turner, V. W. 1968. *The Drums of Affliction*. Oxford: Oxford University Press for the International African Institute.

Turner, V. W. [1969] 1974. *The Ritual Process*. Harmondsworth: Penguin Books.

Turner, V. and E. Bruner. (eds). 1986. *The Anthropology of Experience*. Urbana and Chicago: University of Illinois Press.

Van Binsbergen, W. 1981. *Religious Change in Zambia: exploratory studies*. London: Kegan Paul International.

Van Dijk, R. A. 1992a. 'Young Puritan preachers in post-independence Malawi', *Africa* 62, 159–81.

Van Dijk, R. A. [1992b] 1993. 'Young Born-again preachers in post-independence Malawi: the significance of an extraneous identity', in P. Gifford (ed.), *New Dimensions in African Christianity*. Ibadan: SEFER.

Van Gennep, A. [1909] 1990. *Les Rites de Passage*. Paris: Emile Nourry; trans. M. B. Vizedom and G. L. Caffee. 1960. *The Rites of Passage*, with an introduction by S. T. Kimball, London: Routledge & Kegan Paul.

Vaughan, M. 1991. *Curing their Ills*. Cambridge: Polity Press.

Veliz, C. 1983. 'A world made in England', *Quadrant*, March 1983, no. 187, vol. XXVII, no. 3, 8–19.

Wakeford, J. 1969. *The Cloistered Elite: a sociological analysis of the English public boarding school*. London: Macmillan.

Walker, A. 1987. 'Fundamentalism and modernity: the Restoration movement in Britain', in L. Caplan (ed.), *Studies in Religious Fundamentalism*. London: Macmillan.

Warner, M. 1990. *Alone of All Her Sex: the myth and cult of the Virgin Mary*. London: Picador.

Webber, J. 1987. 'Rethinking fundamentalism: the readjustment of Jewish society in the modern world', in L. Caplan (ed.), *Studies in Religious Fundamentalism*. London: Macmillan.

Weber, M. [1915] 1978. *Economy and Society*, 2 vols, G. Roth and C. Wittich (eds). Berkeley: University of California.

Weber, M. [1921] 1991. 'Essays in sociology', in H. Gerth and C. Wright Mills (eds), *From Max Weber: essays in sociology*. London, Routledge.

Weinberg, I. 1967. *The English Public Schools*. New York: Atherton Press.

Weinstein, D. and M. Weinstein. 1984. 'On the visual constitution of society: the contributions of Georg Simmel and J.-P. Sartre to a sociology of the senses', *History of European Ideas*, vol. 5.

Werbner, R. P. 1989. *Ritual Passage, Sacred Journey*. Washington and Manchester: Smithsonian Institution Press and Manchester University Press.

Werbner, R. P. 1994. 'Allegories in Christian Encounters', paper presented at the Journal of Southern African Studies Conference, University of York, 9–11 September.

Werbner, R. P. 1996. 'Introduction: multiple identities, plural arenas', in R. Werbner and T. Ranger (eds), *Postcolonial Identities in Africa*. London: Zed Books.

Werbner, R. P. 1997. 'The suffering body: passion and ritual allegory in Christian encounters', *Journal of Southern African Studies* 23 (2), 311–24.

White, H. 1981. 'The value of narrativity in the representation of reality', in W. J. T. Mitchell (ed.), *On Narrative*. Chicago: University of Chicago Press.

Wilkinson, R. 1964. *The Prefects: British leadership and the public school tradition*. London: Oxford University Press.

Williams, R. 1958. *Culture and Society, 1780–1950*. London: Chatto and Windus.

Williams, R. 1961. *The Long Revolution*. London: Chatto and Windus.

Willis, P. 1977. *Learning to Labour*. Farnborough: Saxon House.

Wirth, A. G. 1966. *John Dewey as Educator: design for work in education, 1894–1904*. New York: Wiley.

World Bank. 1994. *Zambia Poverty Assessment*. Human Resources Division, Southern Africa Department.

York, G. 1986. *Characteristics of Lasallian Schools*. Romeoville: Christian Brothers.

Young, M. F. D. (ed.). 1971. *Knowledge and Control*. London: Collier Macmillan.

INDEX